CROUCHING TIGER
HIDDEN DRAGON

Chapter 4 ───────────○

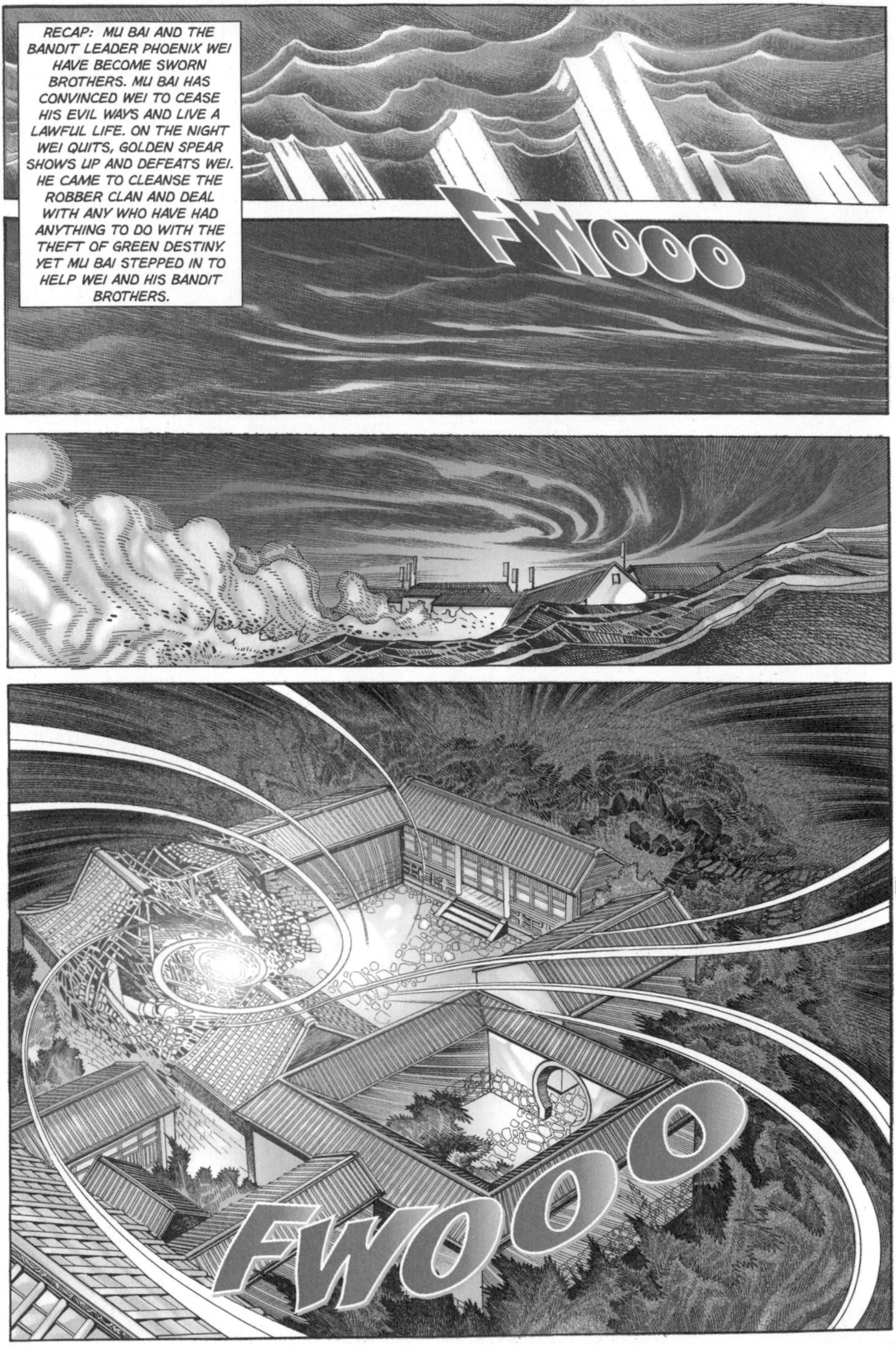
RECAP: MU BAI AND THE BANDIT LEADER PHOENIX WEI HAVE BECOME SWORN BROTHERS. MU BAI HAS CONVINCED WEI TO CEASE HIS EVIL WAYS AND LIVE A LAWFUL LIFE. ON THE NIGHT WEI QUITS, GOLDEN SPEAR SHOWS UP AND DEFEATS WEI. HE CAME TO CLEANSE THE ROBBER CLAN AND DEAL WITH ANY WHO HAVE HAD ANYTHING TO DO WITH THE THEFT OF GREEN DESTINY. YET MU BAI STEPPED IN TO HELP WEI AND HIS BANDIT BROTHERS.
FWOOO
FWOOO

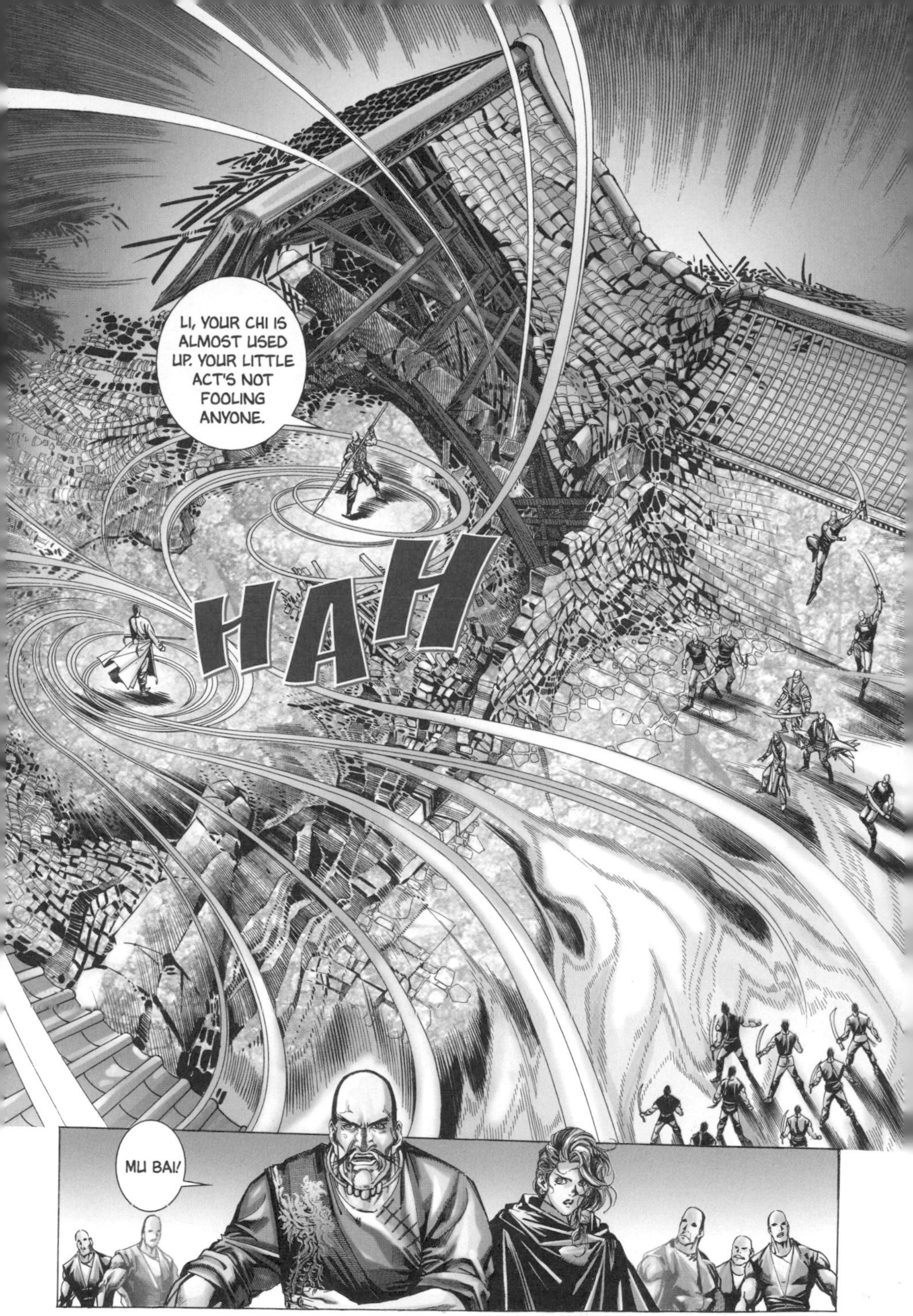
LI, YOUR CHI IS ALMOST USED UP. YOUR LITTLE ACT'S NOT FOOLING ANYONE.
HAH
MU BAI!

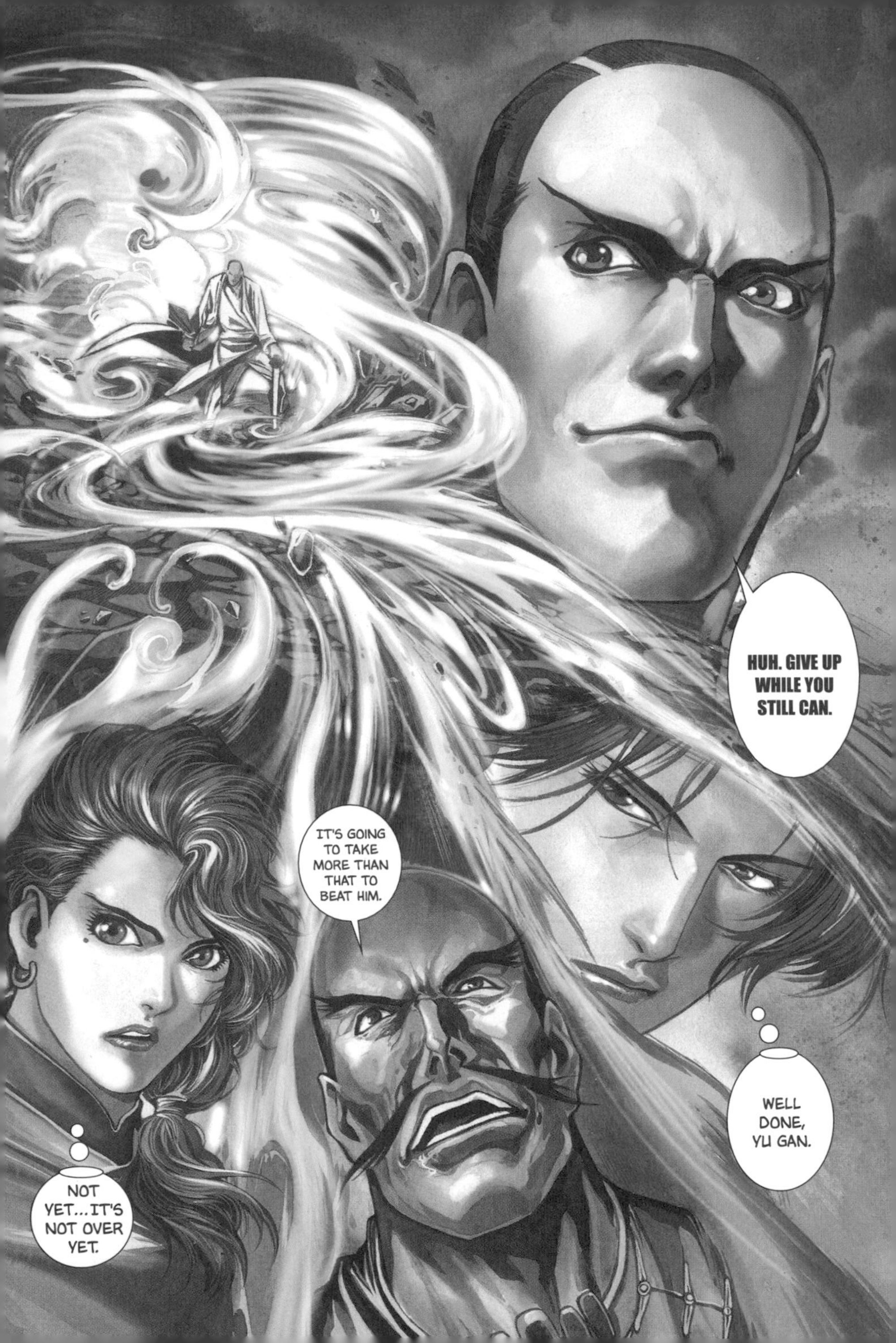
HUH. GIVE UP WHILE YOU STILL CAN.
IT'S GOING TO TAKE MORE THAN THAT TO BEAT HIM.
WELL DONE, YU GAN.
NOT YET...IT'S NOT OVER YET.

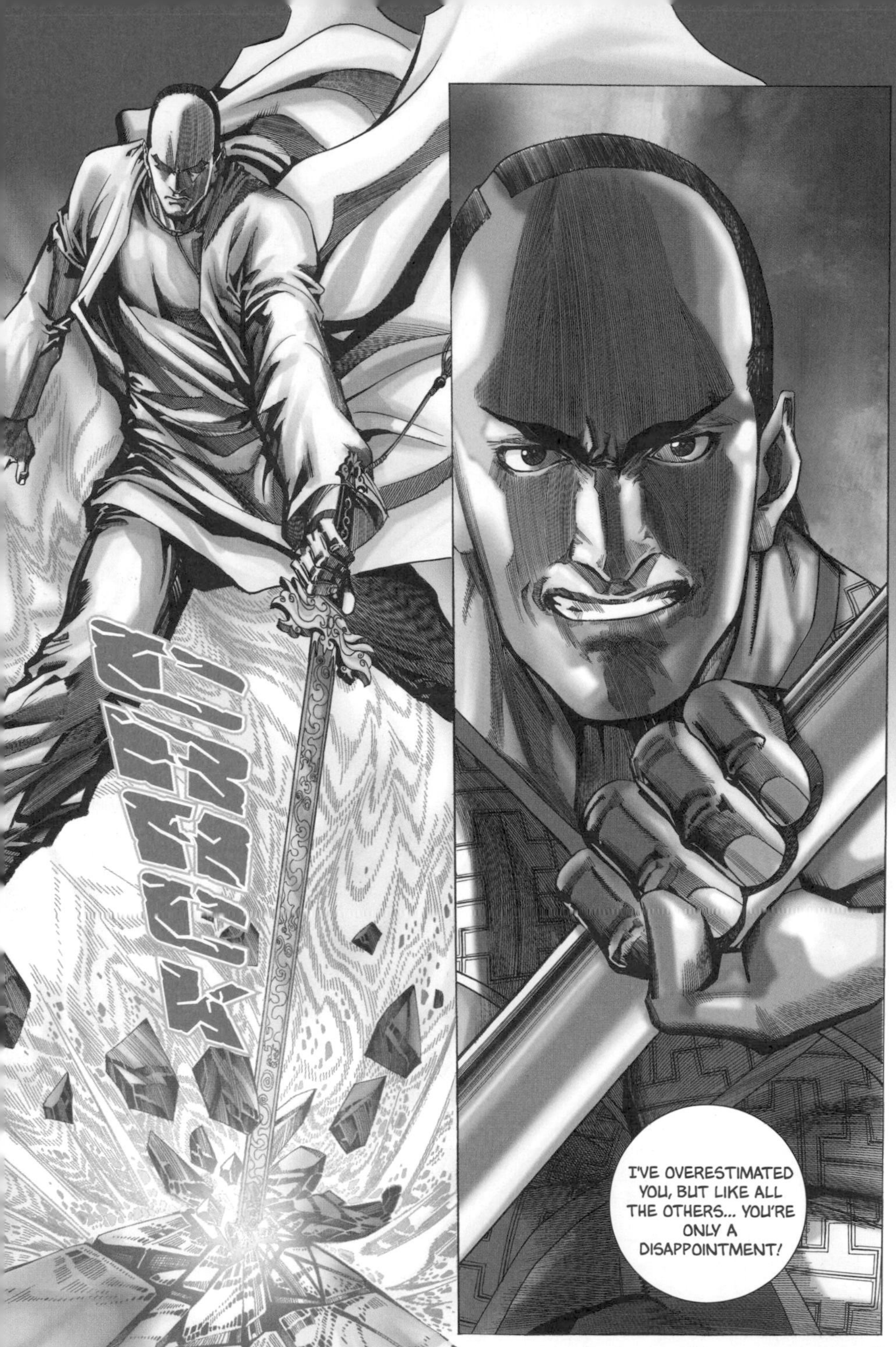
I'VE OVERESTIMATED YOU, BUT LIKE ALL THE OTHERS... YOU'RE ONLY A DISAPPOINTMENT!

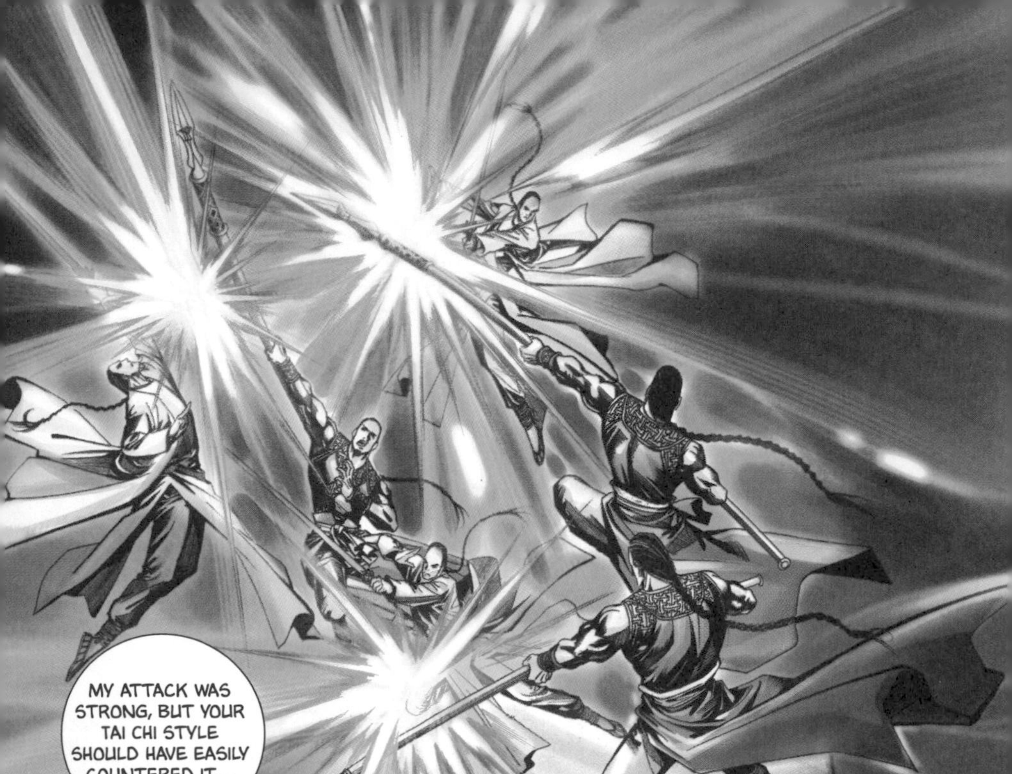
MY ATTACK WAS STRONG, BUT YOUR TAI CHI STYLE SHOULD HAVE EASILY COUNTERED IT...
YOU WERE SO PREDICTABLE, I READ YOU LIKE A BOOK!
YOU KNEW I WAS TRYING TO WEAR YOU DOWN AND ALL YOU HAD TO DO WAS EVADE MY ATTACKS, BUT YOU COULDN'T DO EVEN THAT.

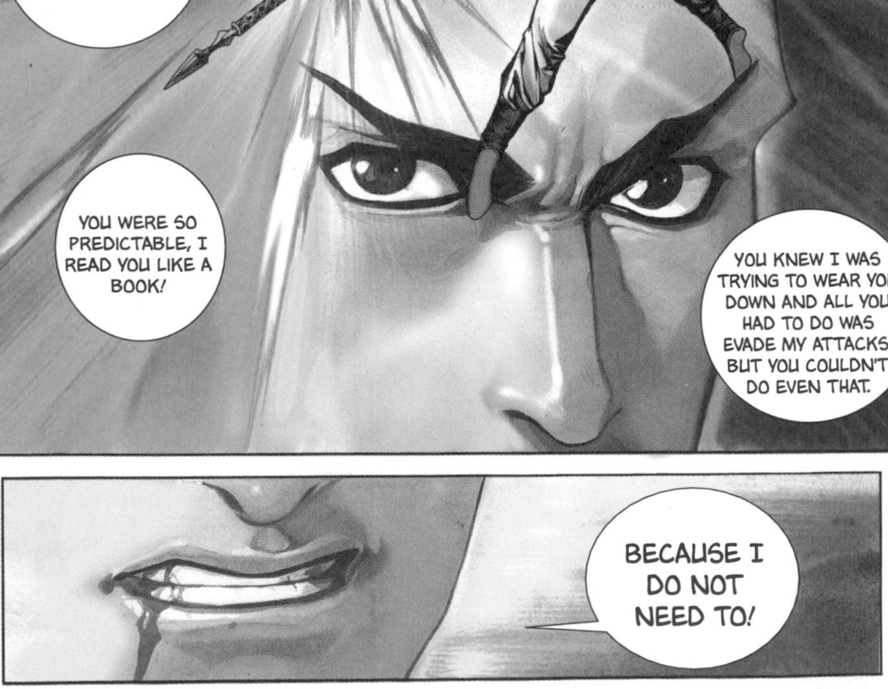
BECAUSE I DO NOT NEED TO!

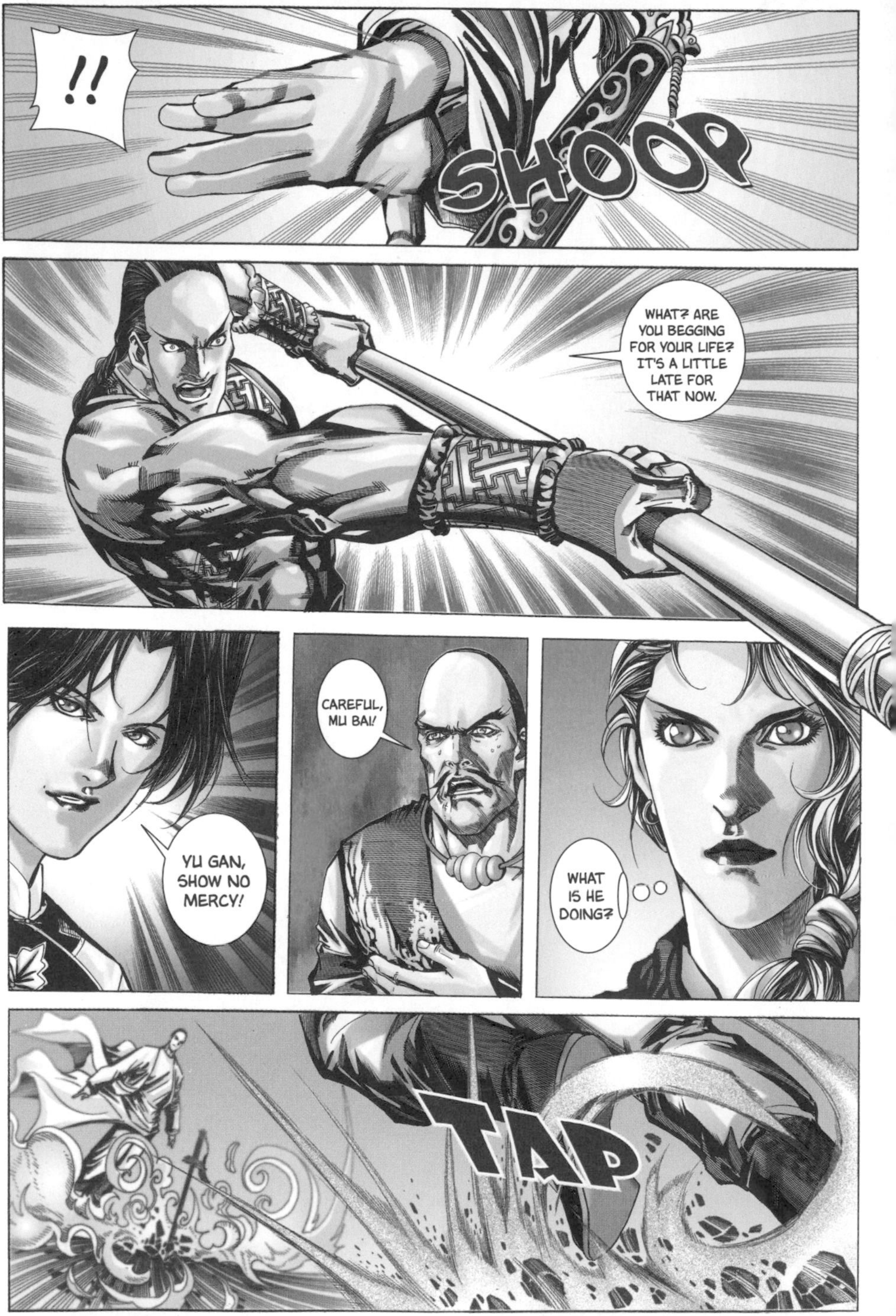
!!
SHOOP
WHAT? ARE YOU BEGGING FOR YOUR LIFE? IT'S A LITTLE LATE FOR THAT NOW.
YU GAN, SHOW NO MERCY!
CAREFUL, MU BAI!
WHAT IS HE DOING?
TAP

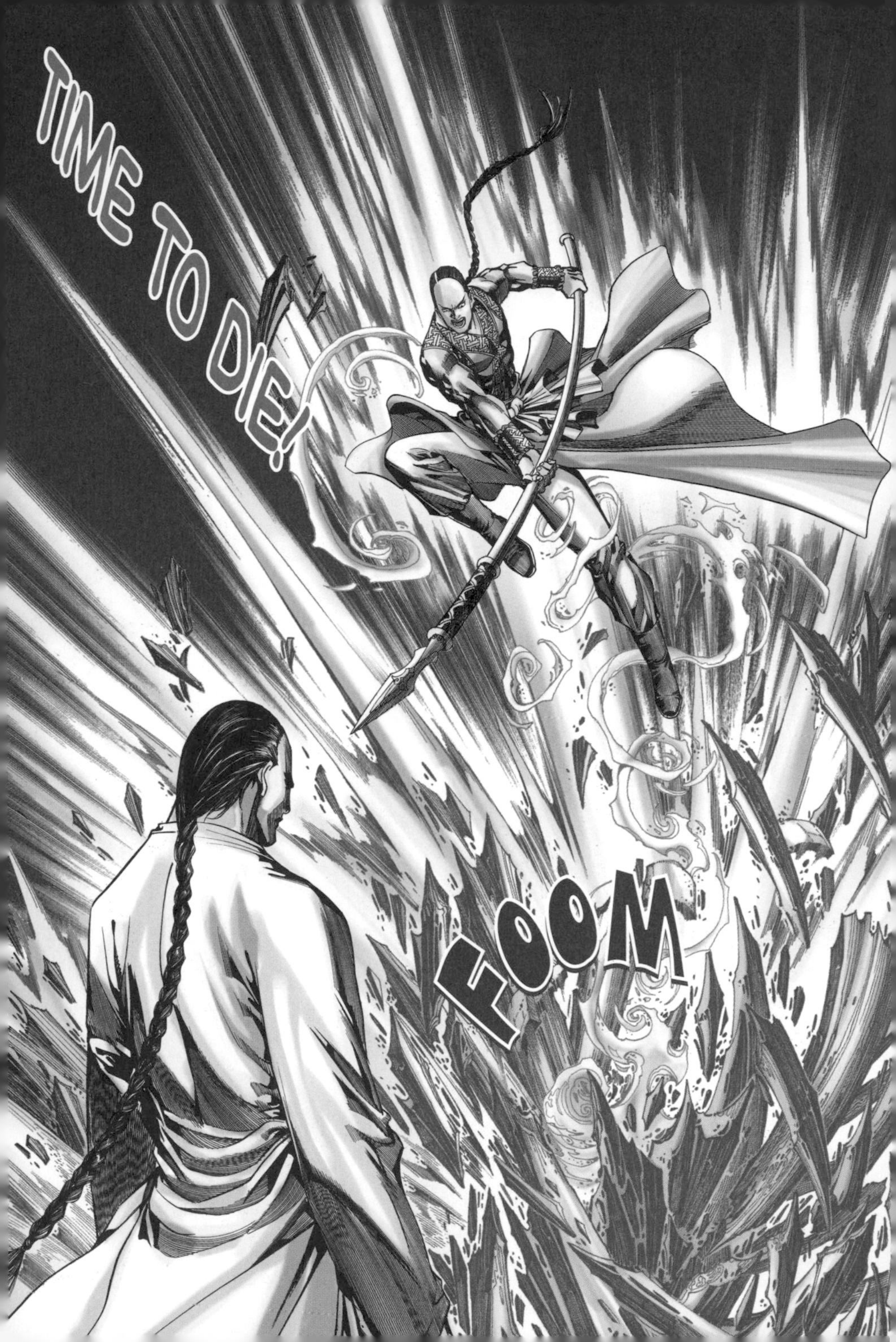
TIME TO DIE!
FOOM

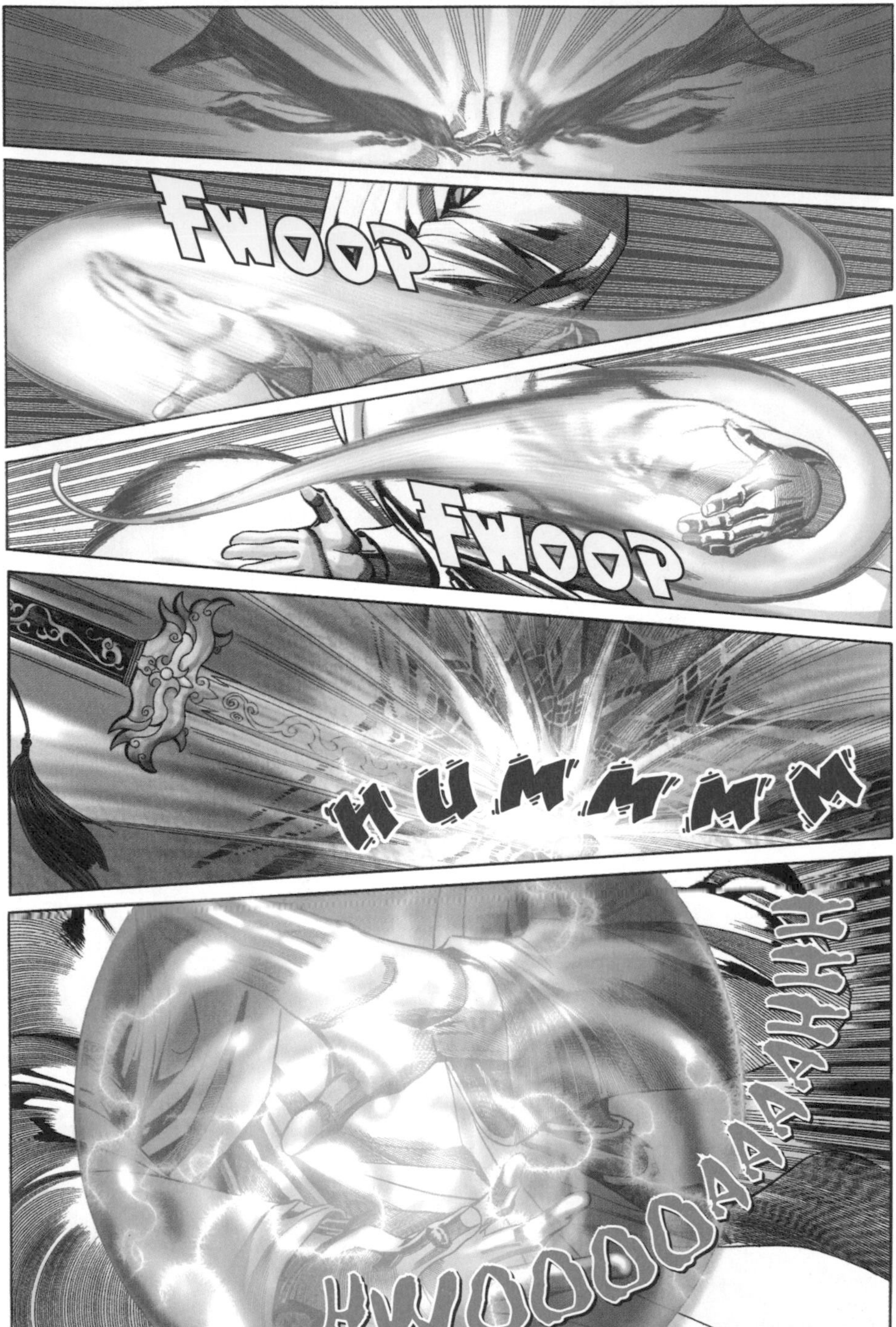
FWOOP
FWOOP
HUMMMMM
HWOOOOAAAAHHH

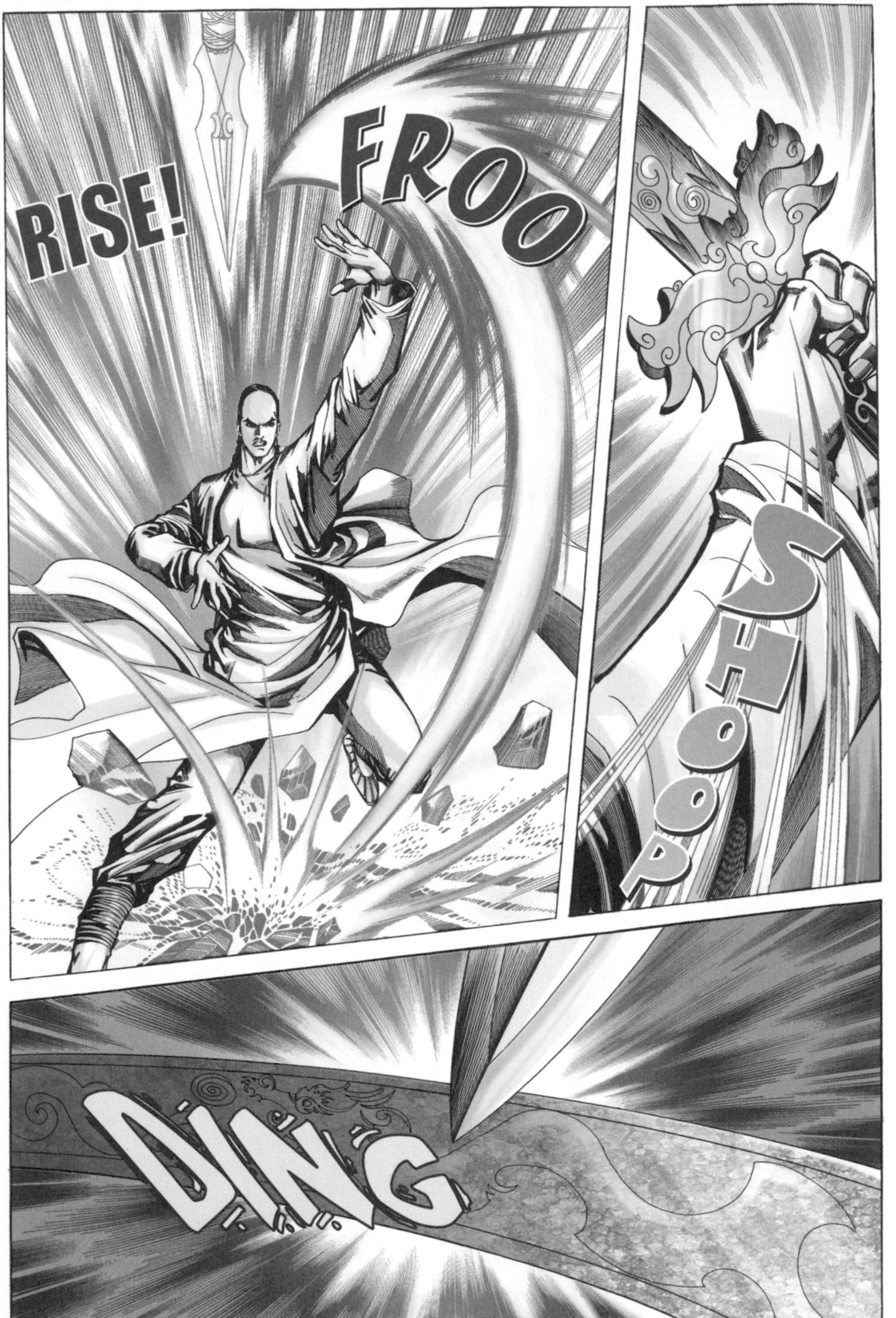
RISE!
FROO
SHOOP
DING

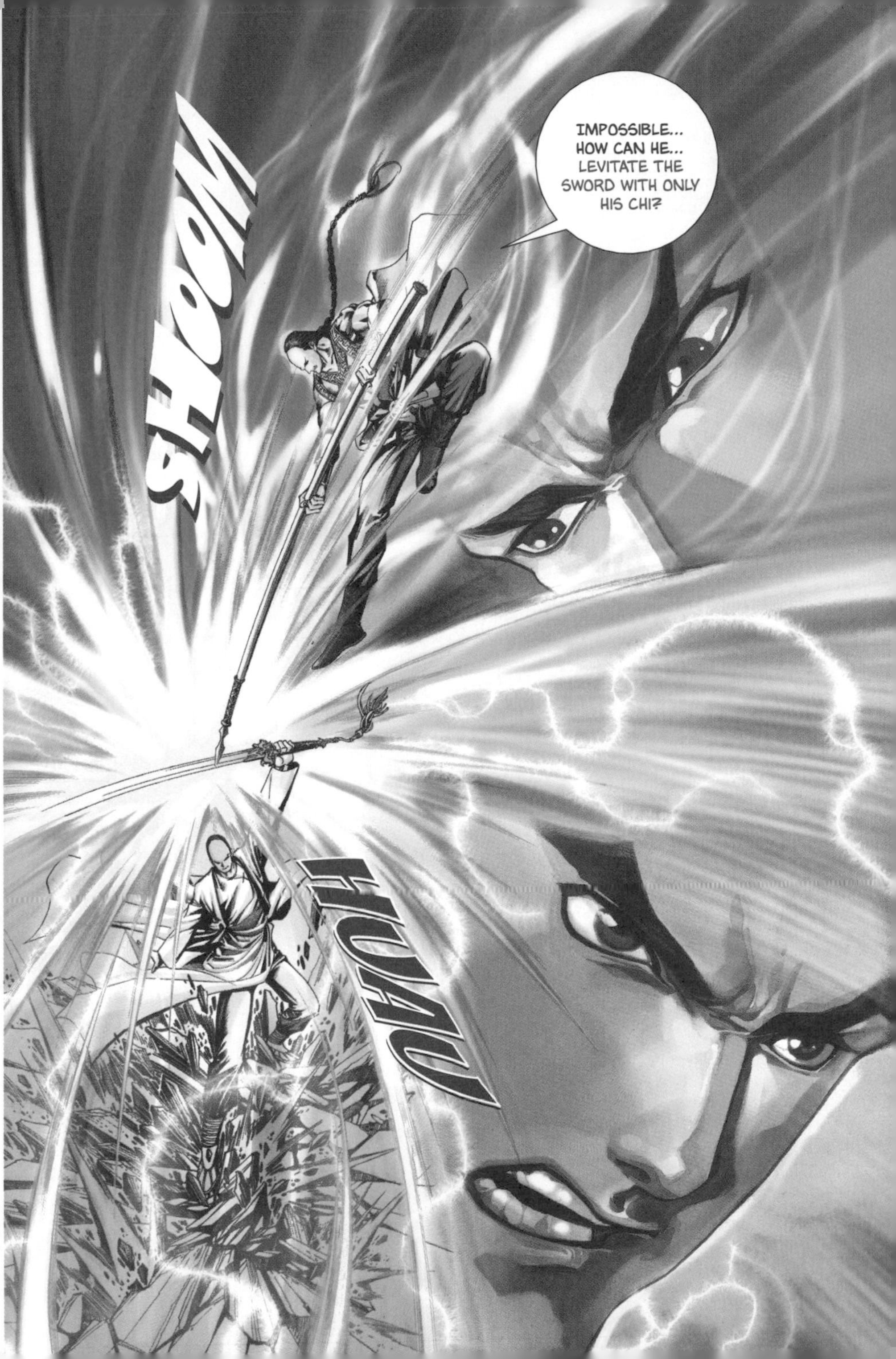
SHOOM
IMPOSSIBLE... HOW CAN HE... LEVITATE THE SWORD WITH ONLY HIS CHI?
HUAU

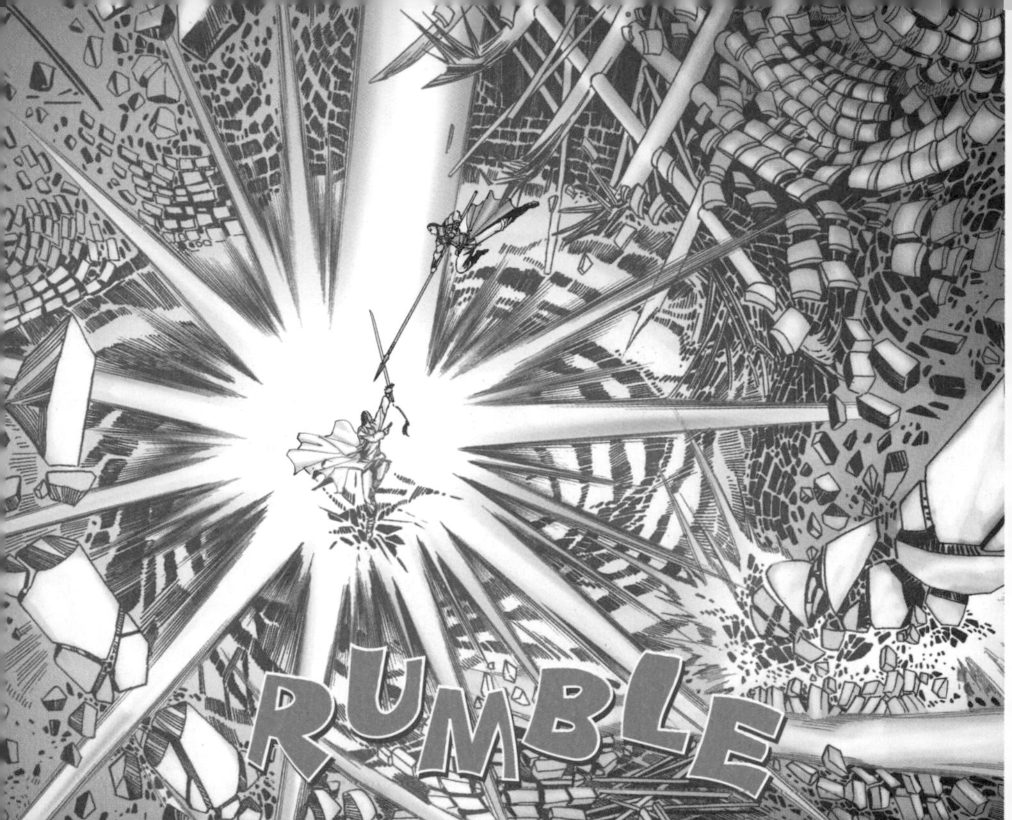
RUMBLE
MU BAI'S CHI SUDDENLY SPIKES TO INCREDIBLE PROPORTIONS. HIS CHI LEVITATES GREEN DESTINY INTO HIS OWN HAND AND BLOCKS GOLDEN SPEAR'S DEADLY STRIKE. HIS CHI IS SO STRONG. LIKE A VACUUM, IT PREVENTS GOLDEN SPEAR FROM ESCAPING...

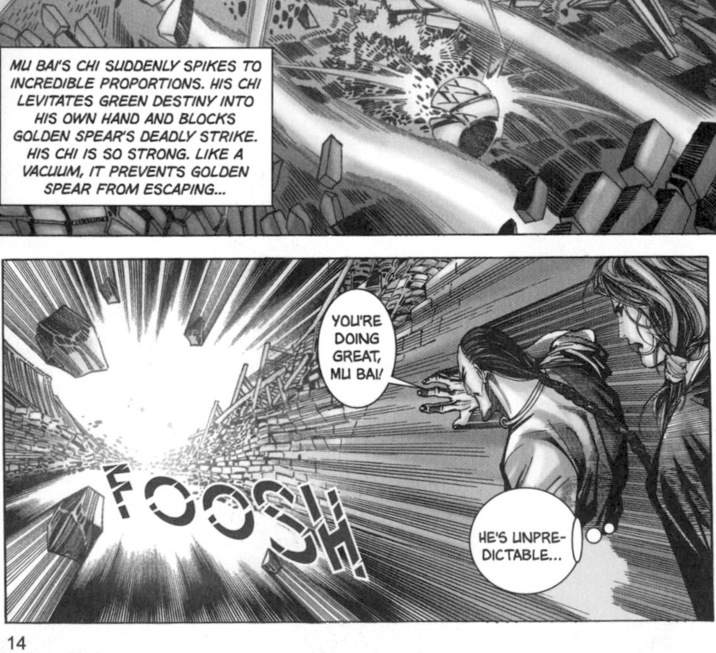
YOU'RE DOING GREAT, MU BAI!
FOOSH
HE'S UNPRE-DICTABLE...

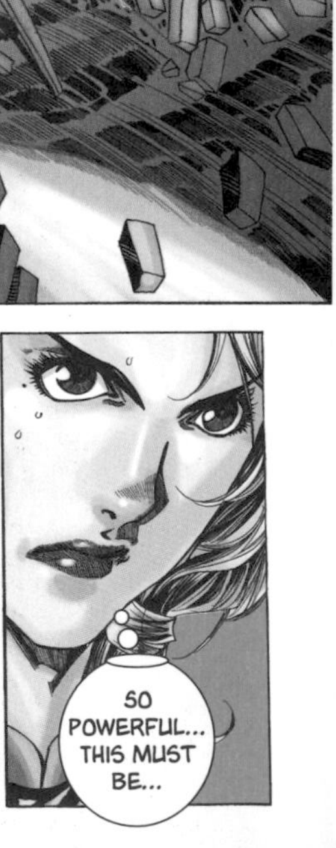
SO POWERFUL... THIS MUST BE...

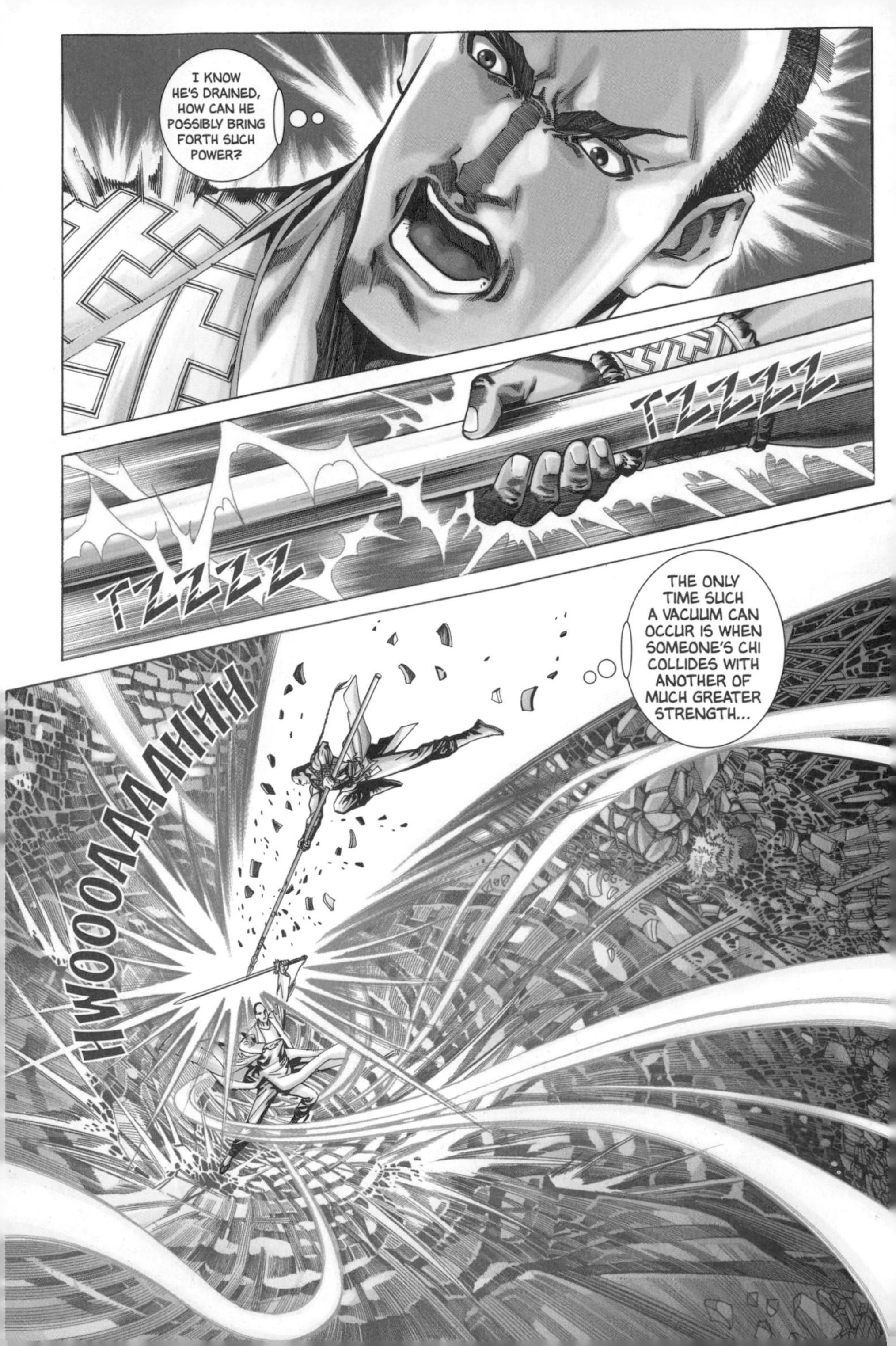
I KNOW HE'S DRAINED, HOW CAN HE POSSIBLY BRING FORTH SUCH POWER?
TZZZZZ
TZZZZZ
THE ONLY TIME SUCH A VACUUM CAN OCCUR IS WHEN SOMEONE'S CHI COLLIDES WITH ANOTHER OF MUCH GREATER STRENGTH...
HWOOOAAAAHHH

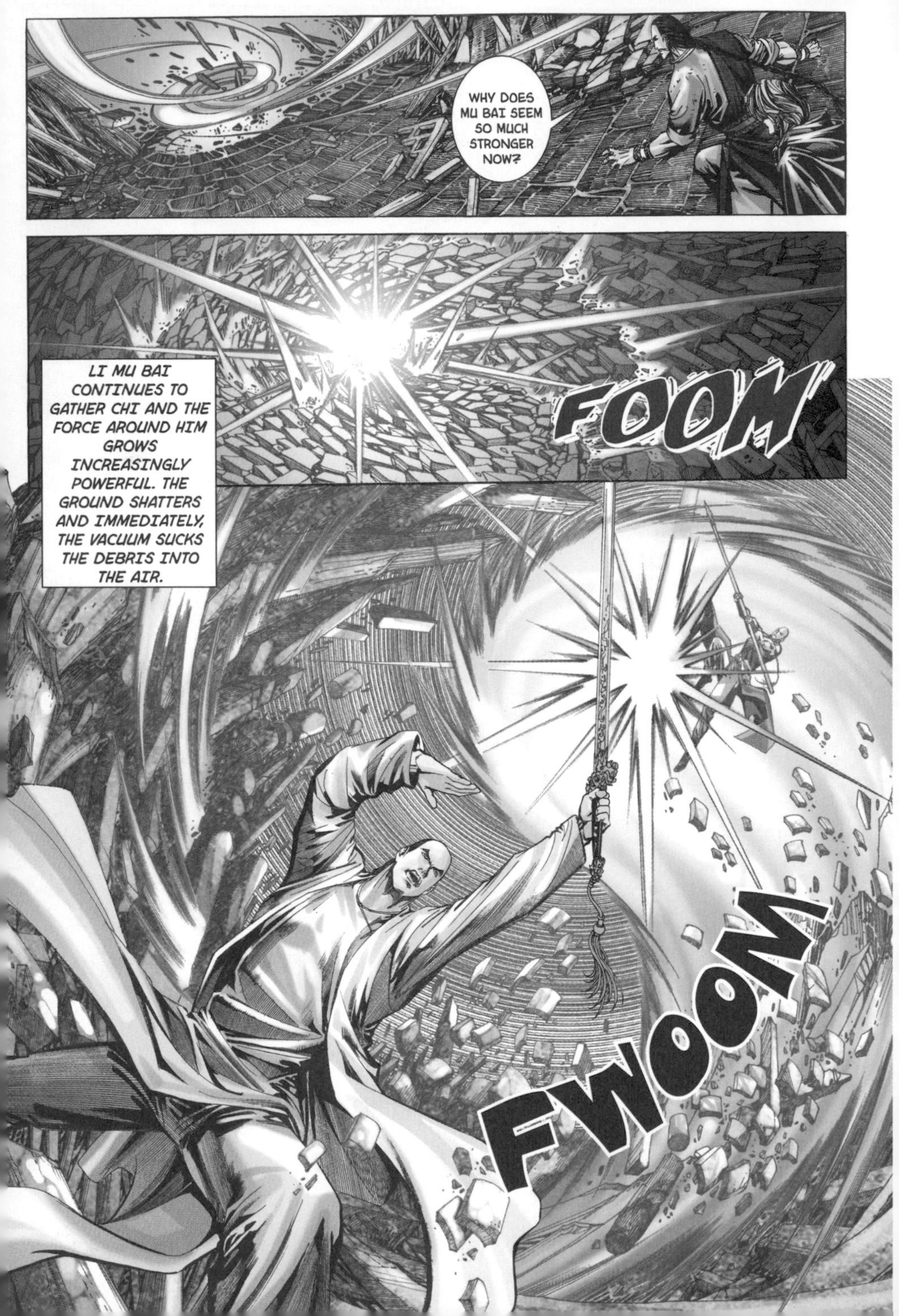
WHY DOES MU BAI SEEM SO MUCH STRONGER NOW?
LI MU BAI CONTINUES TO GATHER CHI AND THE FORCE AROUND HIM GROWS INCREASINGLY POWERFUL. THE GROUND SHATTERS AND IMMEDIATELY, THE VACUUM SUCKS THE DEBRIS INTO THE AIR.
FOOM
FWOOM

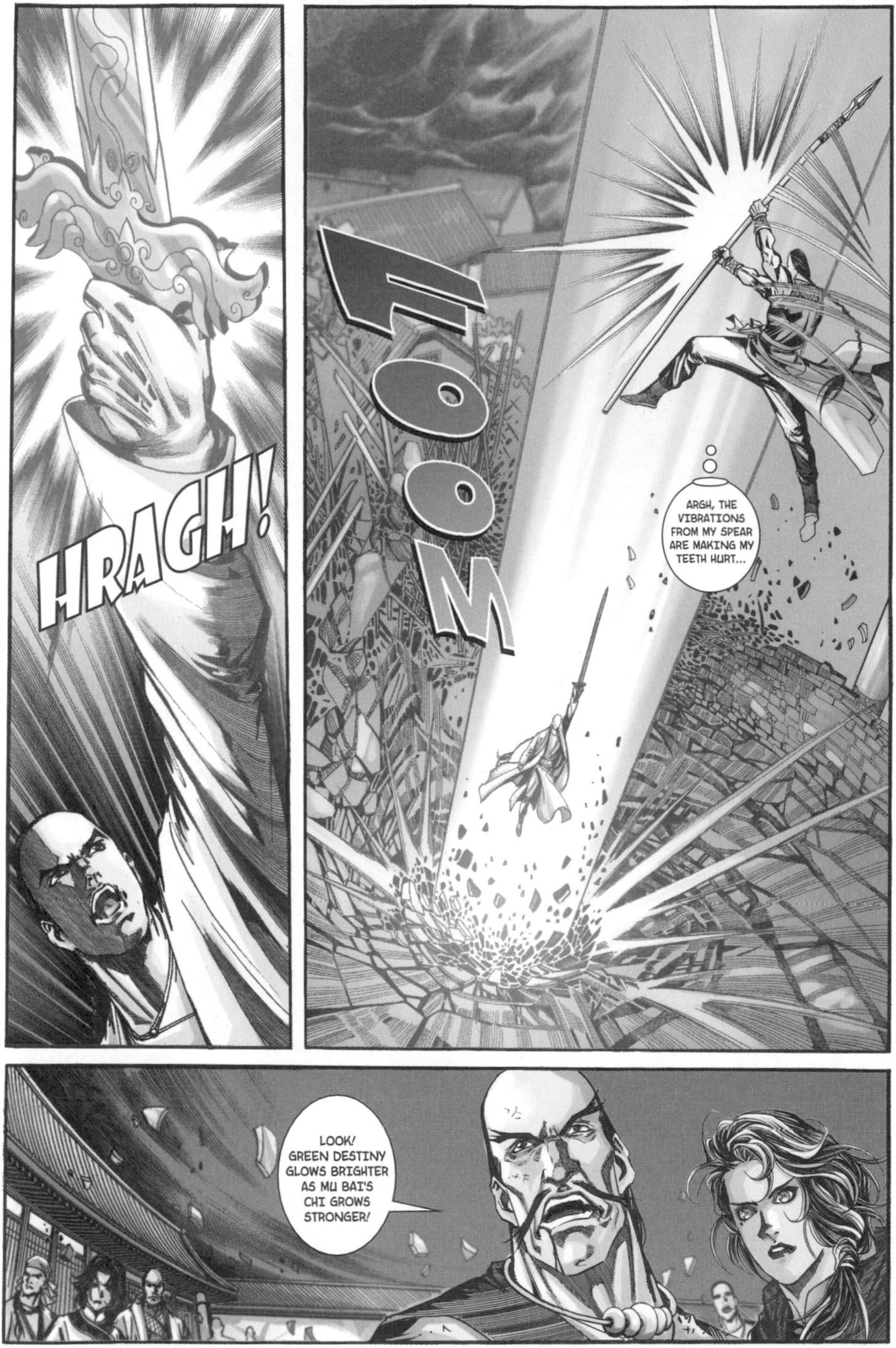
HRAGH!
FOOOM
ARGH, THE VIBRATIONS FROM MY SPEAR ARE MAKING MY TEETH HURT...
LOOK! GREEN DESTINY GLOWS BRIGHTER AS MU BAI'S CHI GROWS STRONGER!

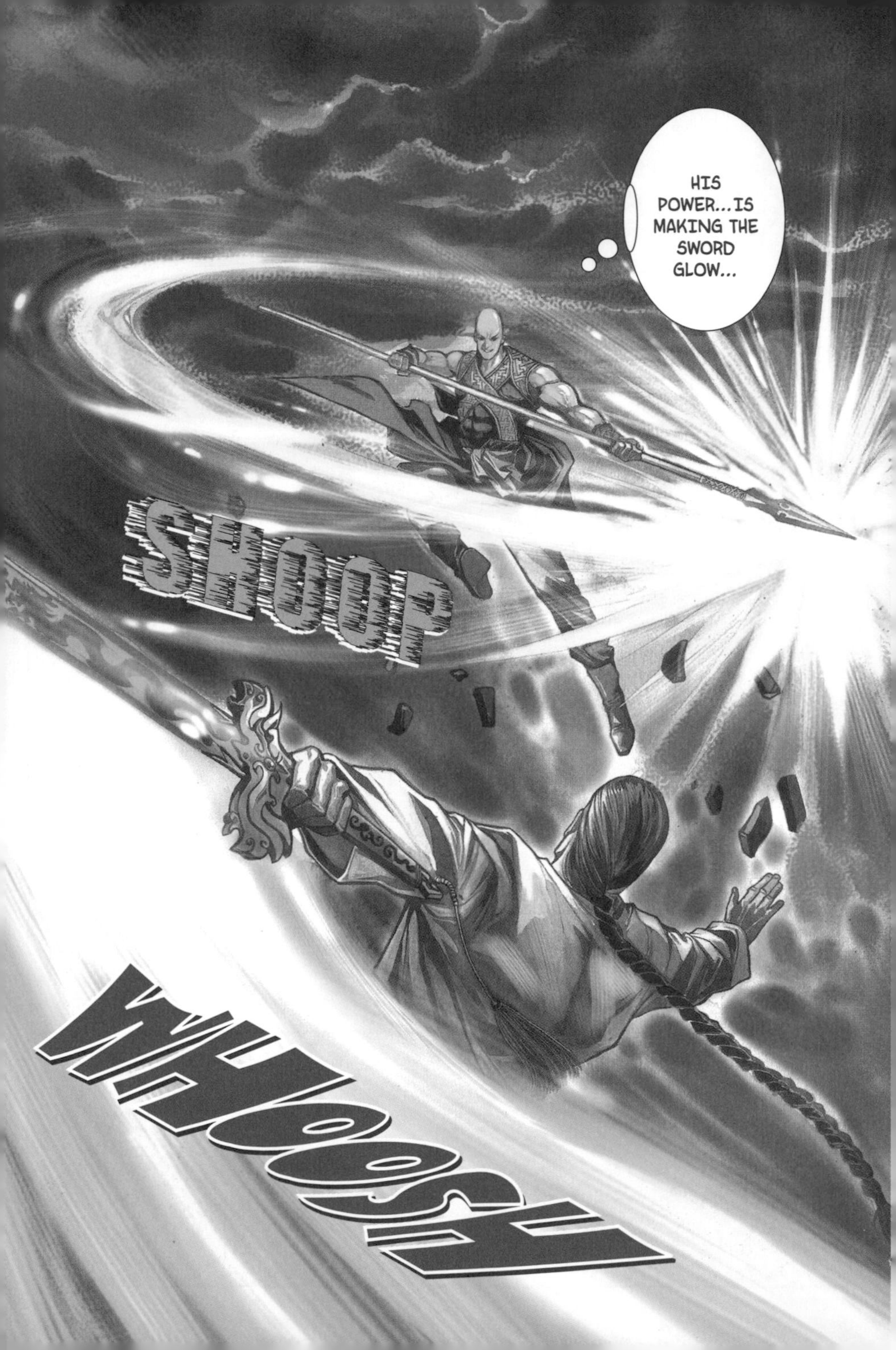
HIS POWER...IS MAKING THE SWORD GLOW...
SHOOP
WHOOSH

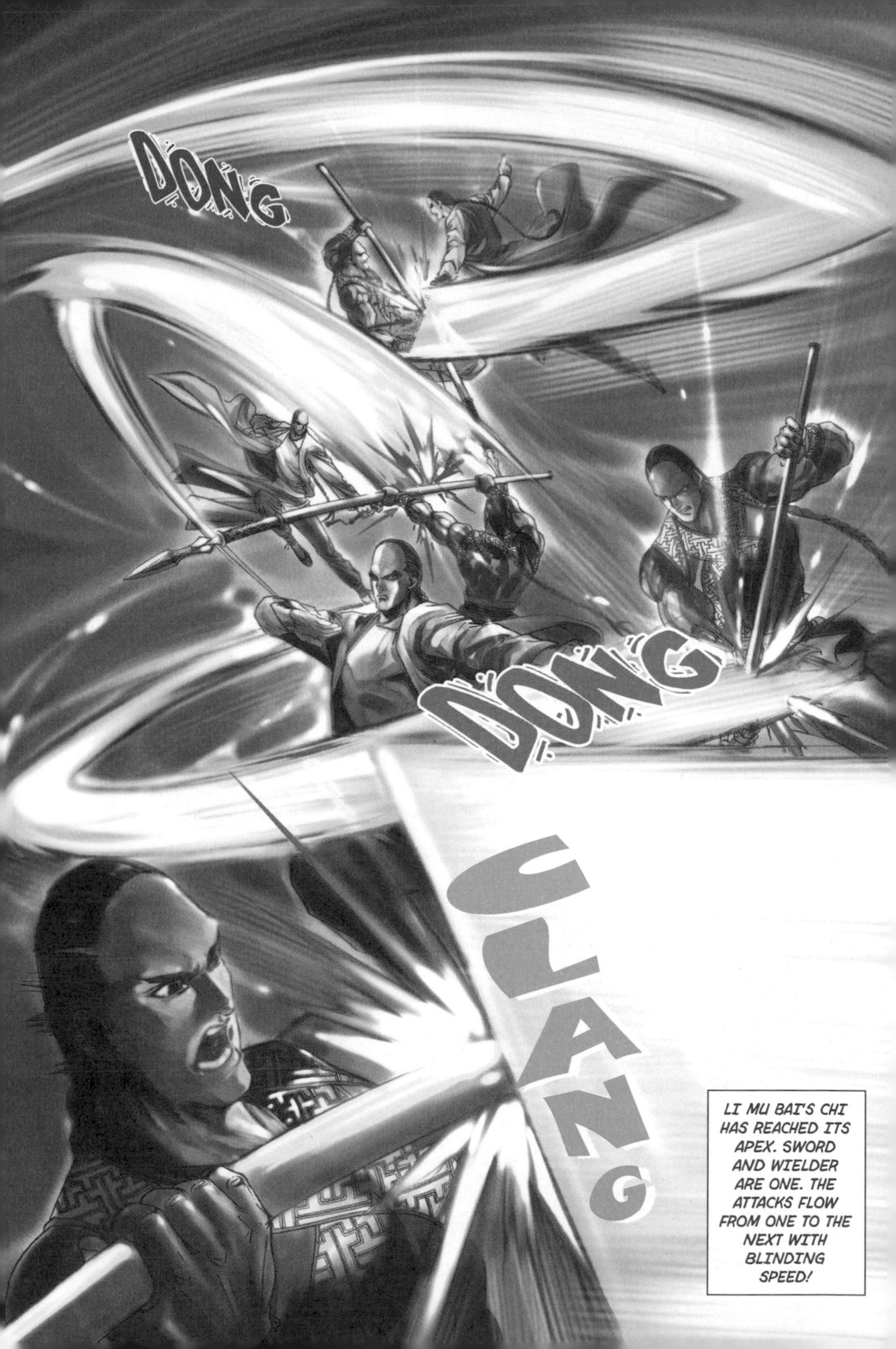
DONG
DONG
CLANG
LI MU BAI'S CHI HAS REACHED ITS APEX. SWORD AND WIELDER ARE ONE. THE ATTACKS FLOW FROM ONE TO THE NEXT WITH BLINDING SPEED!

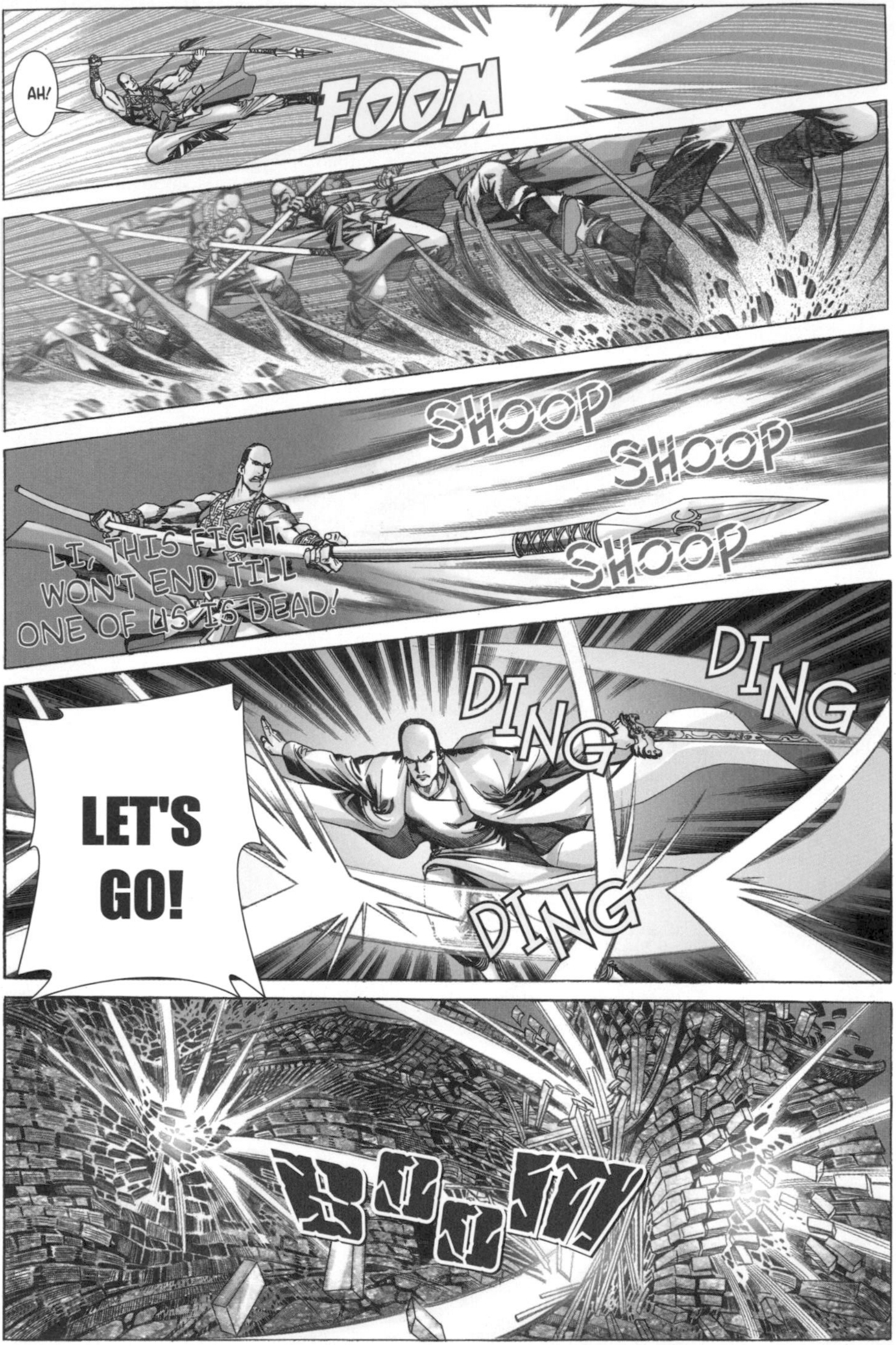
AH!
FOOM
SHOOP
SHOOP
SHOOP
LI, THIS FIGHT WON'T END TILL ONE OF US IS DEAD!
DING
DING
DING
LET'S GO!

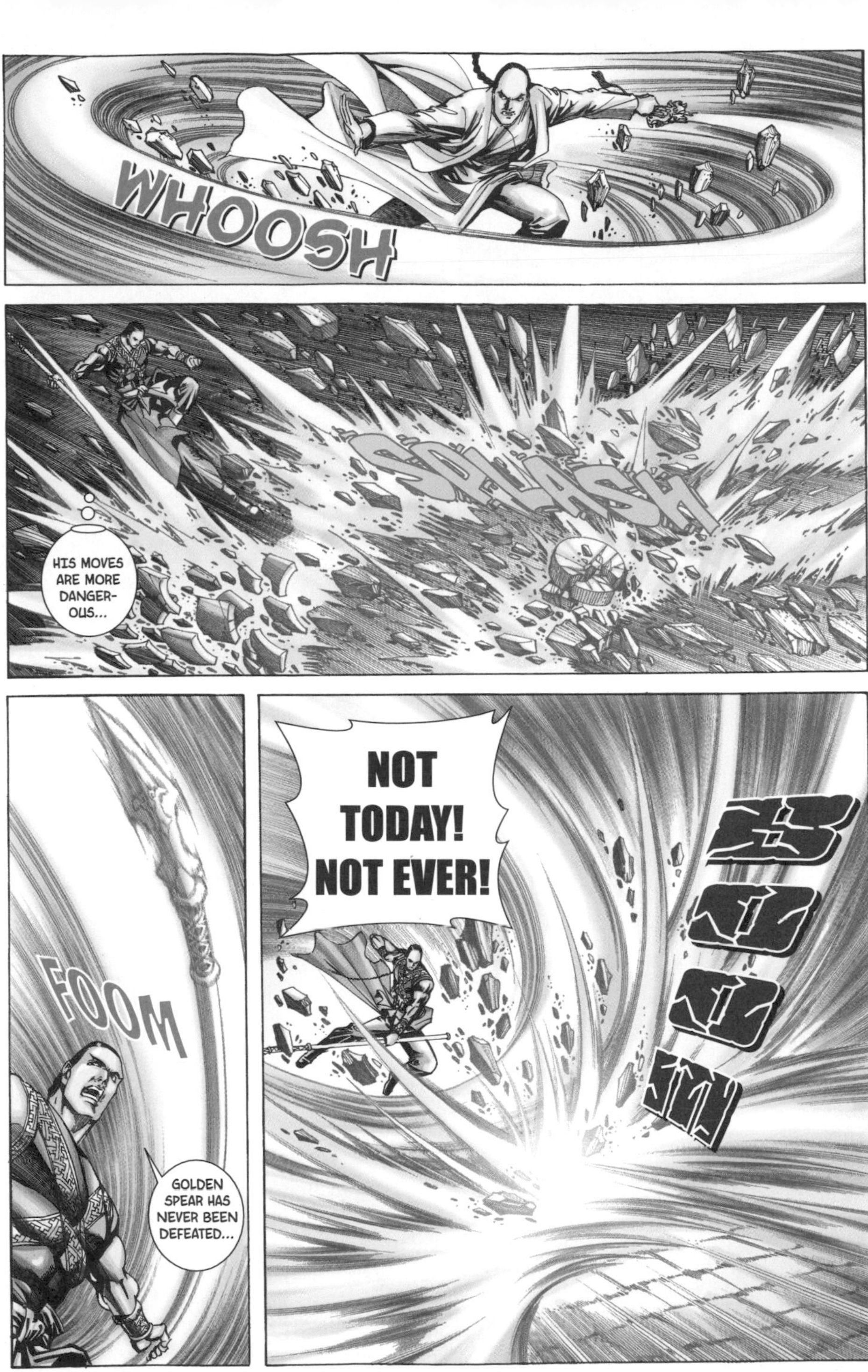
WHOOSH
SPLASH
HIS MOVES ARE MORE DANGER-OUS...
FOOM
GOLDEN SPEAR HAS NEVER BEEN DEFEATED...
NOT TODAY! NOT EVER!

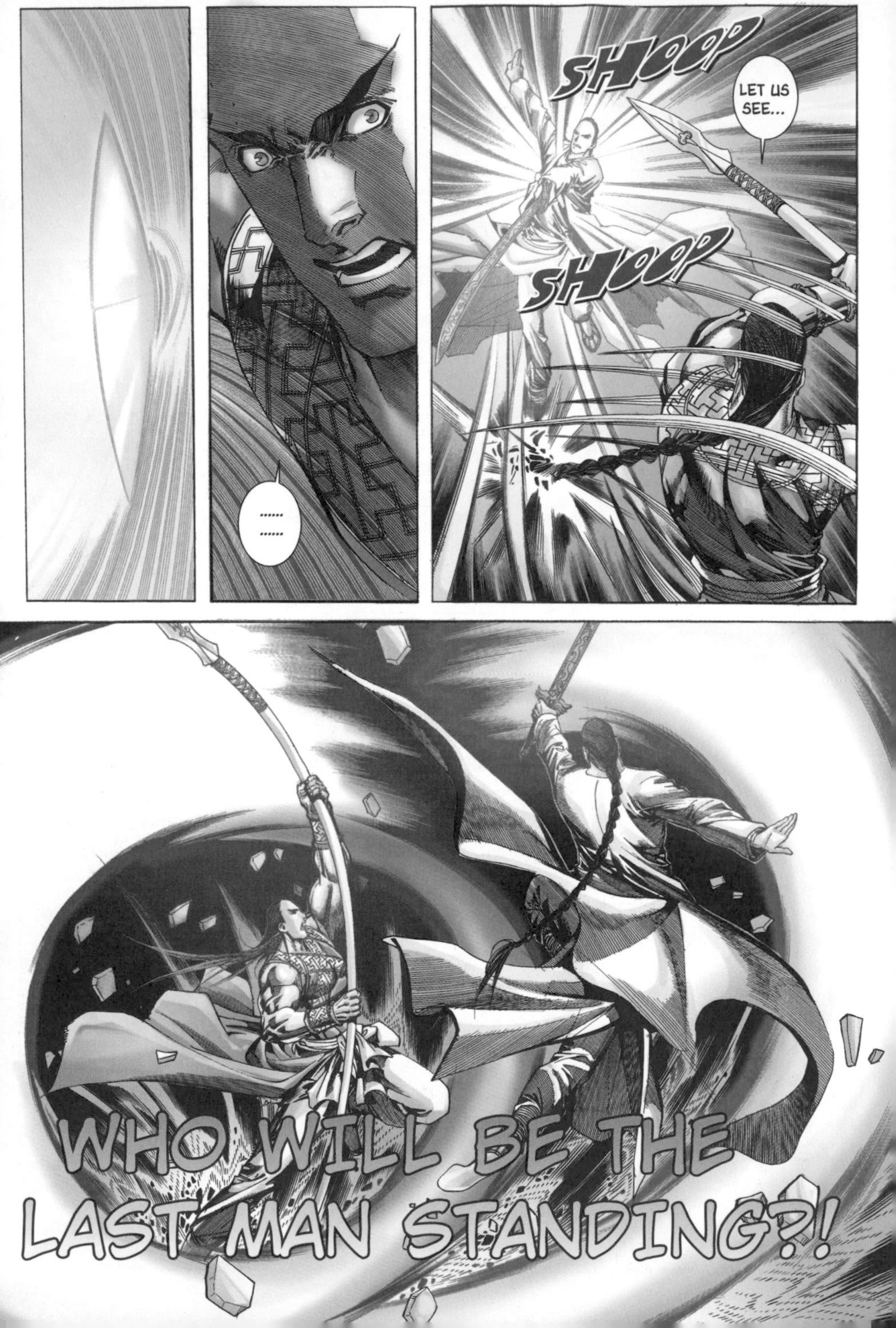
......
......
SHOOP
SHOOP
LET US SEE...
WHO WILL BE THE LAST MAN STANDING?!

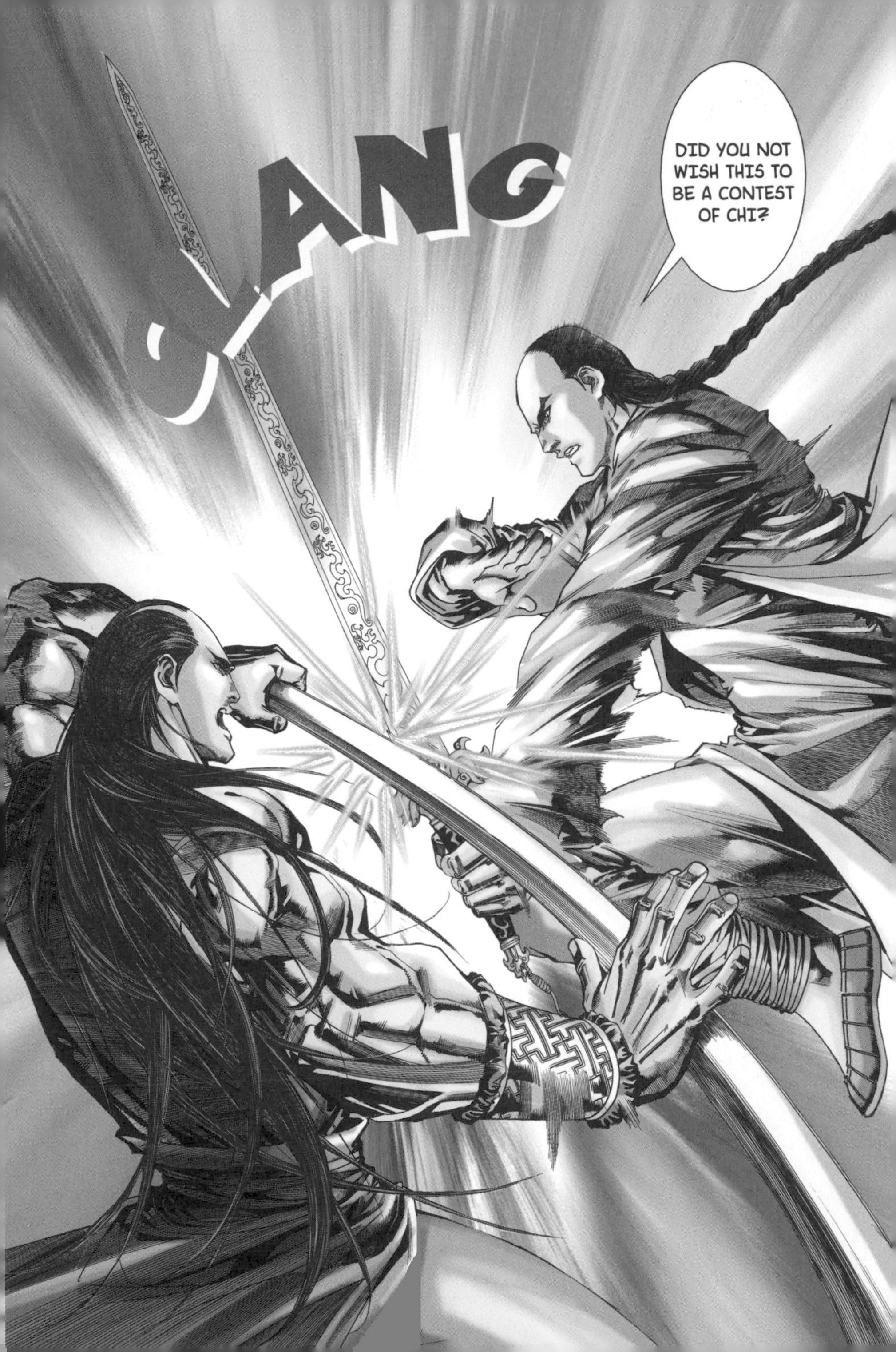
CLANG
DID YOU NOT WISH THIS TO BE A CONTEST OF CHI?

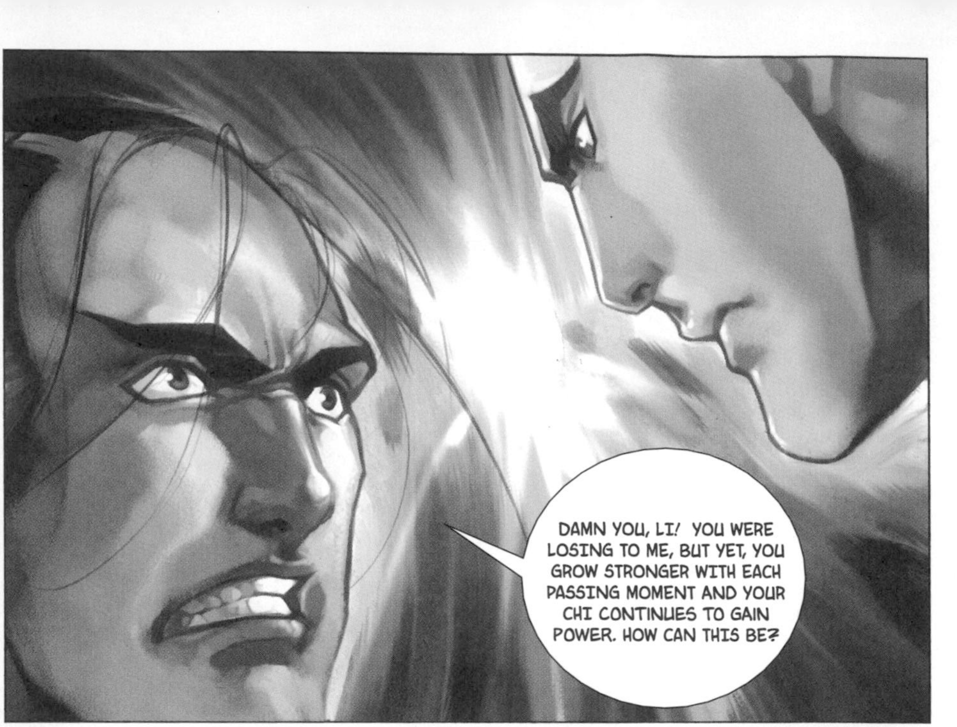
DAMN YOU, LI! YOU WERE LOSING TO ME, BUT YET, YOU GROW STRONGER WITH EACH PASSING MOMENT AND YOUR CHI CONTINUES TO GAIN POWER. HOW CAN THIS BE?

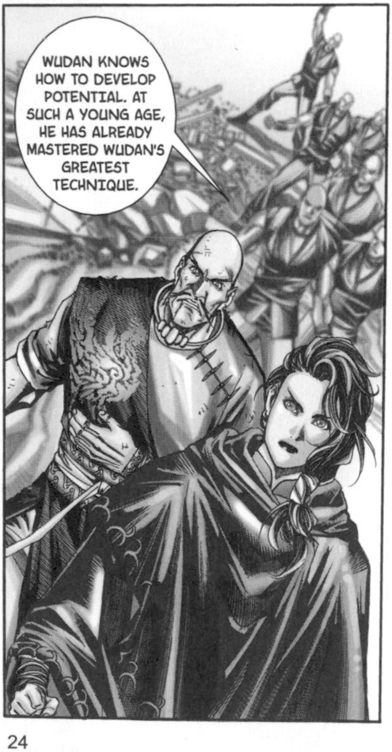
WUDAN KNOWS HOW TO DEVELOP POTENTIAL. AT SUCH A YOUNG AGE, HE HAS ALREADY MASTERED WUDAN'S GREATEST TECHNIQUE.

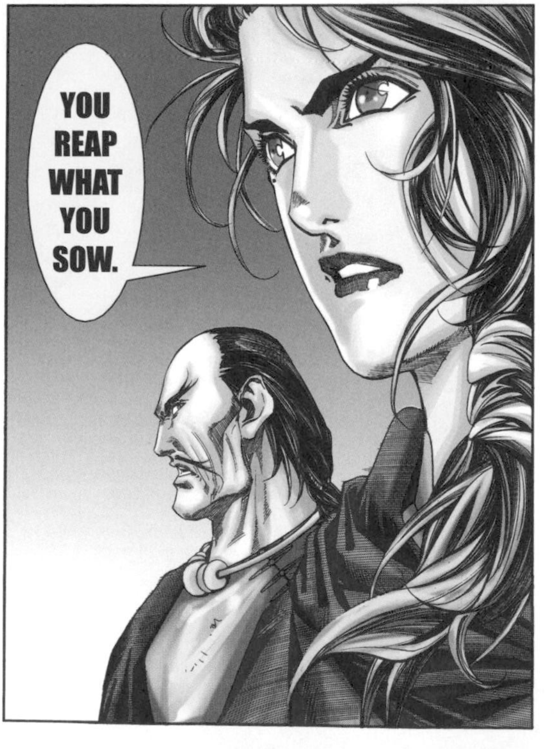
YOU REAP WHAT YOU SOW.

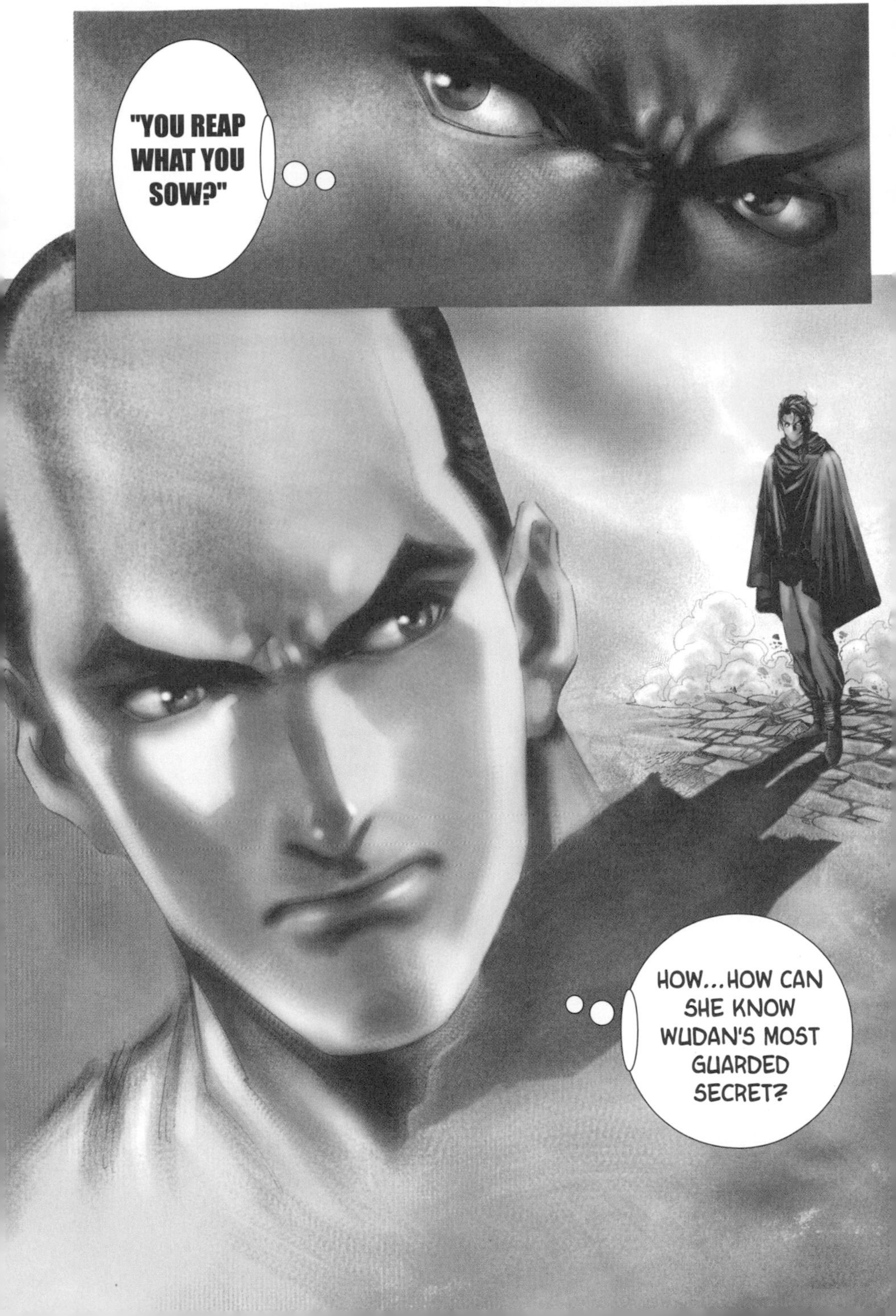
"YOU REAP WHAT YOU SOW?"
HOW...HOW CAN SHE KNOW WUDAN'S MOST GUARDED SECRET?

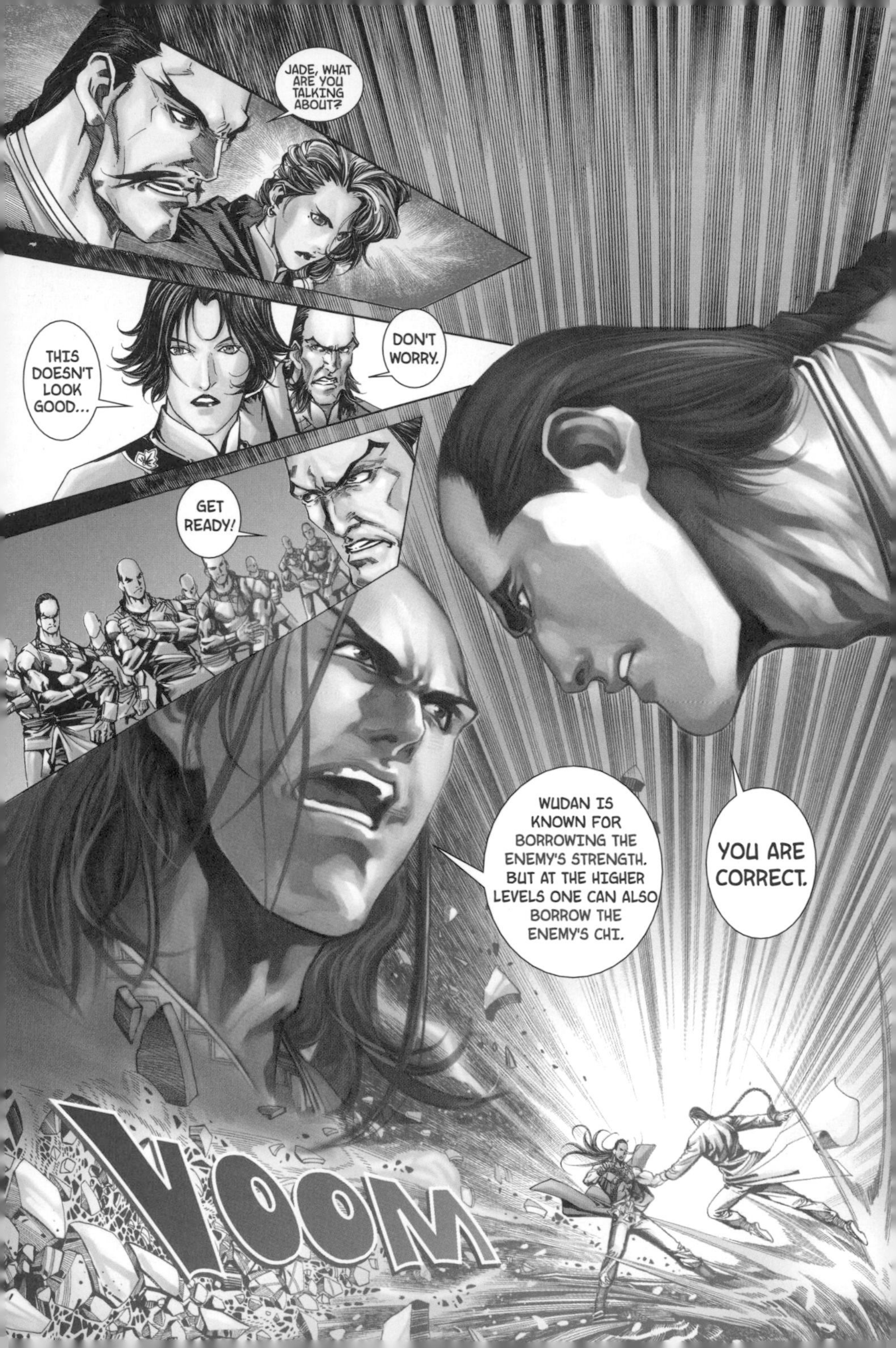
JADE, WHAT ARE YOU TALKING ABOUT?
THIS DOESN'T LOOK GOOD...
DON'T WORRY.
GET READY!
WUDAN IS KNOWN FOR BORROWING THE ENEMY'S STRENGTH. BUT AT THE HIGHER LEVELS ONE CAN ALSO BORROW THE ENEMY'S CHI.
YOU ARE CORRECT.
VOOM

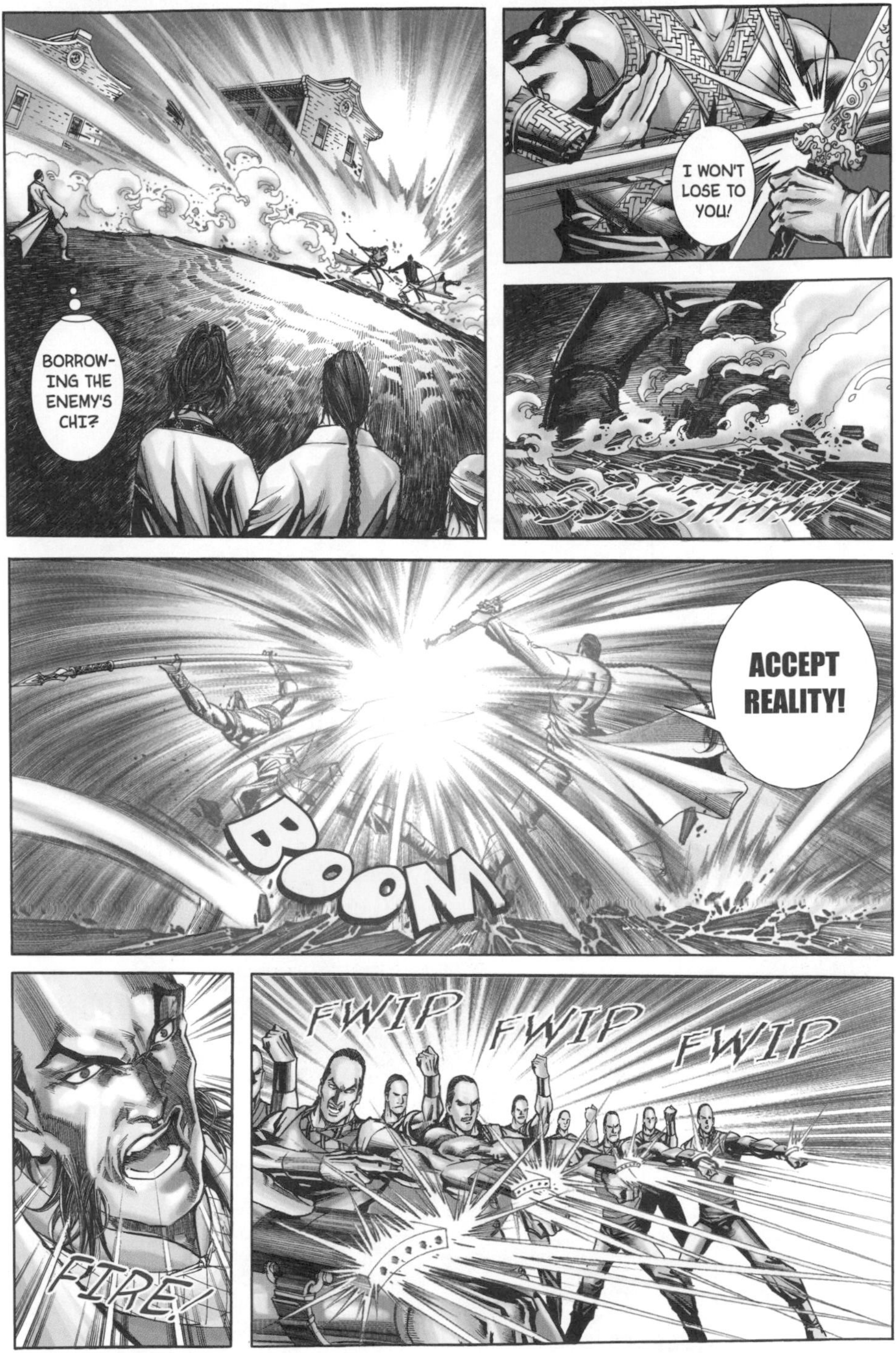
BORROWING THE ENEMY'S CHI?
I WON'T LOSE TO YOU!
ACCEPT REALITY!
BOOM
FIRE!
FWIP
FWIP
FWIP

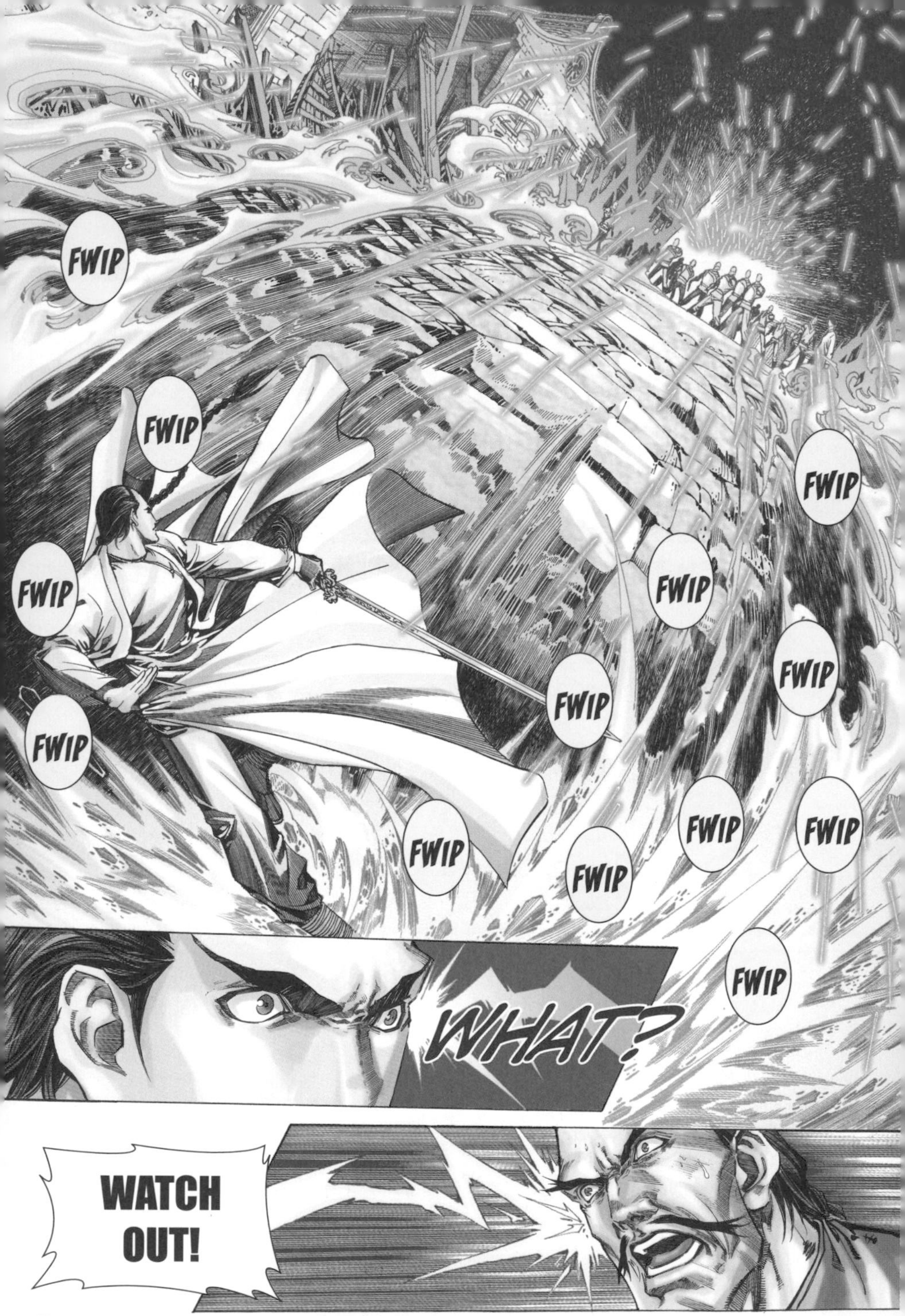
FWIP
FWIP
FWIP
FWIP
FWIP
FWIP
FWIP
FWIP
FWIP
FWIP
FWIP
FWIP
FWIP
WHAT?
WATCH OUT!

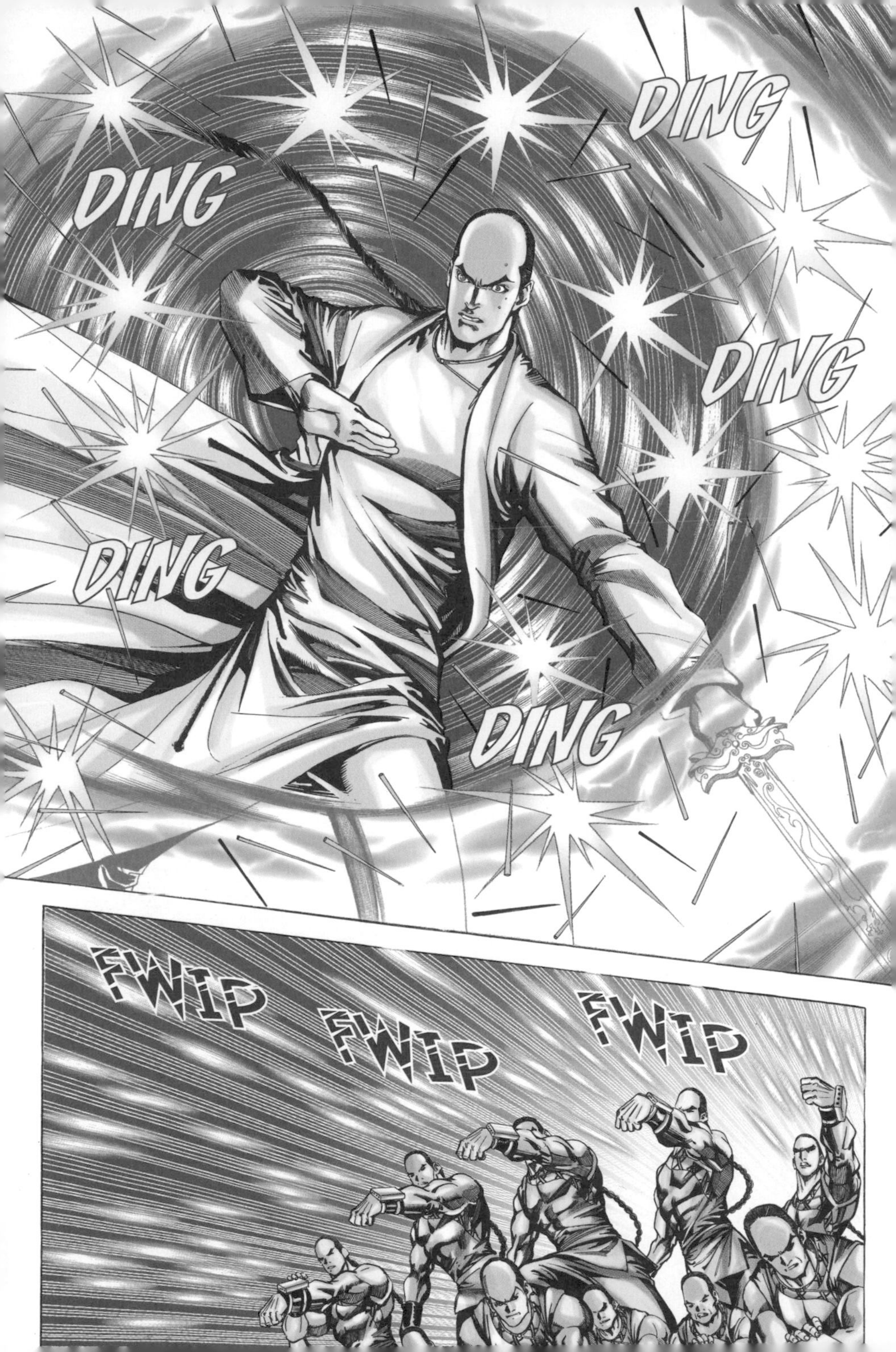
DING
DING
DING
DING
DING
FWIP
FWIP
FWIP

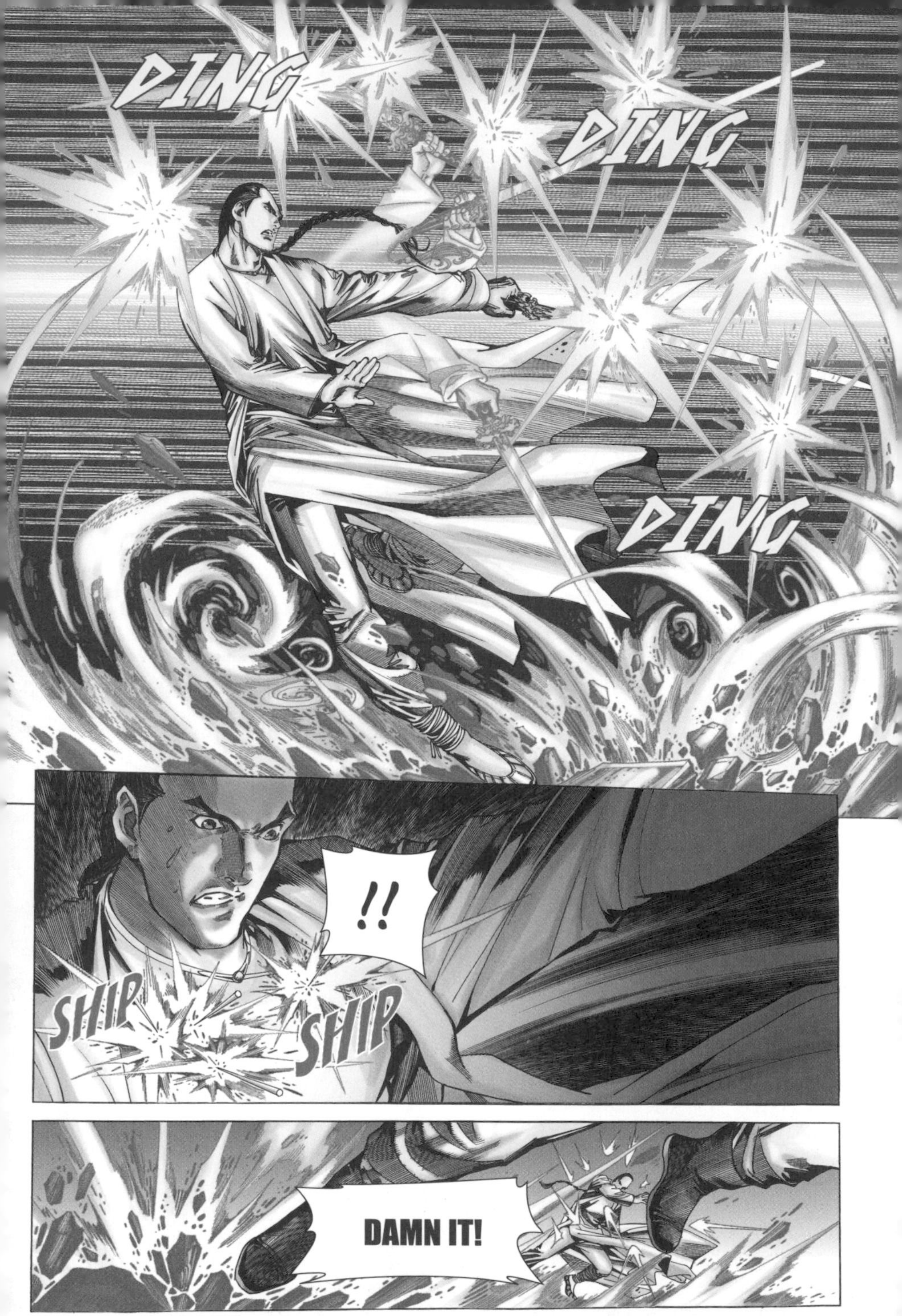
DING
DING
DING
!!
SHIP
SHIP
DAMN IT!

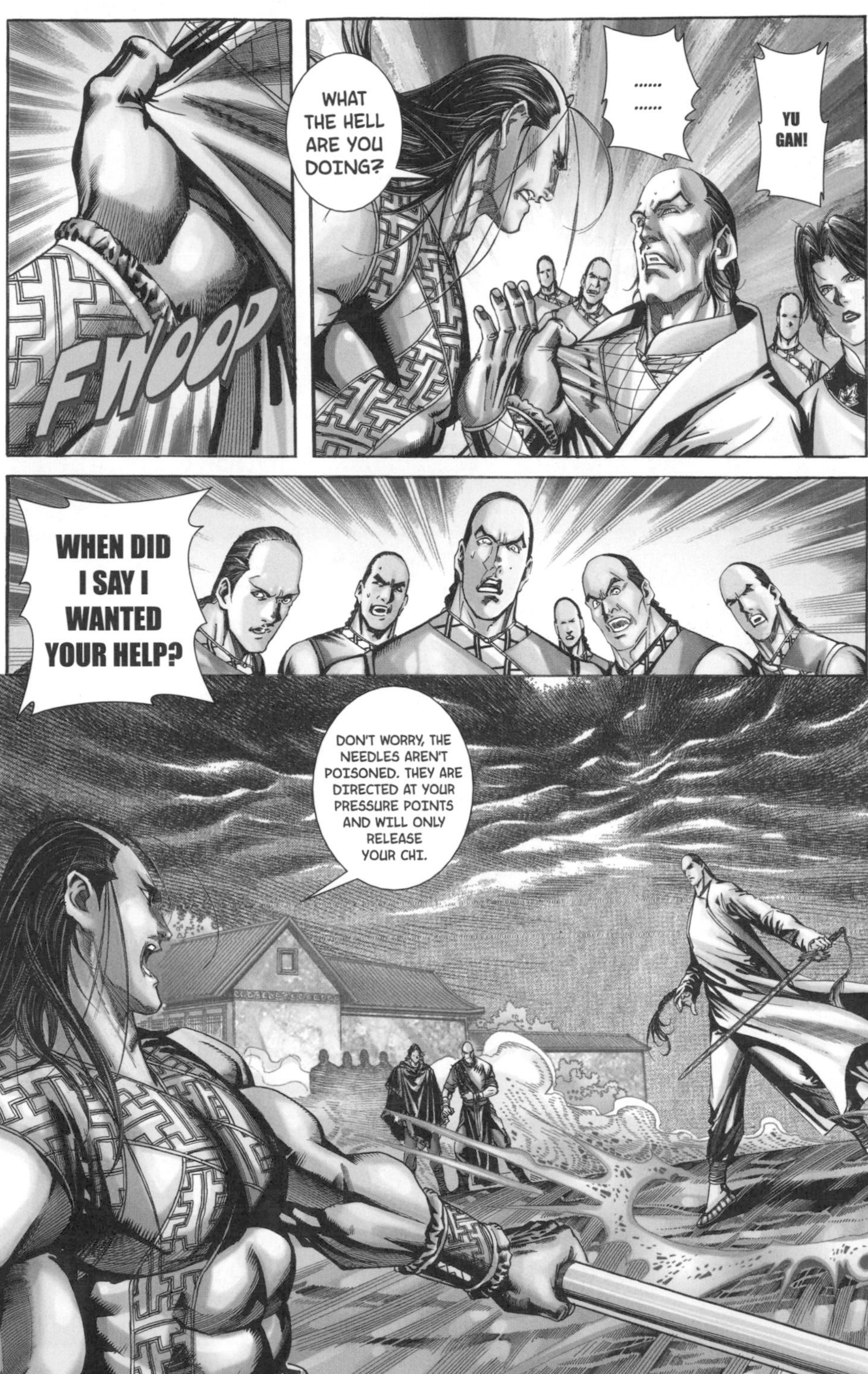
FWOOP
WHAT THE HELL ARE YOU DOING?
......
......
YU GAN!
WHEN DID I SAY I WANTED YOUR HELP?
DON'T WORRY, THE NEEDLES AREN'T POISONED. THEY ARE DIRECTED AT YOUR PRESSURE POINTS AND WILL ONLY RELEASE YOUR CHI.

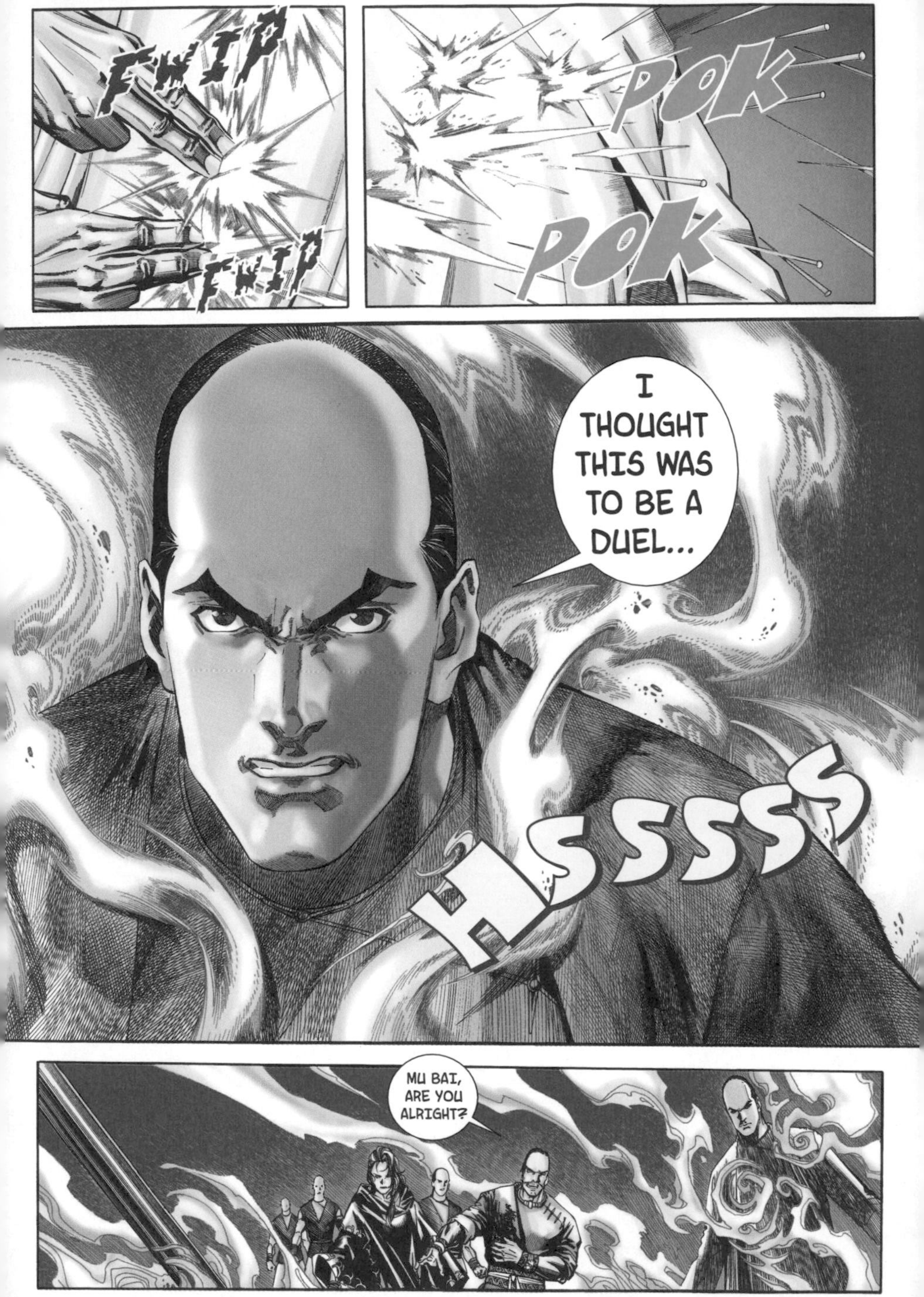
FWIP
FWIP
POK
POK
I THOUGHT THIS WAS TO BE A DUEL...
HSSSSS
MU BAI, ARE YOU ALRIGHT?

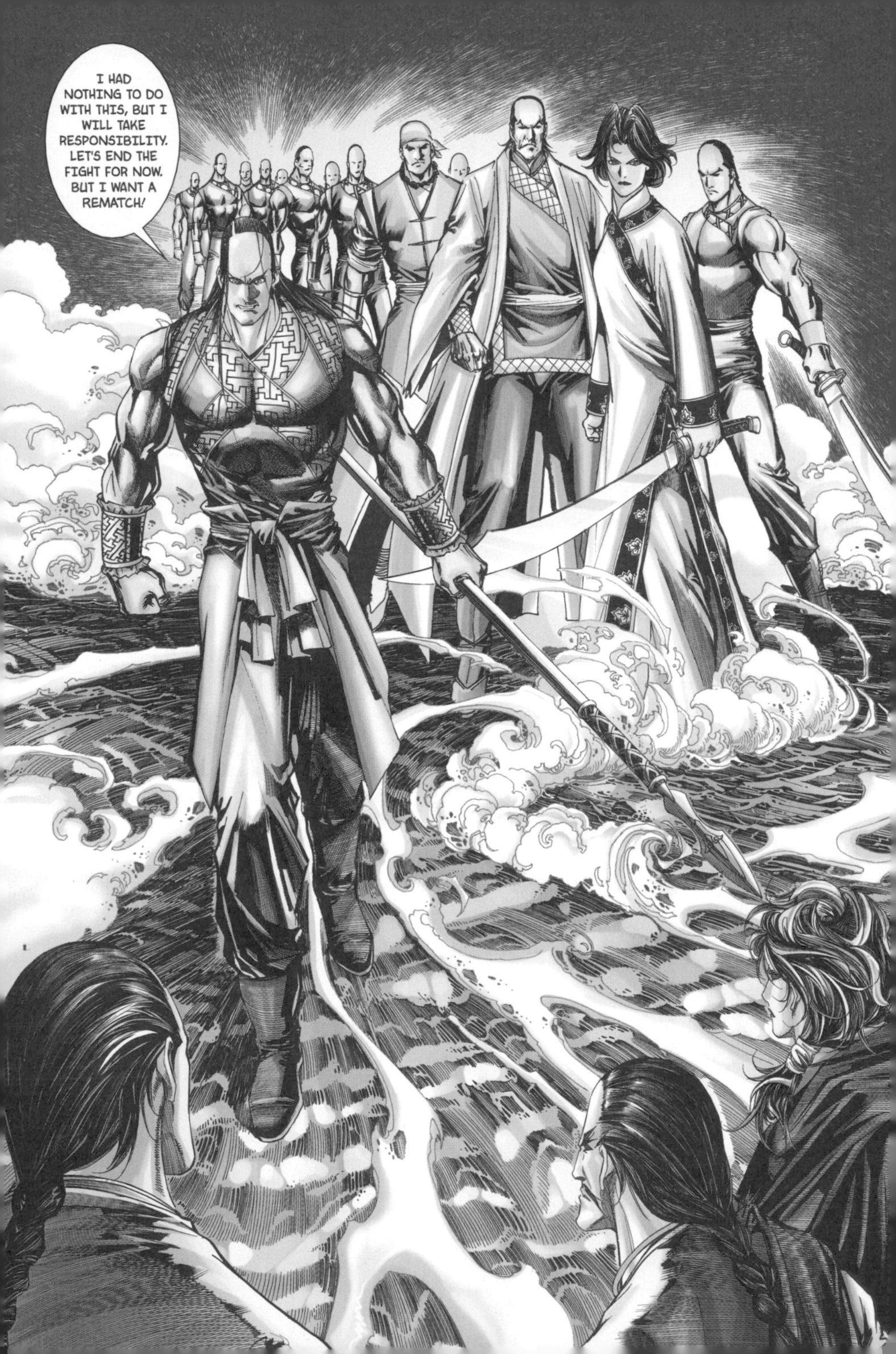
I HAD NOTHING TO DO WITH THIS, BUT I WILL TAKE RESPONSIBILITY. LET'S END THE FIGHT FOR NOW. BUT I WANT A REMATCH!

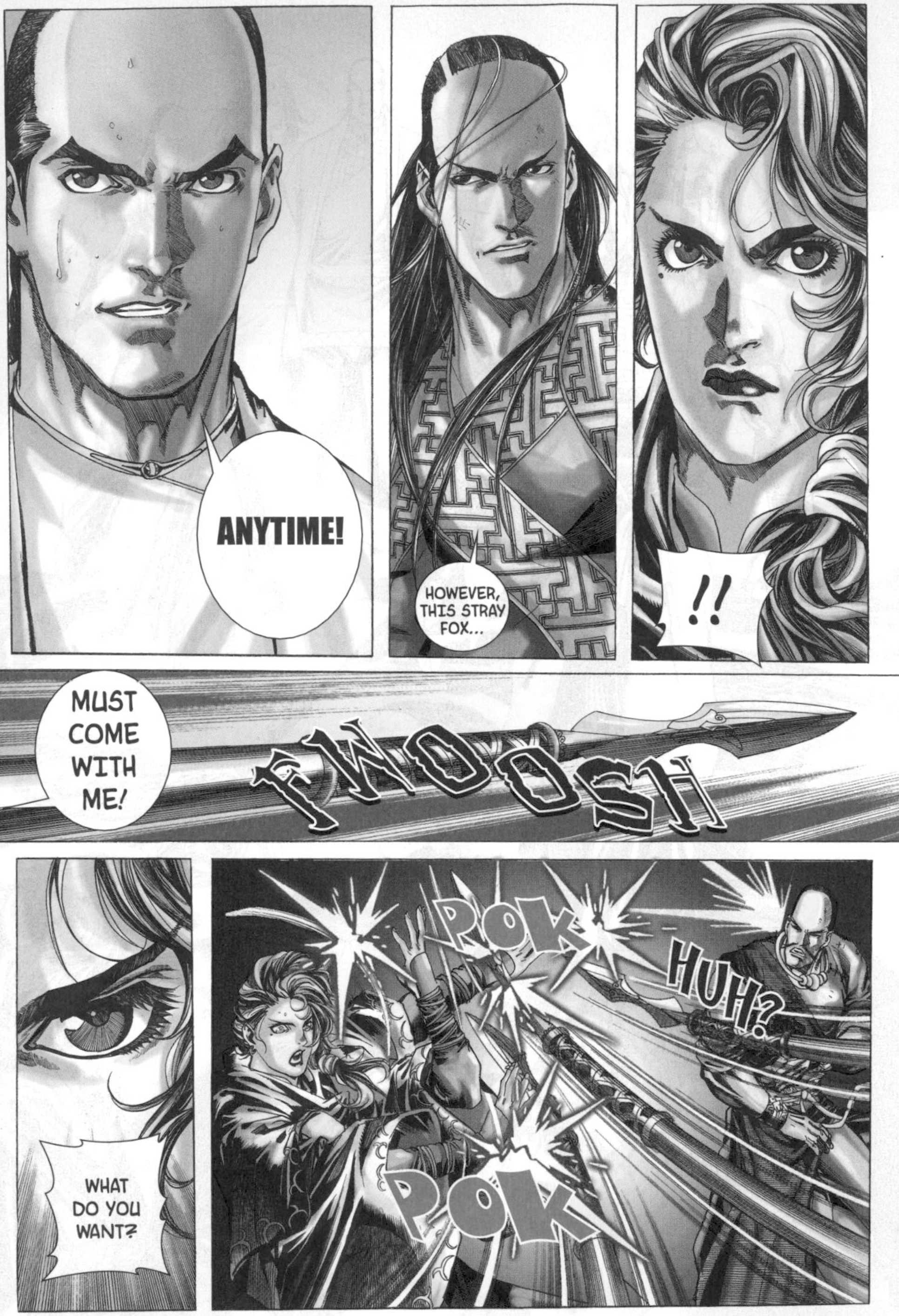
ANYTIME!
HOWEVER, THIS STRAY FOX...
!!
MUST COME WITH ME!
FWOOSH
WHAT DO YOU WANT?
POK
HUH?
POK

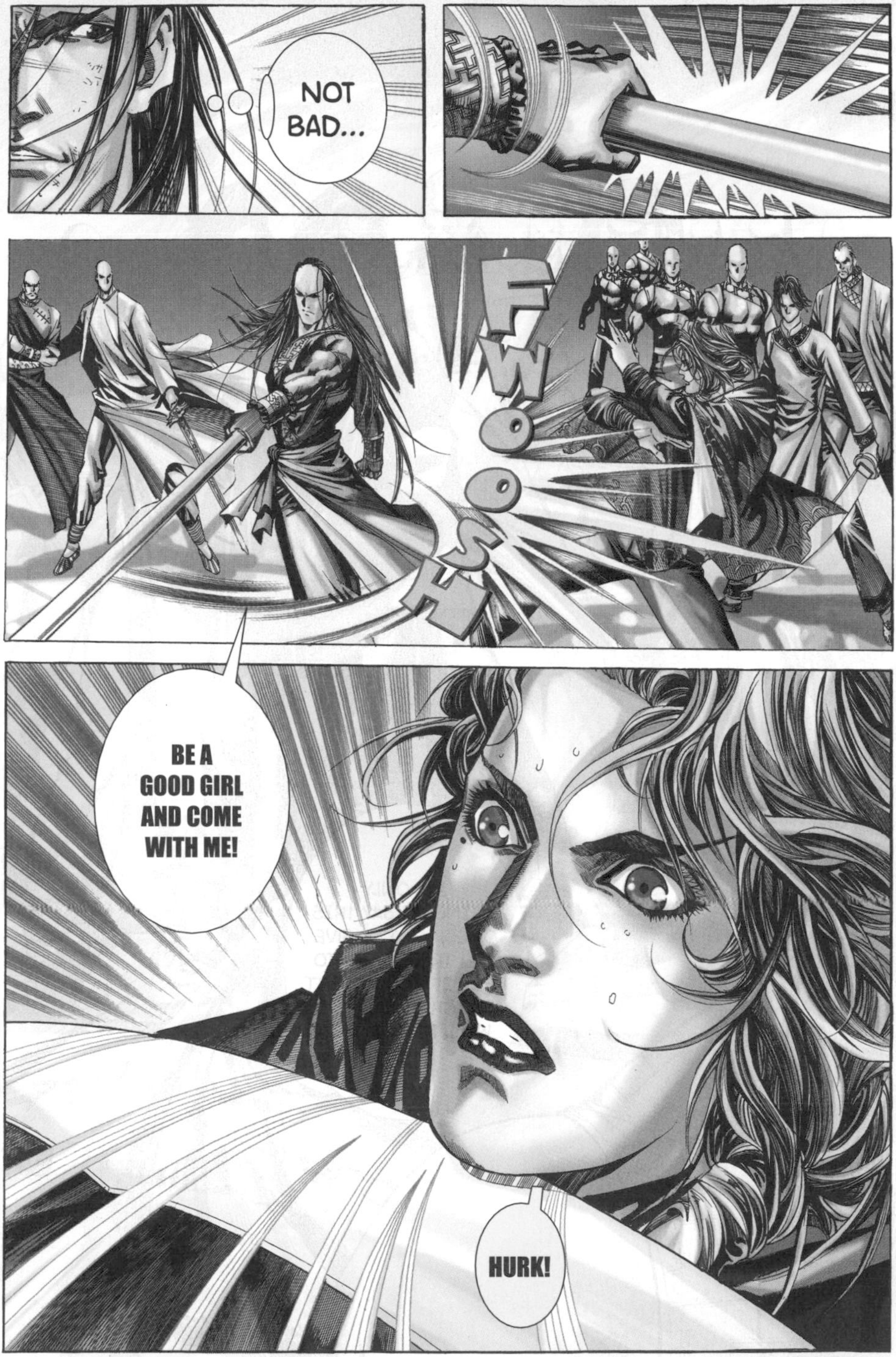
NOT BAD...
FWOOSH
BE A GOOD GIRL AND COME WITH ME!
HURK!

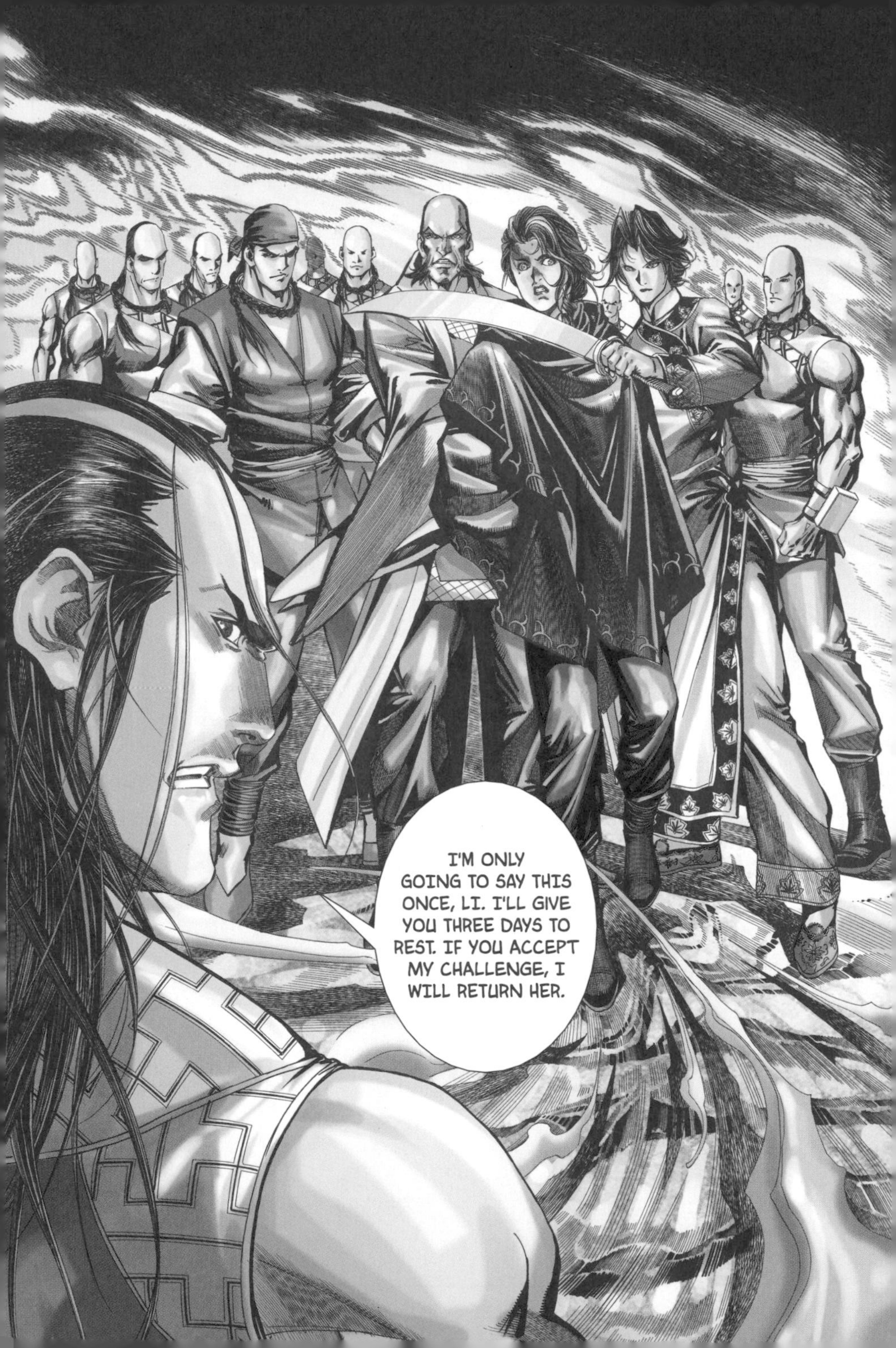
I'M ONLY GOING TO SAY THIS ONCE, LI. I'LL GIVE YOU THREE DAYS TO REST. IF YOU ACCEPT MY CHALLENGE, I WILL RETURN HER.

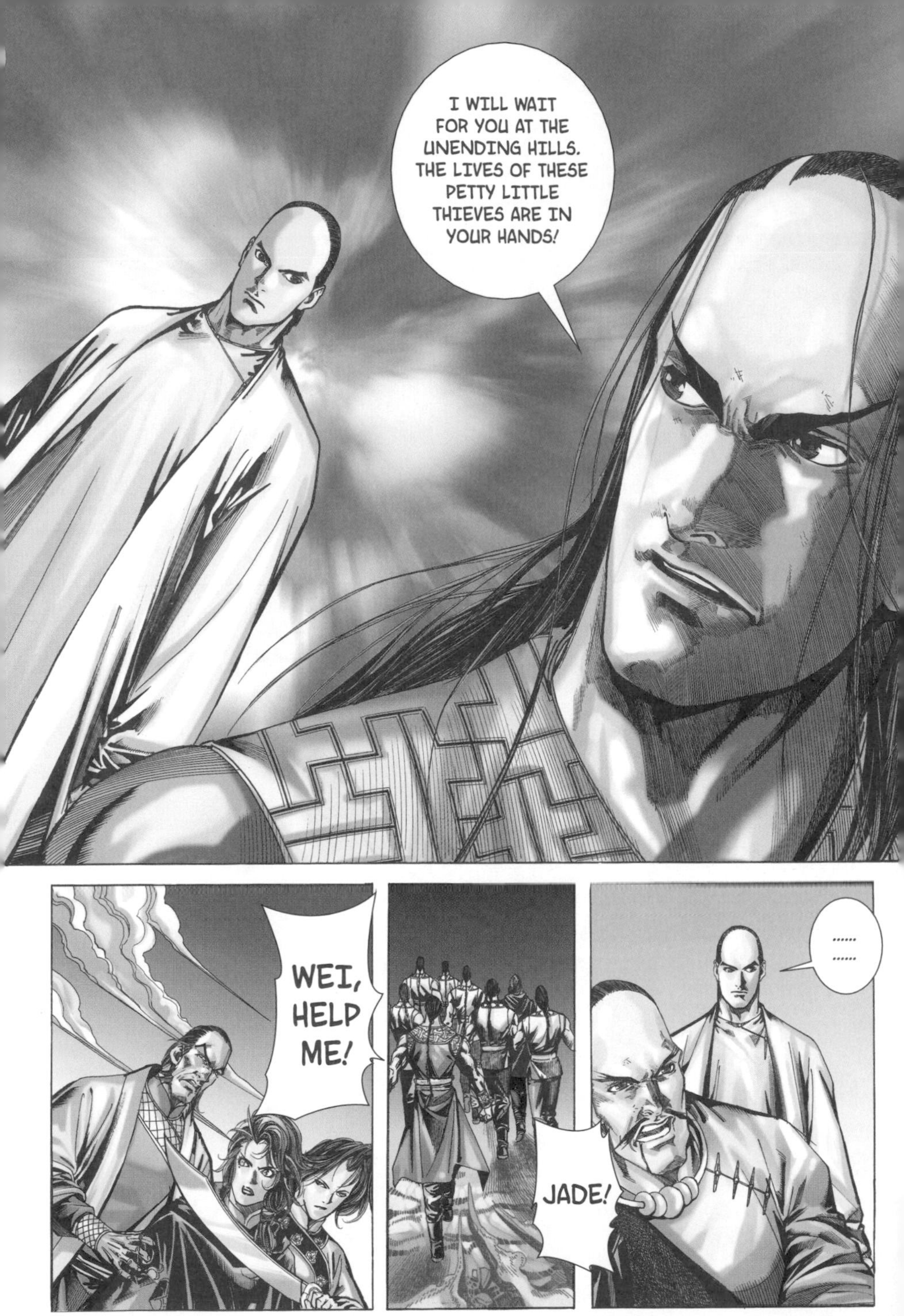
I WILL WAIT FOR YOU AT THE UNENDING HILLS. THE LIVES OF THESE PETTY LITTLE THIEVES ARE IN YOUR HANDS!
WEI, HELP ME!
......
......
JADE!

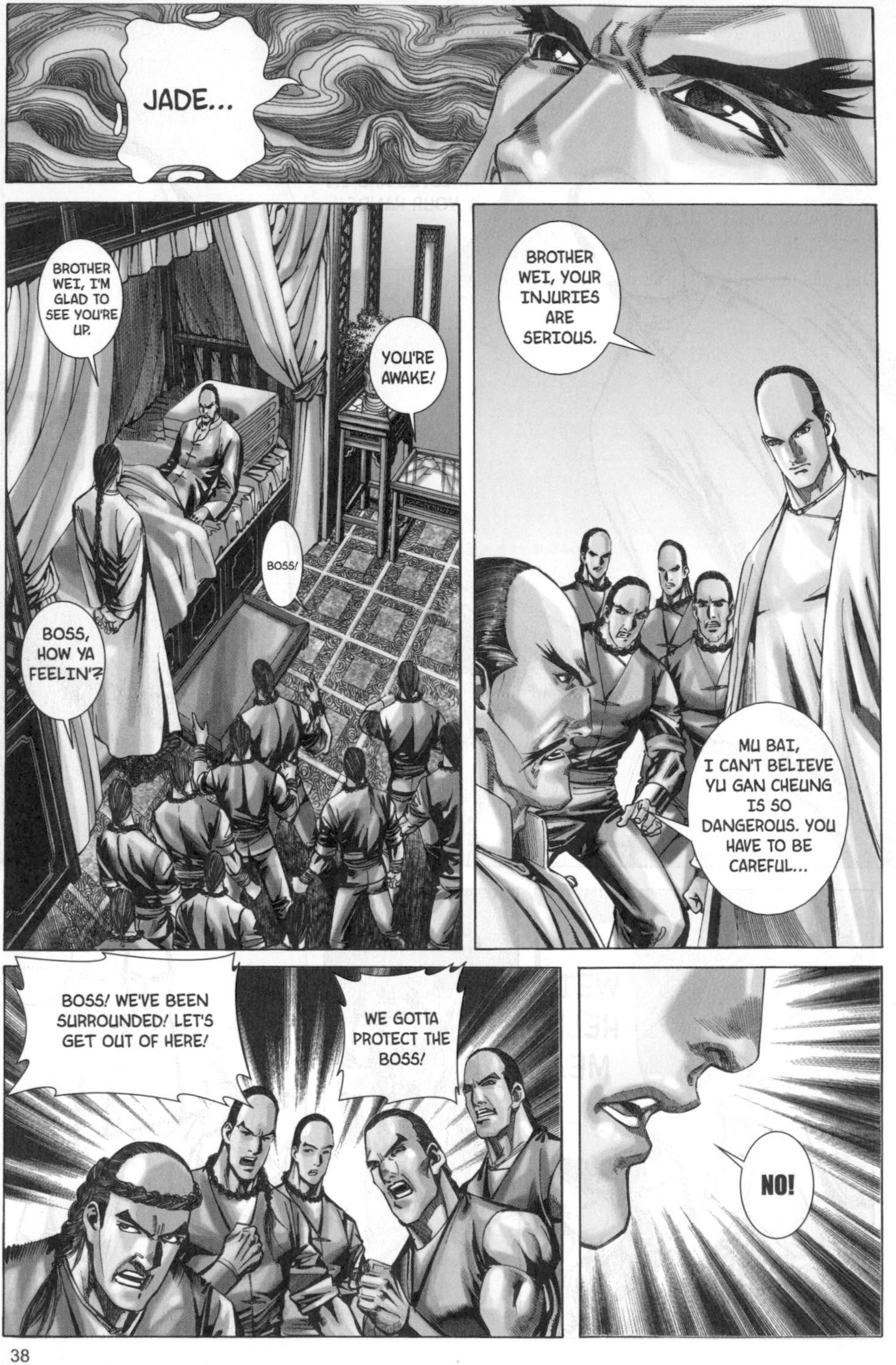
JADE...
BROTHER WEI, I'M GLAD TO SEE YOU'RE UP.
YOU'RE AWAKE!
BOSS!
BOSS, HOW YA FEELIN'?
BROTHER WEI, YOUR INJURIES ARE SERIOUS.
MU BAI, I CAN'T BELIEVE YU GAN CHEUNG IS SO DANGEROUS. YOU HAVE TO BE CAREFUL...
BOSS! WE'VE BEEN SURROUNDED! LET'S GET OUT OF HERE!
WE GOTTA PROTECT THE BOSS!
NO!

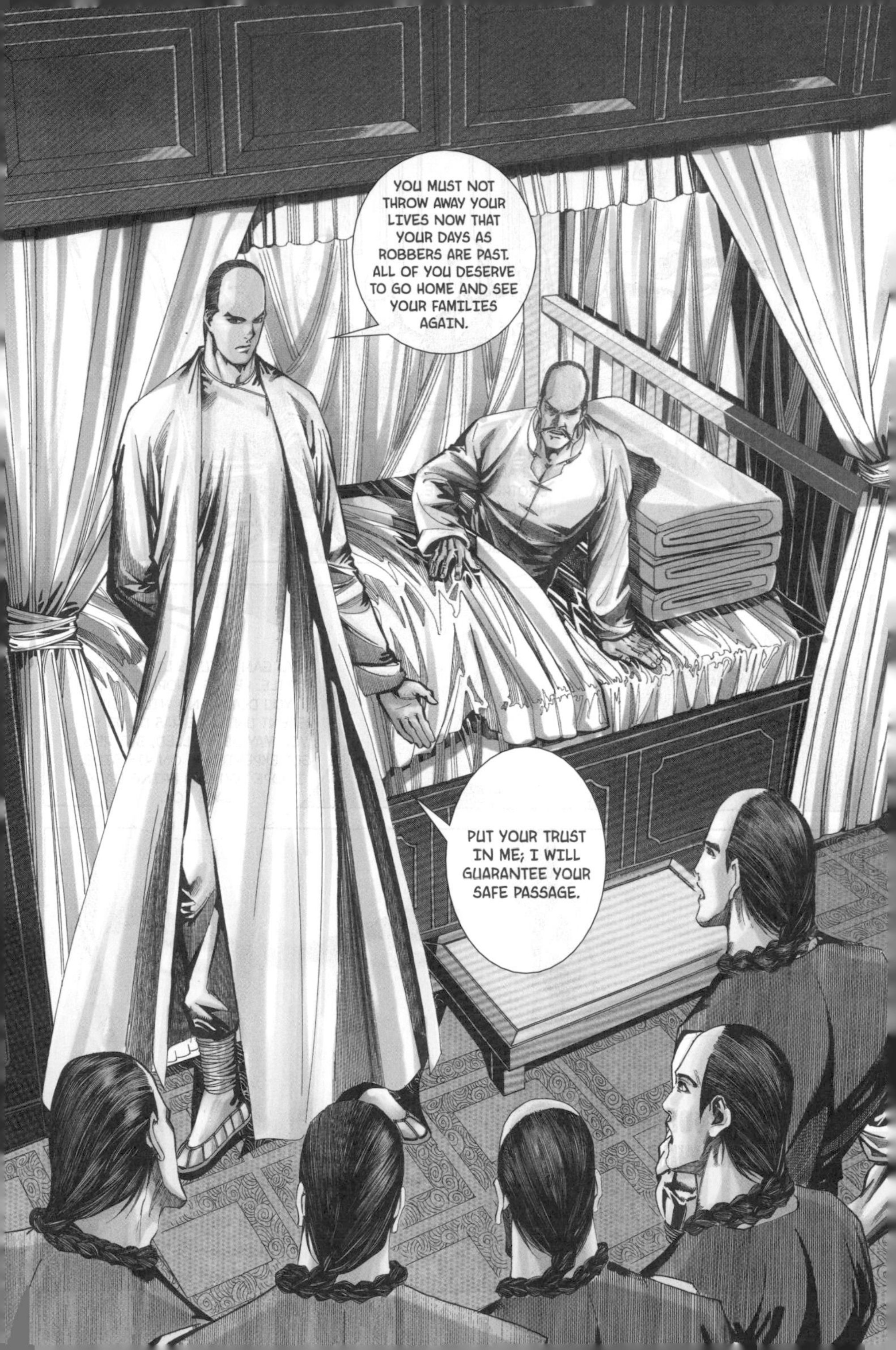
YOU MUST NOT THROW AWAY YOUR LIVES NOW THAT YOUR DAYS AS ROBBERS ARE PAST. ALL OF YOU DESERVE TO GO HOME AND SEE YOUR FAMILIES AGAIN.
PUT YOUR TRUST IN ME; I WILL GUARANTEE YOUR SAFE PASSAGE.

MU BAI IS RIGHT. YOU ALL ARE LIKE BROTHERS TO ME. HAVE FAITH IN HIM, HE'LL SEE US THROUGH THIS.

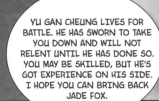

YU GAN CHEUNG LIVES FOR BATTLE. HE HAS SWORN TO TAKE YOU DOWN AND WILL NOT RELENT UNTIL HE HAS DONE SO. YOU MAY BE SKILLED, BUT HE'S GOT EXPERIENCE ON HIS SIDE. I HOPE YOU CAN BRING BACK JADE FOX.

DON'T WORRY. I WILL WIN!

THE GREEN DESTINY SWORD IS TRULY MAGNIFICENT, IT MOVES LIKE AN EXTENSION OF MY ARM...
HM! JADE FOX... HOW CAN SHE KNOW WUDAN'S MOST GUARDED SECRET?
ACCORDING TO RUMOR, ONE OF THE GRANDMASTER'S DISCIPLES, THE DEAF MASTER, HAD FALLEN IN LOVE WITH A WOMAN. HE LEFT WUDAN AND TOOK WITH HIM A SACRED RELIC OF WUDAN, "THE BOOK OF SACRED FORMS." NO ONE HAS HEARD FROM HIM SINCE. I WONDER IF JADE FOX IS LINKED TO HIM!

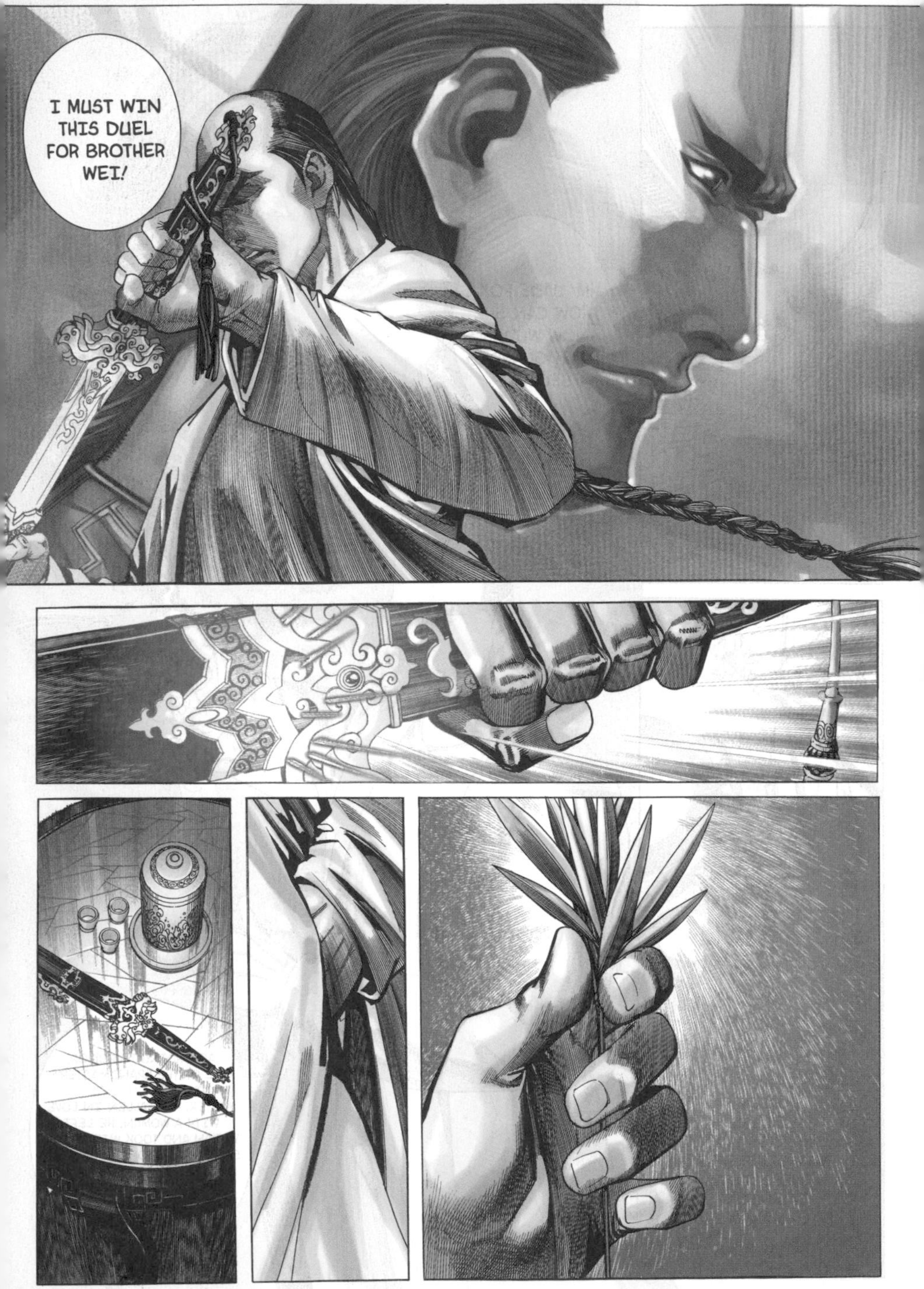
I MUST WIN THIS DUEL FOR BROTHER WEI!

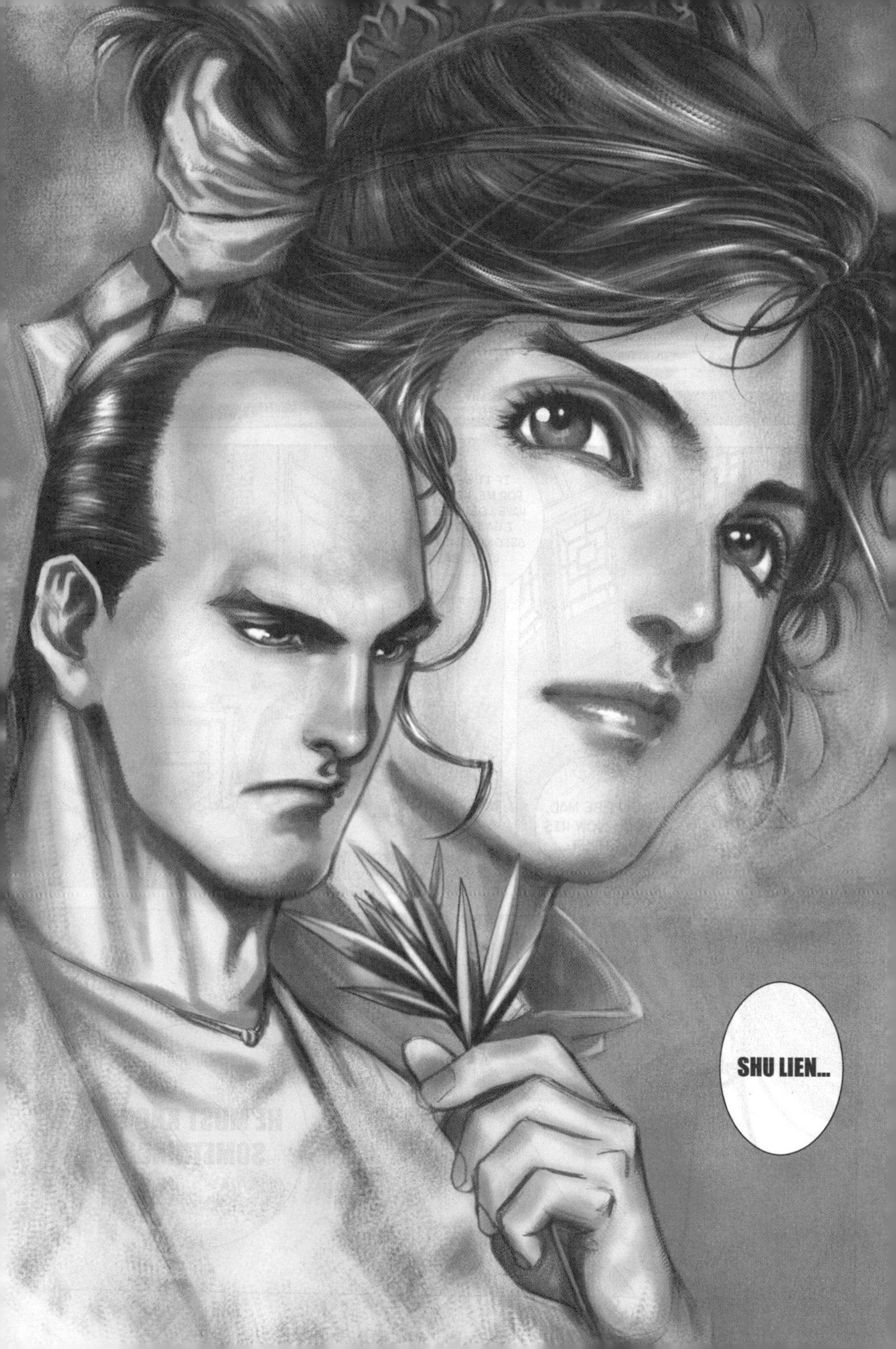
SHU LIEN...

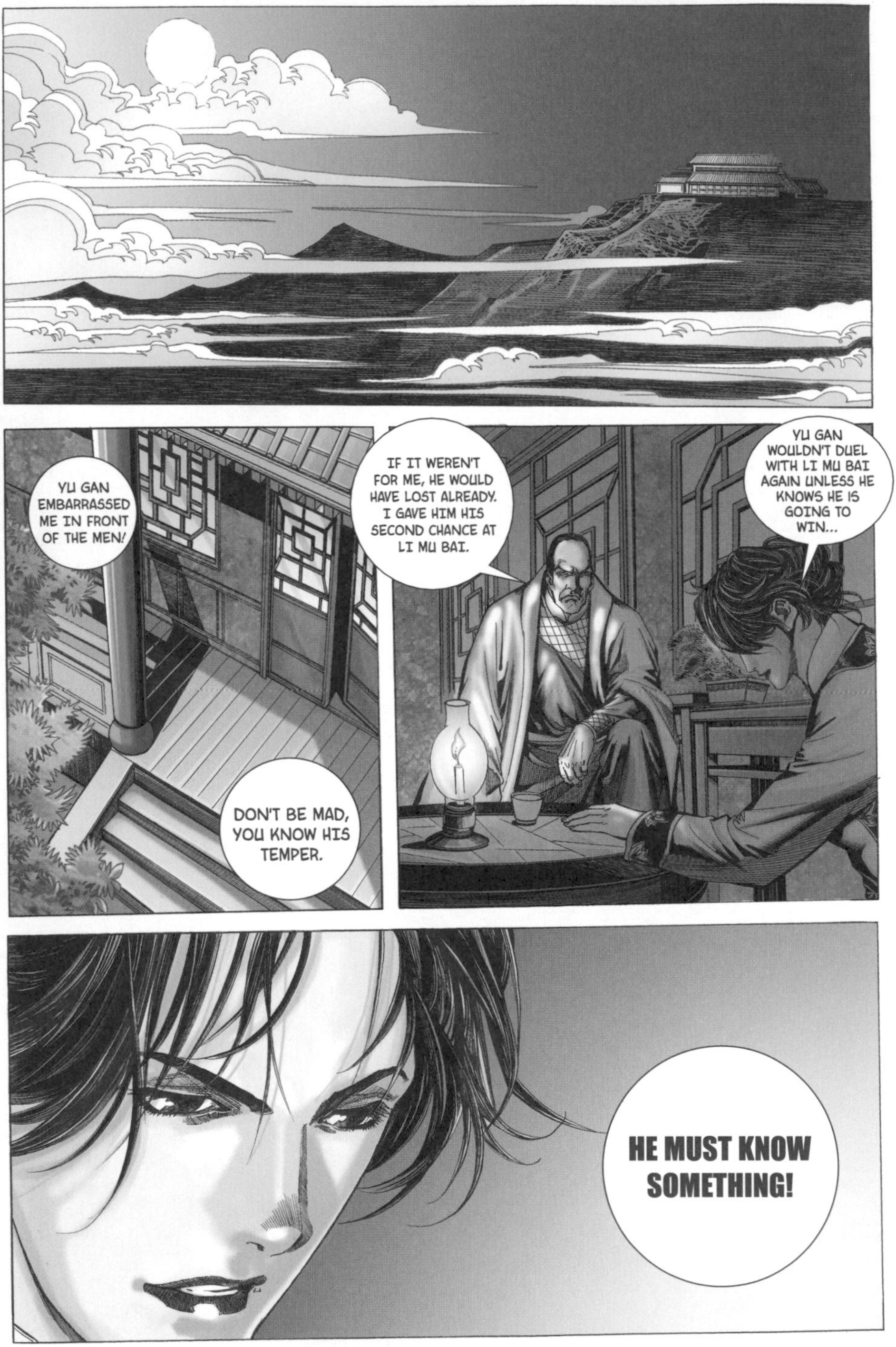
YU GAN EMBARRASSED ME IN FRONT OF THE MEN!
DON'T BE MAD, YOU KNOW HIS TEMPER.
IF IT WEREN'T FOR ME, HE WOULD HAVE LOST ALREADY. I GAVE HIM HIS SECOND CHANCE AT LI MU BAI.
YU GAN WOULDN'T DUEL WITH LI MU BAI AGAIN UNLESS HE KNOWS HE IS GOING TO WIN...
HE MUST KNOW SOMETHING!

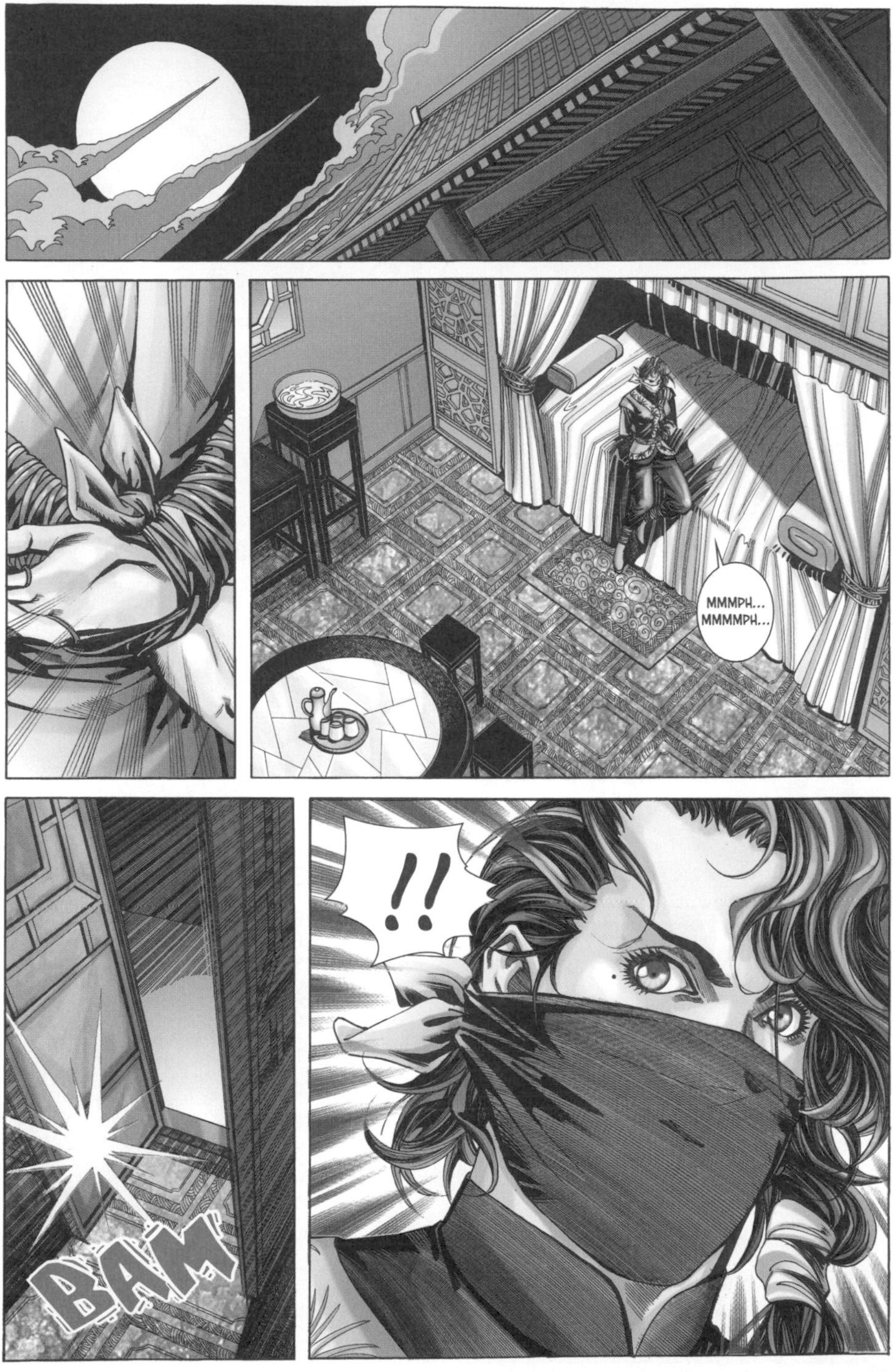
MMMPH...
MMMMPH...
!!
BAM

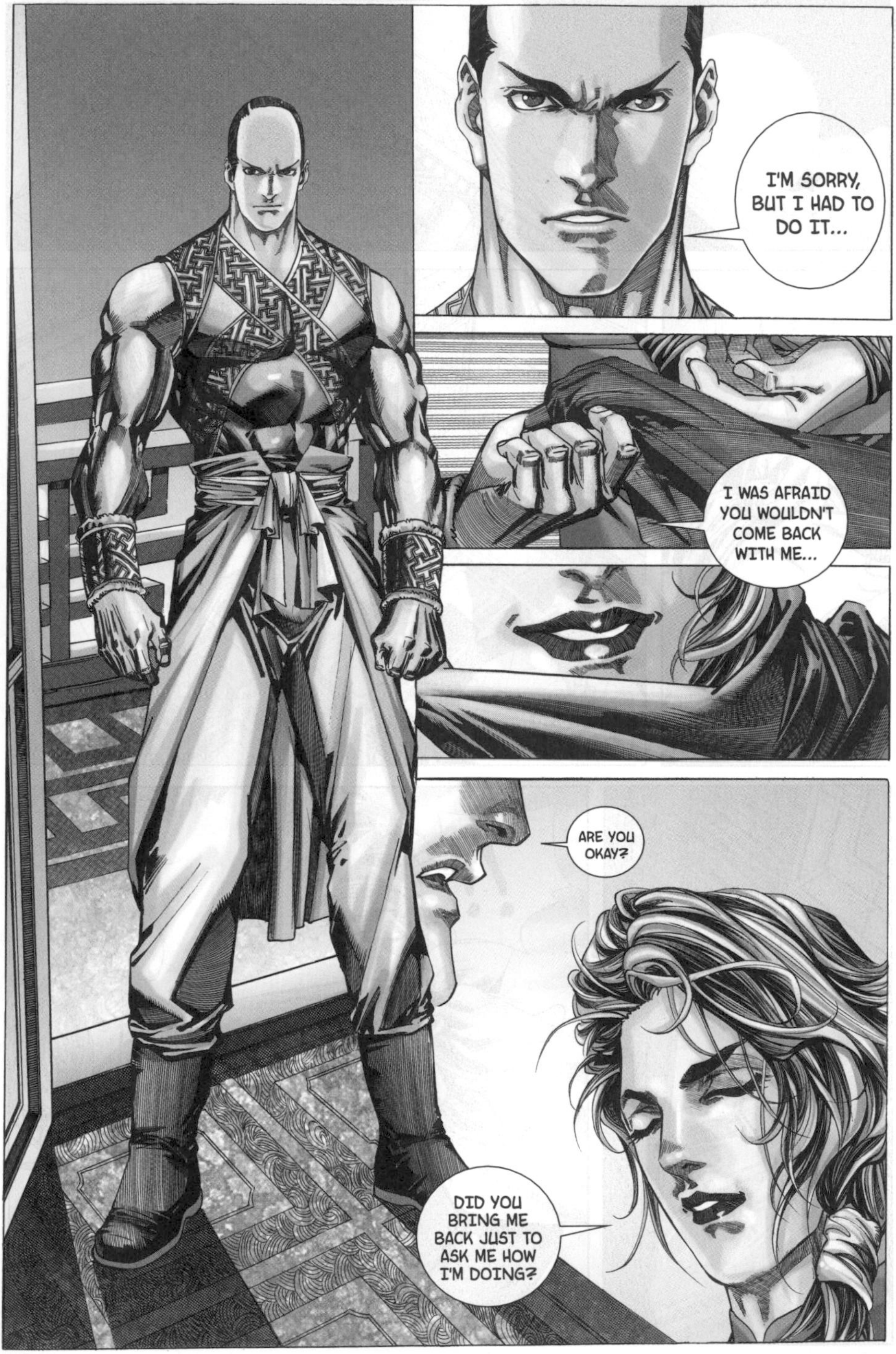
I'M SORRY, BUT I HAD TO DO IT...
I WAS AFRAID YOU WOULDN'T COME BACK WITH ME...
ARE YOU OKAY?
DID YOU BRING ME BACK JUST TO ASK ME HOW I'M DOING?

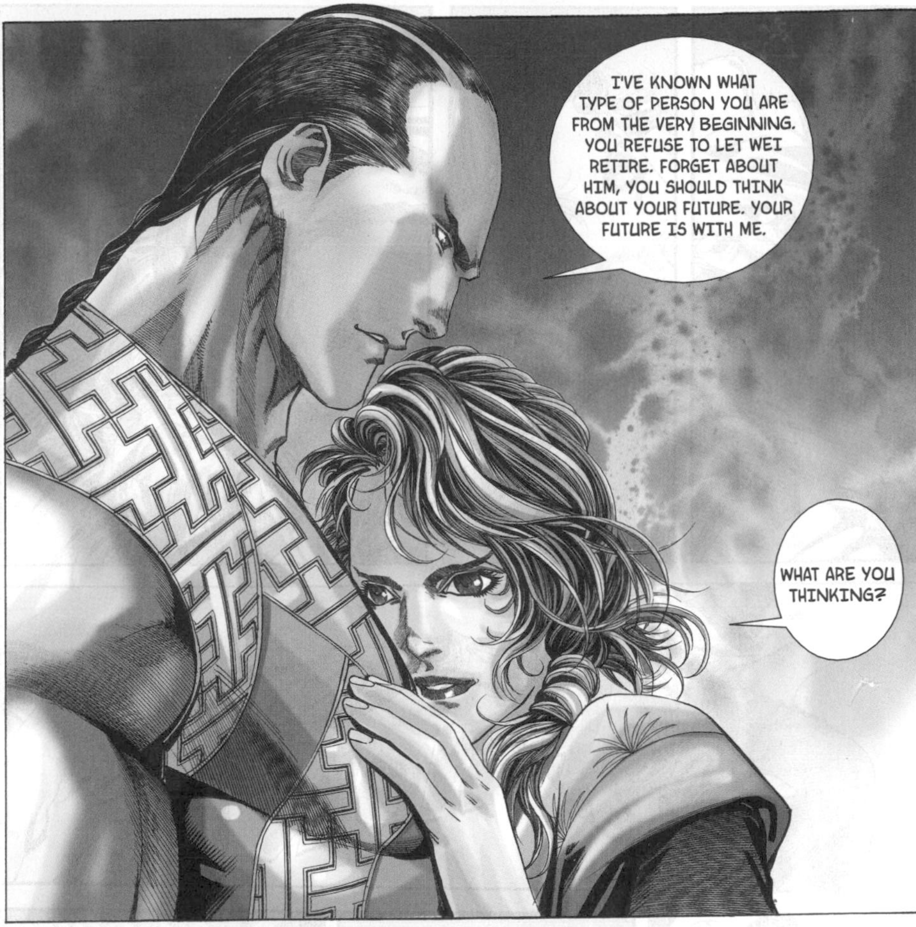
I'VE KNOWN WHAT TYPE OF PERSON YOU ARE FROM THE VERY BEGINNING. YOU REFUSE TO LET WEI RETIRE. FORGET ABOUT HIM, YOU SHOULD THINK ABOUT YOUR FUTURE. YOUR FUTURE IS WITH ME.
WHAT ARE YOU THINKING?
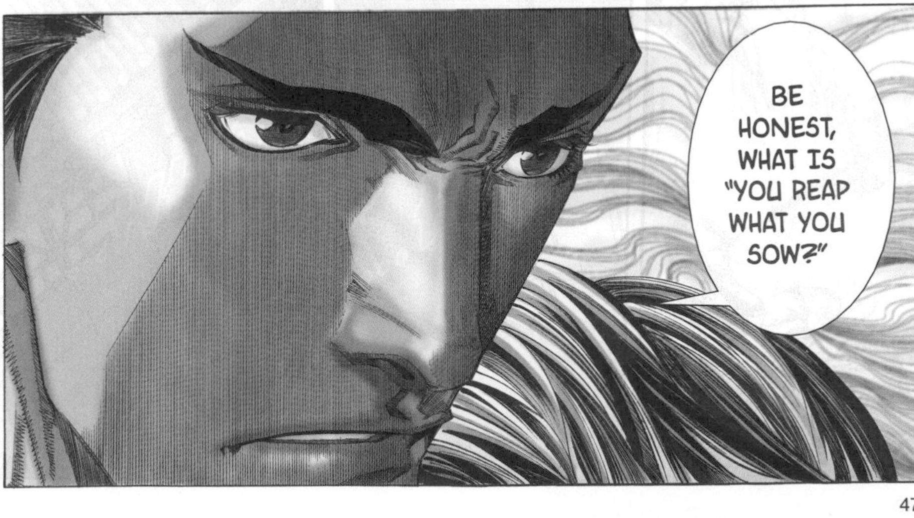
BE HONEST, WHAT IS "YOU REAP WHAT YOU SOW?"

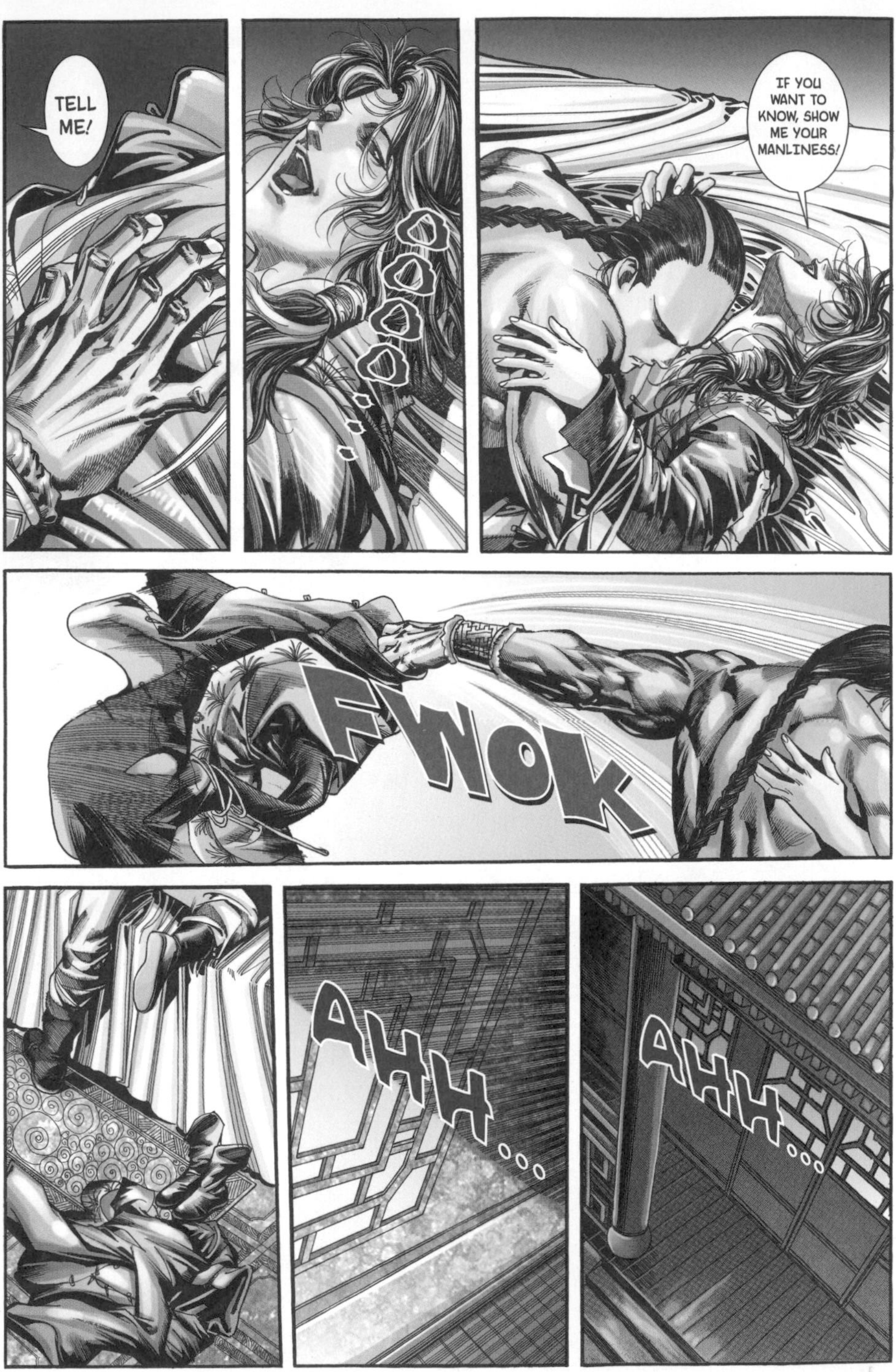
TELL ME!
IF YOU WANT TO KNOW, SHOW ME YOUR MANLINESS!
FWOK
AHH...
AHH...

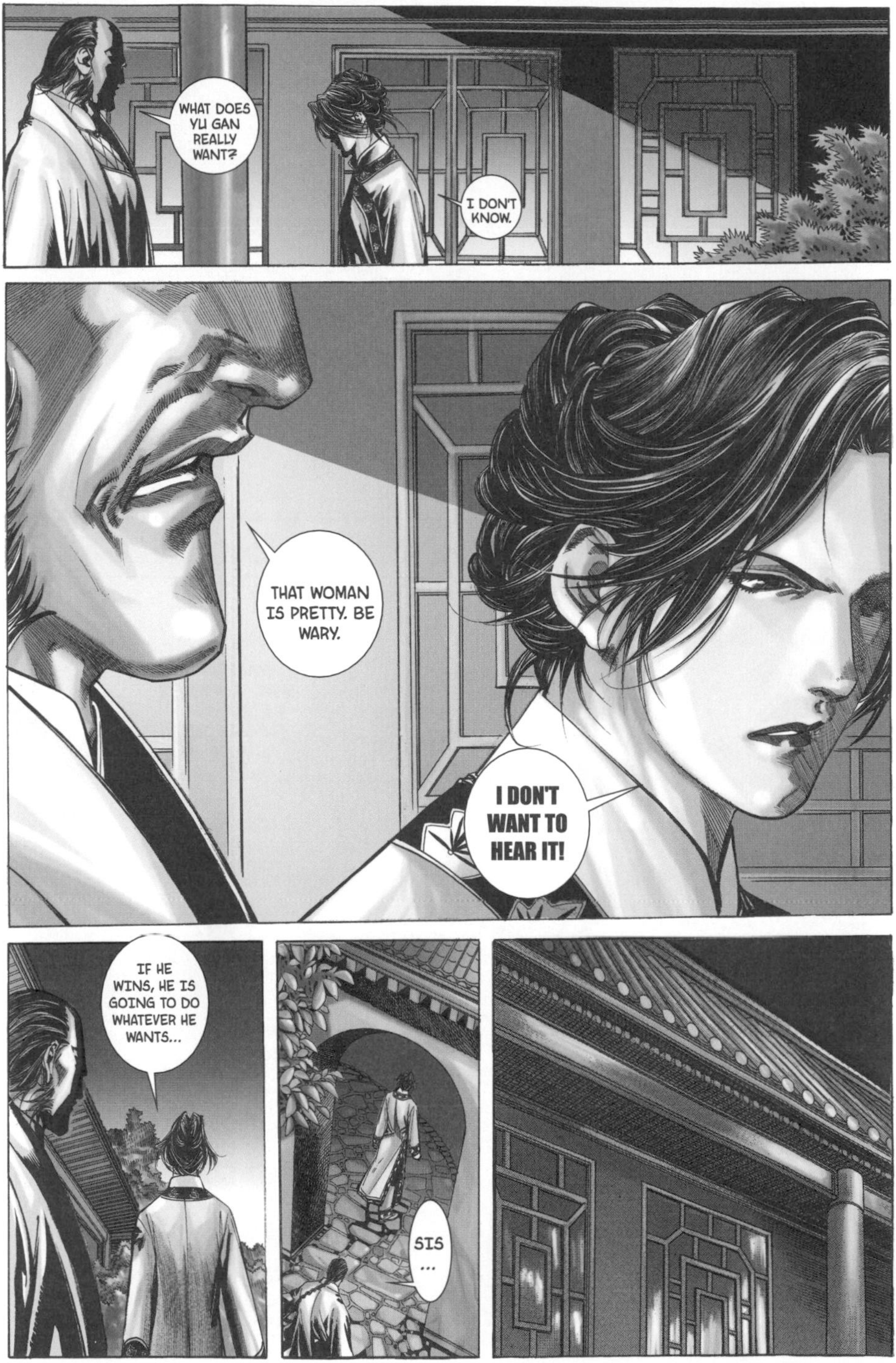
WHAT DOES YU GAN REALLY WANT?
I DON'T KNOW.
THAT WOMAN IS PRETTY. BE WARY.
I DON'T WANT TO HEAR IT!
IF HE WINS, HE IS GOING TO DO WHATEVER HE WANTS...
SIS ...

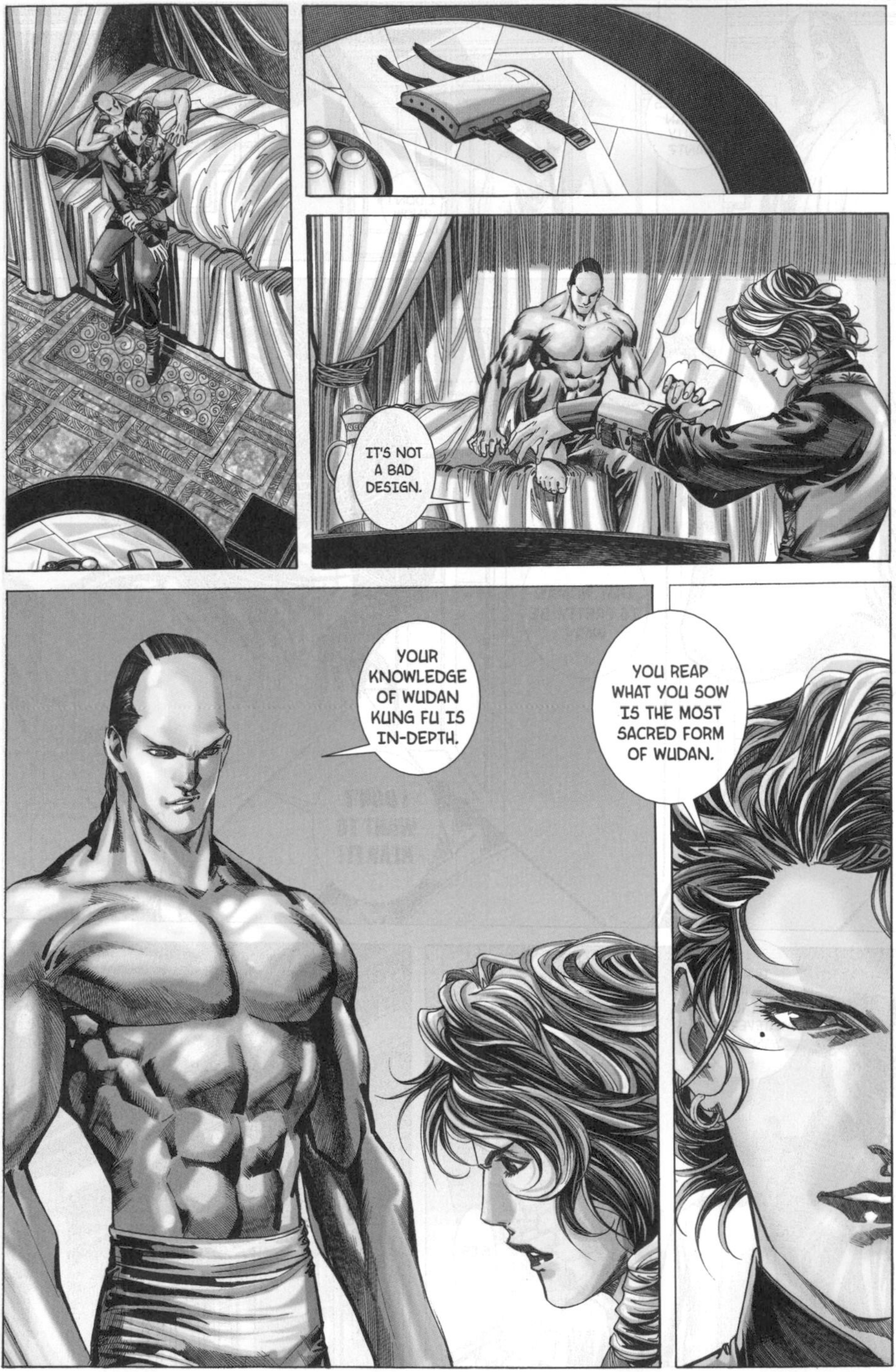
IT'S NOT A BAD DESIGN.
YOUR KNOWLEDGE OF WUDAN KUNG FU IS IN-DEPTH.
YOU REAP WHAT YOU SOW IS THE MOST SACRED FORM OF WUDAN.

IMAGINE YOU THREW A ROCK AT YOUR OPPONENT. YOU WANT TO HIT HIM IN THE HEAD, BUT INSTEAD HE CATCHES THE ROCK AND STRIKES YOU IN THE HEAD.
ABSORBING YOUR OPPONENT'S CHI AND USING IT AGAINST YOUR OPPONENT...
BUT, A ROCK IS DIFFERENT FROM CHI. A ROCK HAS PHYSICAL FORM AND YOU CAN SEE WHERE IT IS...

HOWEVER, WHEN HE ABSORBS YOUR CHI, YOU WON'T KNOW IT. WHEN YOU THINK THAT HE IS INJURED...
YOU WILL PRESS YOUR ATTACK AND HE WILL ONLY ABSORB MORE CHI. WHEN HE HAS ABSORBED ENOUGH INTERNAL ENERGY, HE WILL INITIATE A FULL RETALIATION...
BY THEN, IT WILL BE TOO LATE!
SO... ABSORBING AN ENEMY'S CHI IS REALLY POSSIBLE...

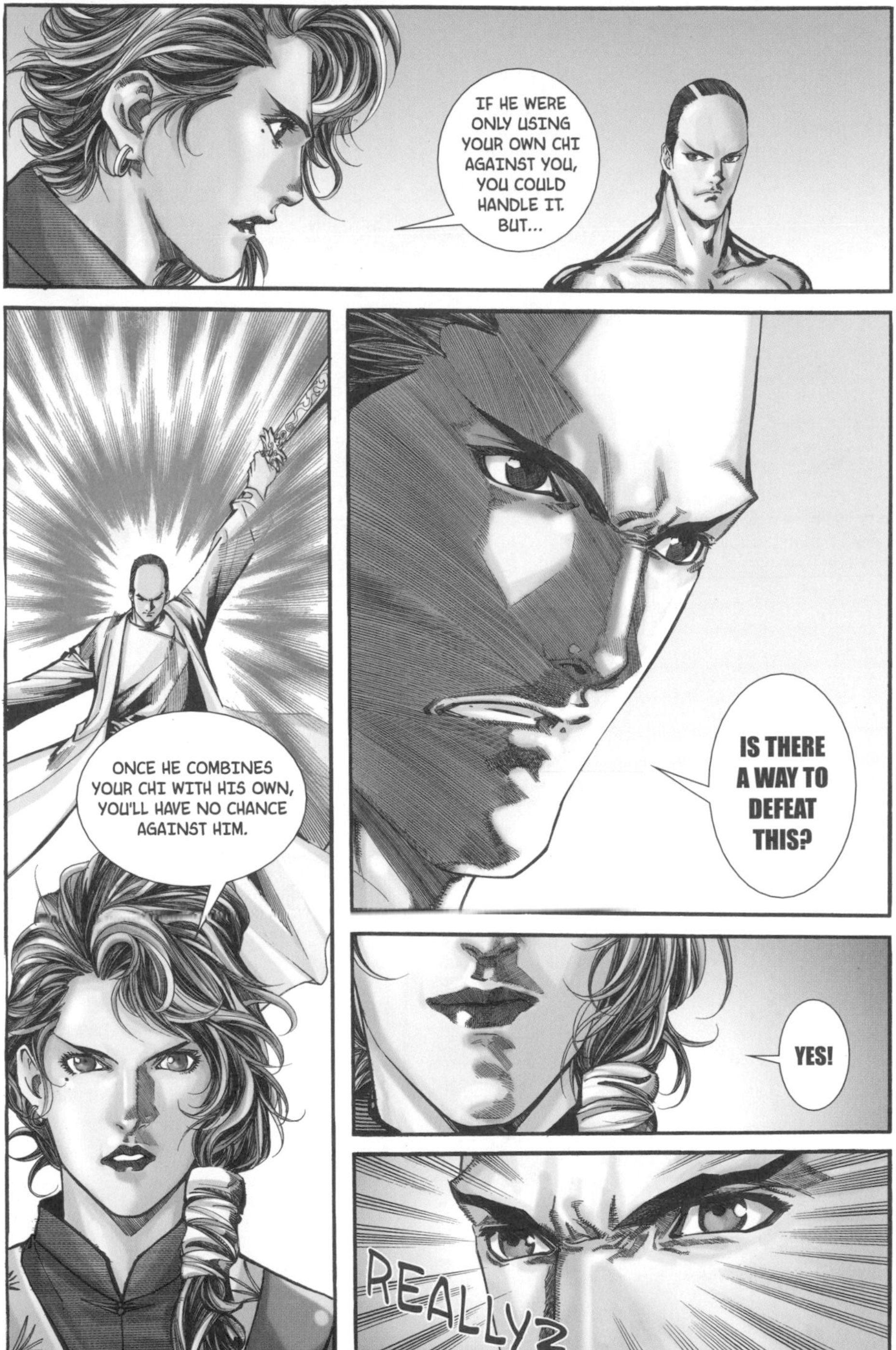
IF HE WERE ONLY USING YOUR OWN CHI AGAINST YOU, YOU COULD HANDLE IT. BUT...
ONCE HE COMBINES YOUR CHI WITH HIS OWN, YOU'LL HAVE NO CHANCE AGAINST HIM.
IS THERE A WAY TO DEFEAT THIS?
YES!
REALLY?

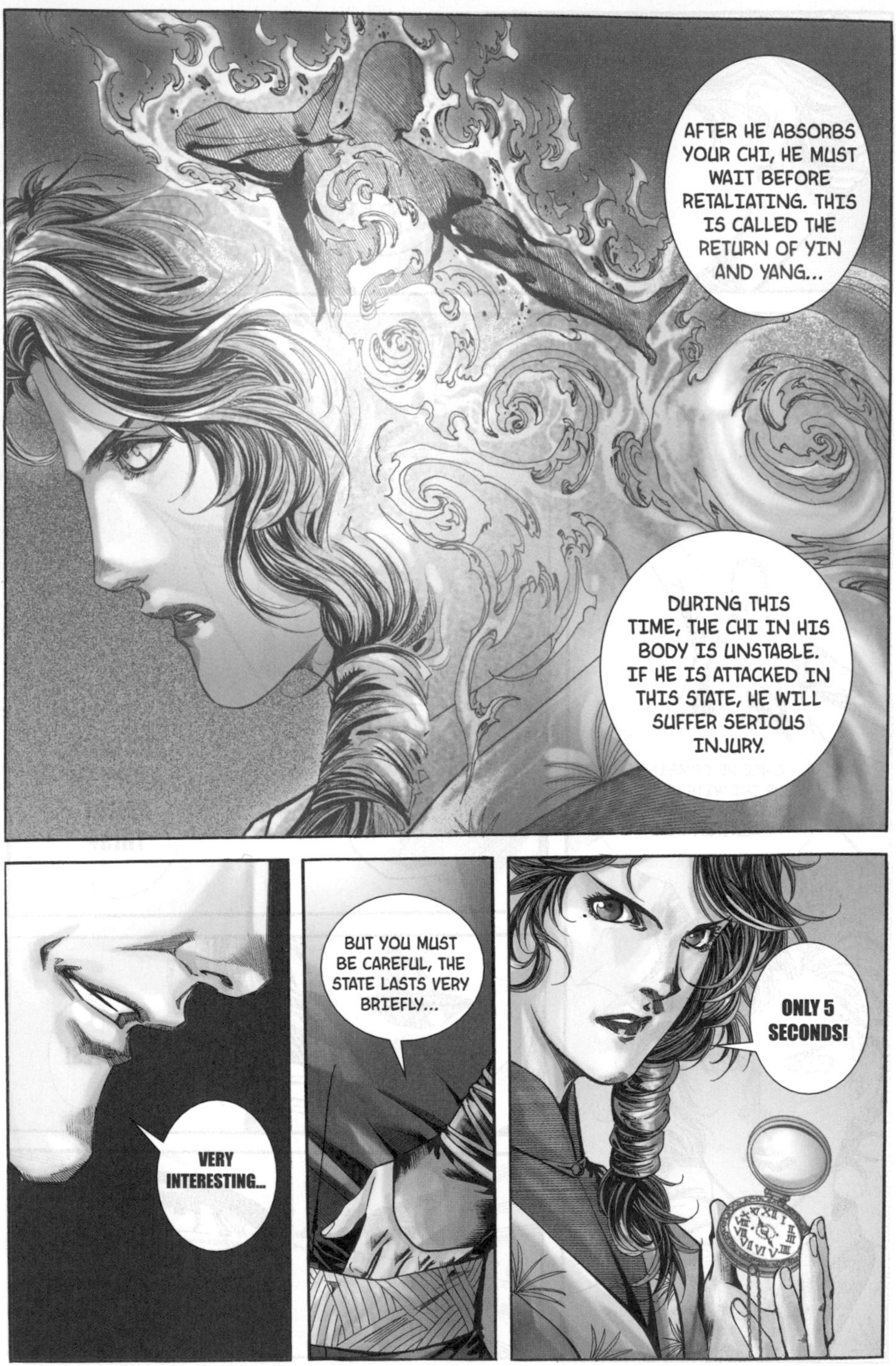
AFTER HE ABSORBS YOUR CHI, HE MUST WAIT BEFORE RETALIATING. THIS IS CALLED THE RETURN OF YIN AND YANG...
DURING THIS TIME, THE CHI IN HIS BODY IS UNSTABLE. IF HE IS ATTACKED IN THIS STATE, HE WILL SUFFER SERIOUS INJURY.
VERY INTERESTING...
BUT YOU MUST BE CAREFUL, THE STATE LASTS VERY BRIEFLY...
ONLY 5 SECONDS!

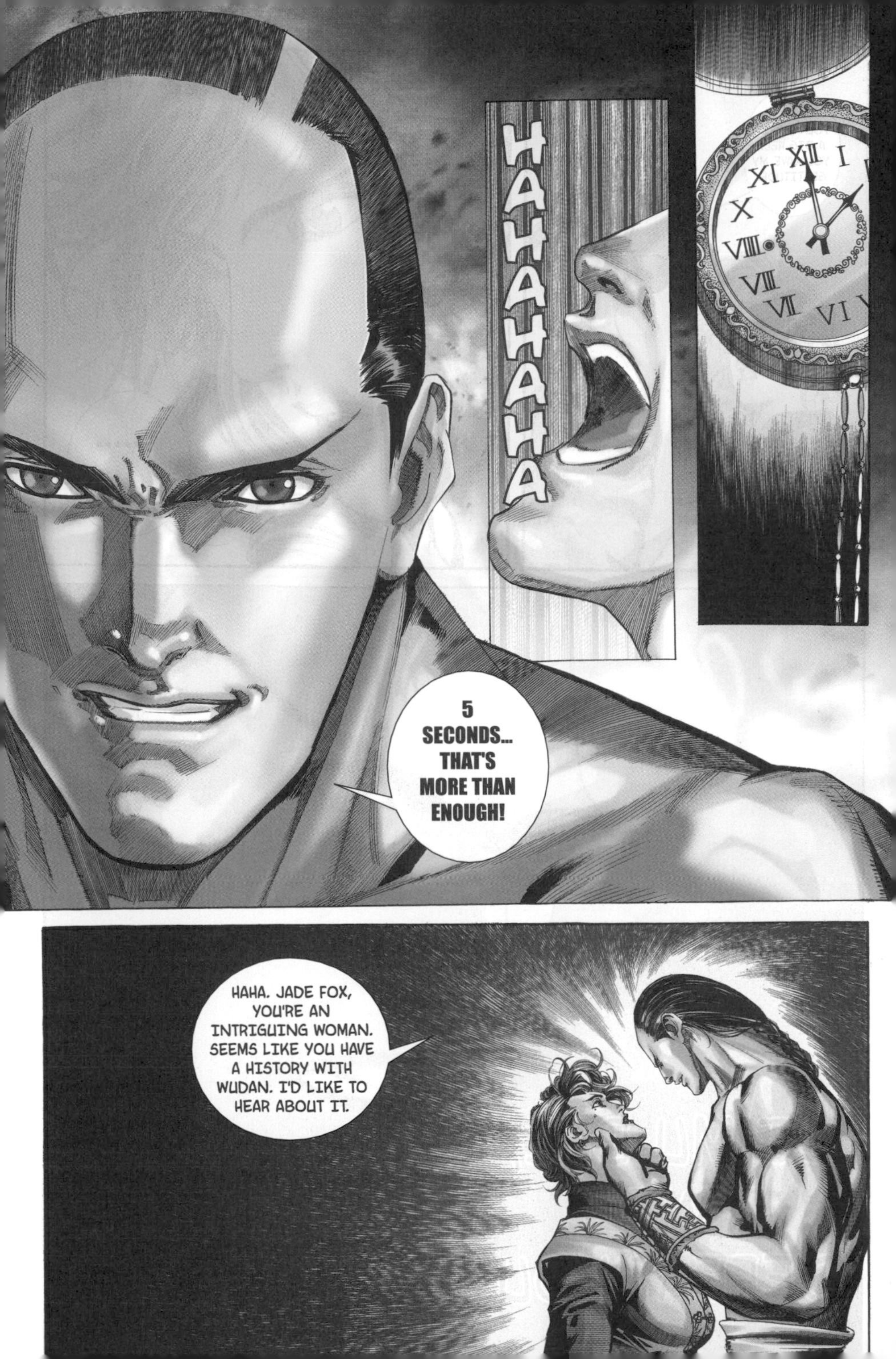
HAHAHAHAHA
5 SECONDS... THAT'S MORE THAN ENOUGH!
HAHA. JADE FOX, YOU'RE AN INTRIGUING WOMAN. SEEMS LIKE YOU HAVE A HISTORY WITH WUDAN. I'D LIKE TO HEAR ABOUT IT.

YOU'VE BEEN A BIG HELP. YOU HAVE MY GRATITUDE!
....
LI MU BAI, I WILL DEFEAT YOU!

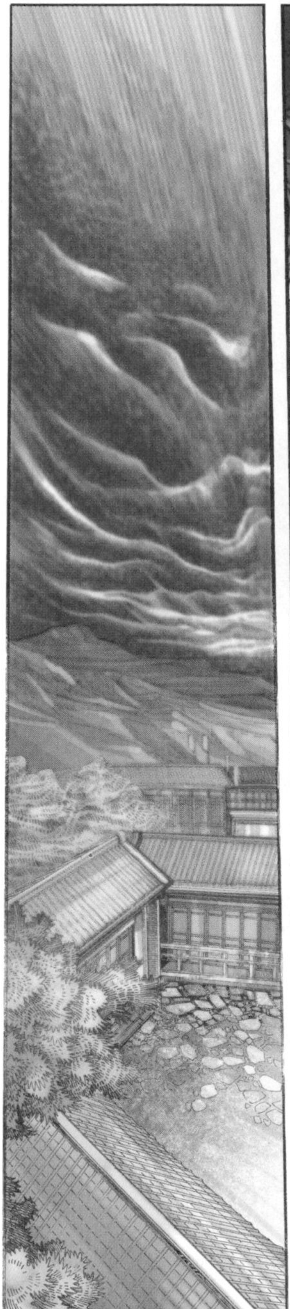

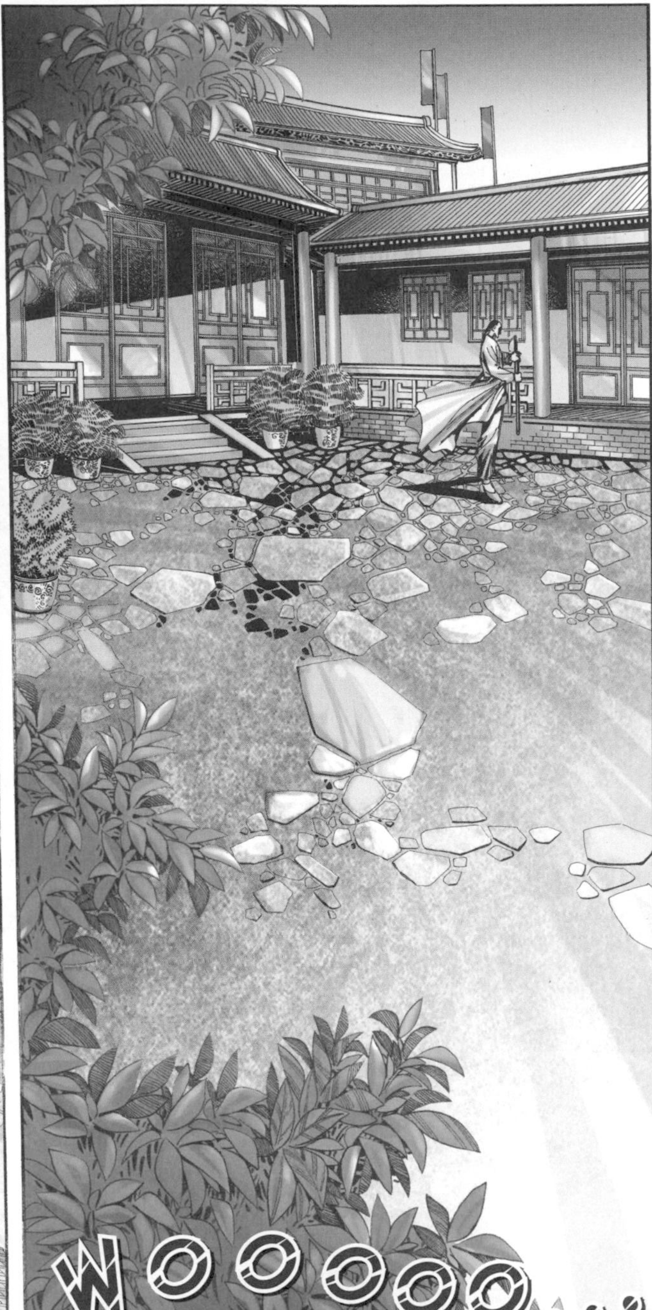
WOOOOOO...

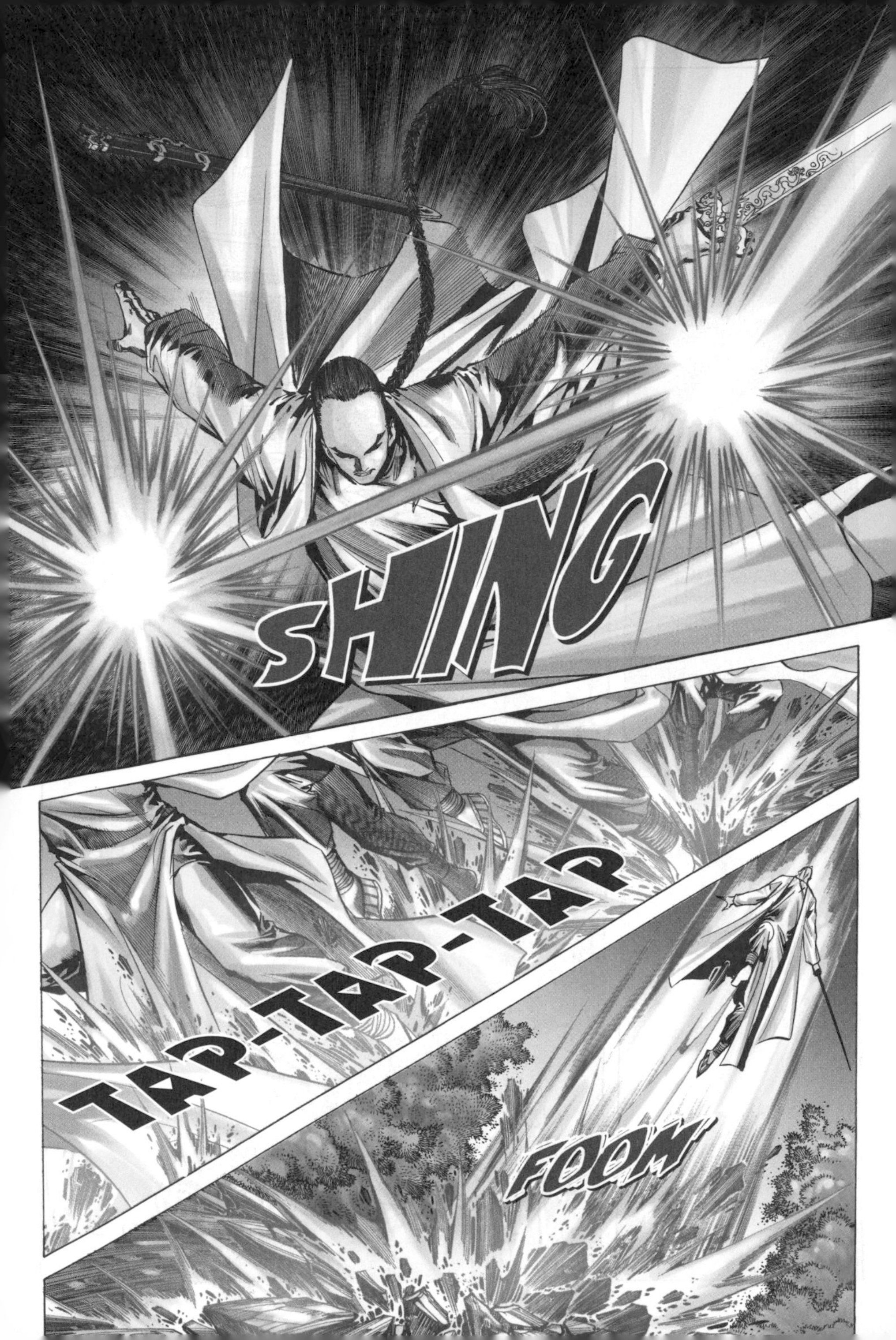
SHING
TAP-TAP-TAP
FOOM

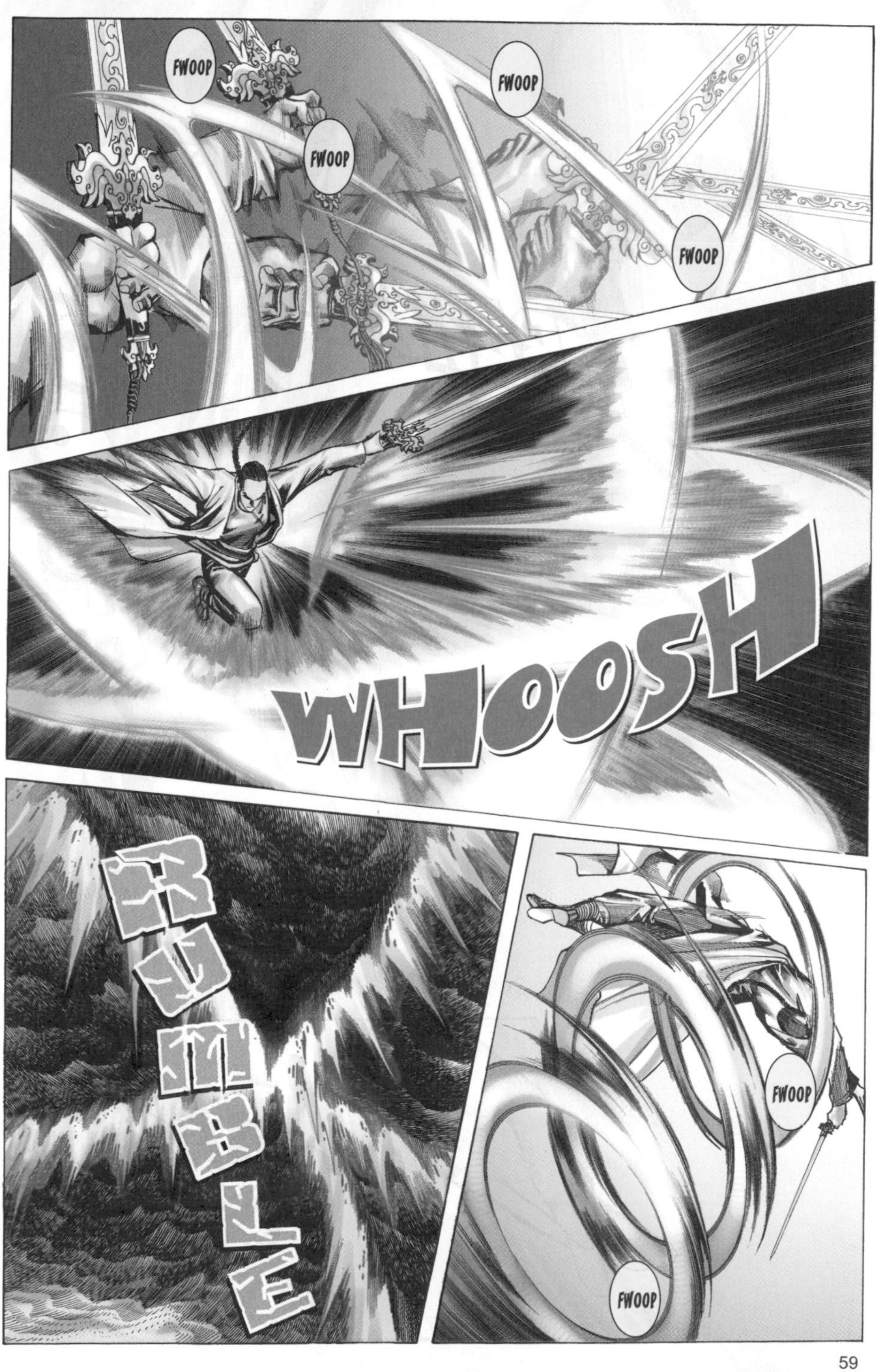
FWOOP
FWOOP
FWOOP
FWOOP
WHOOSH
RUMBLE
FWOOP
FWOOP

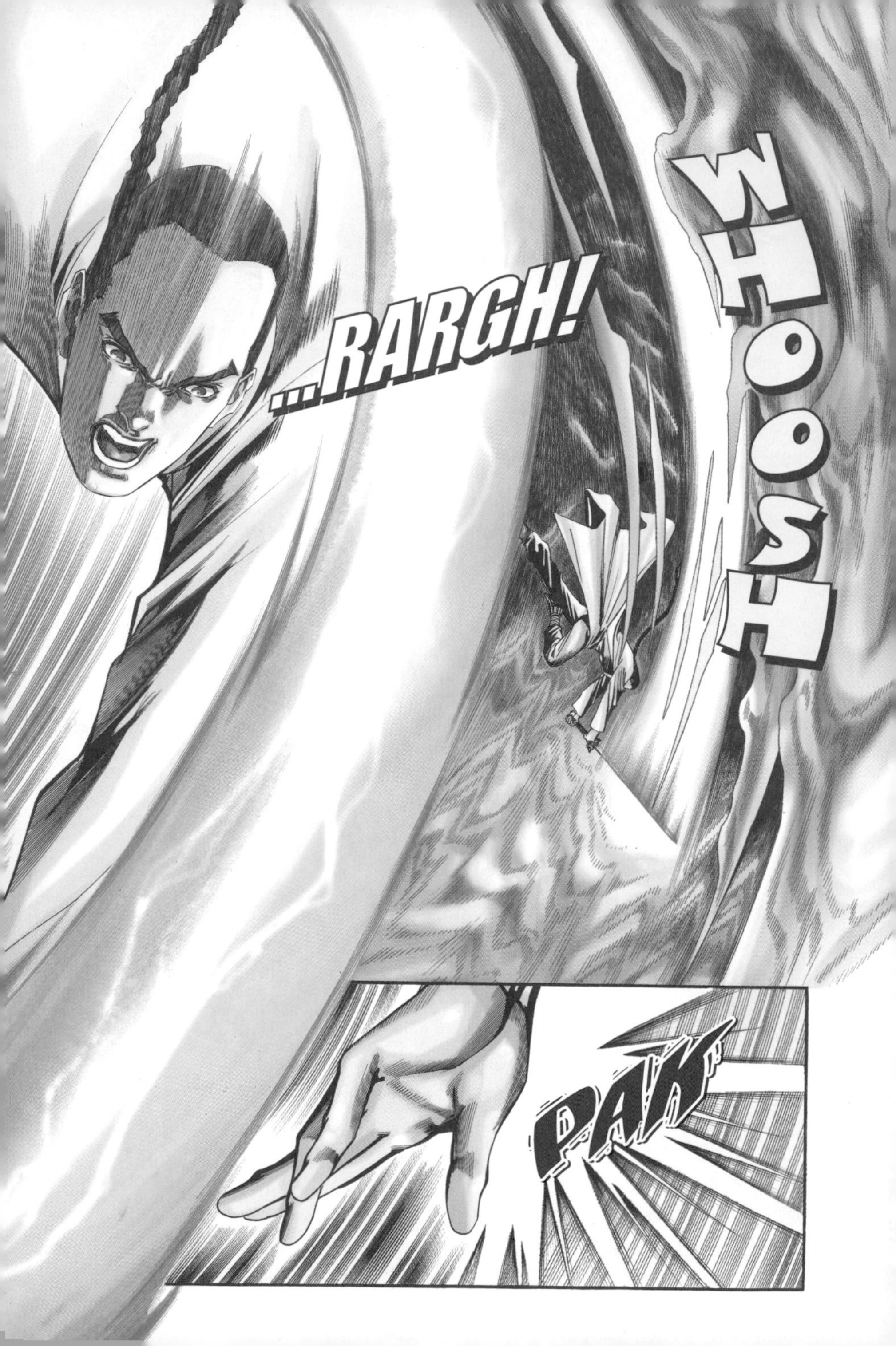
WHOOSH
...RARGH!
PAK

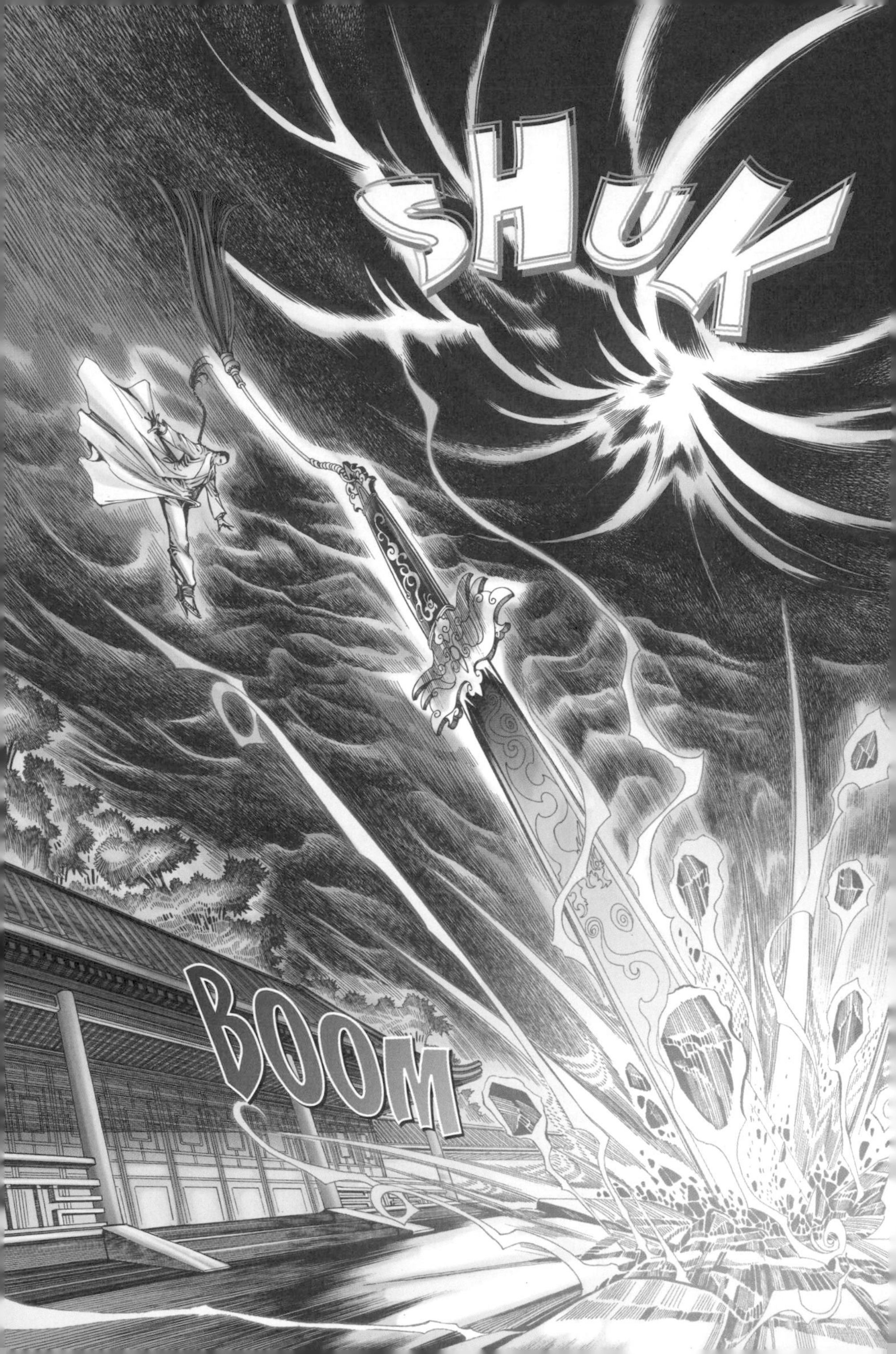
SHUK
BOOM

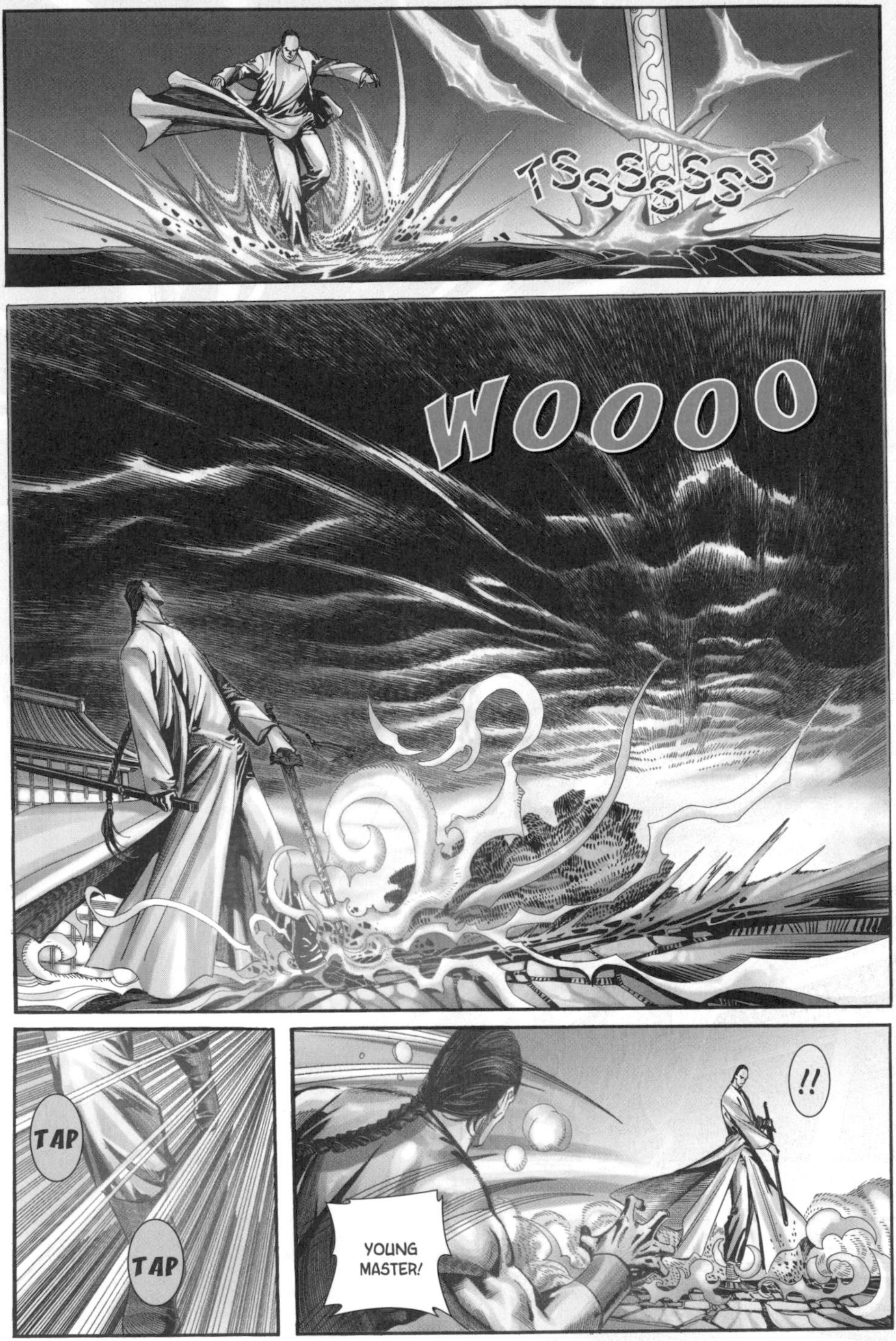
TSSSSSSS
WOOOO
TAP
TAP
!!
YOUNG MASTER!

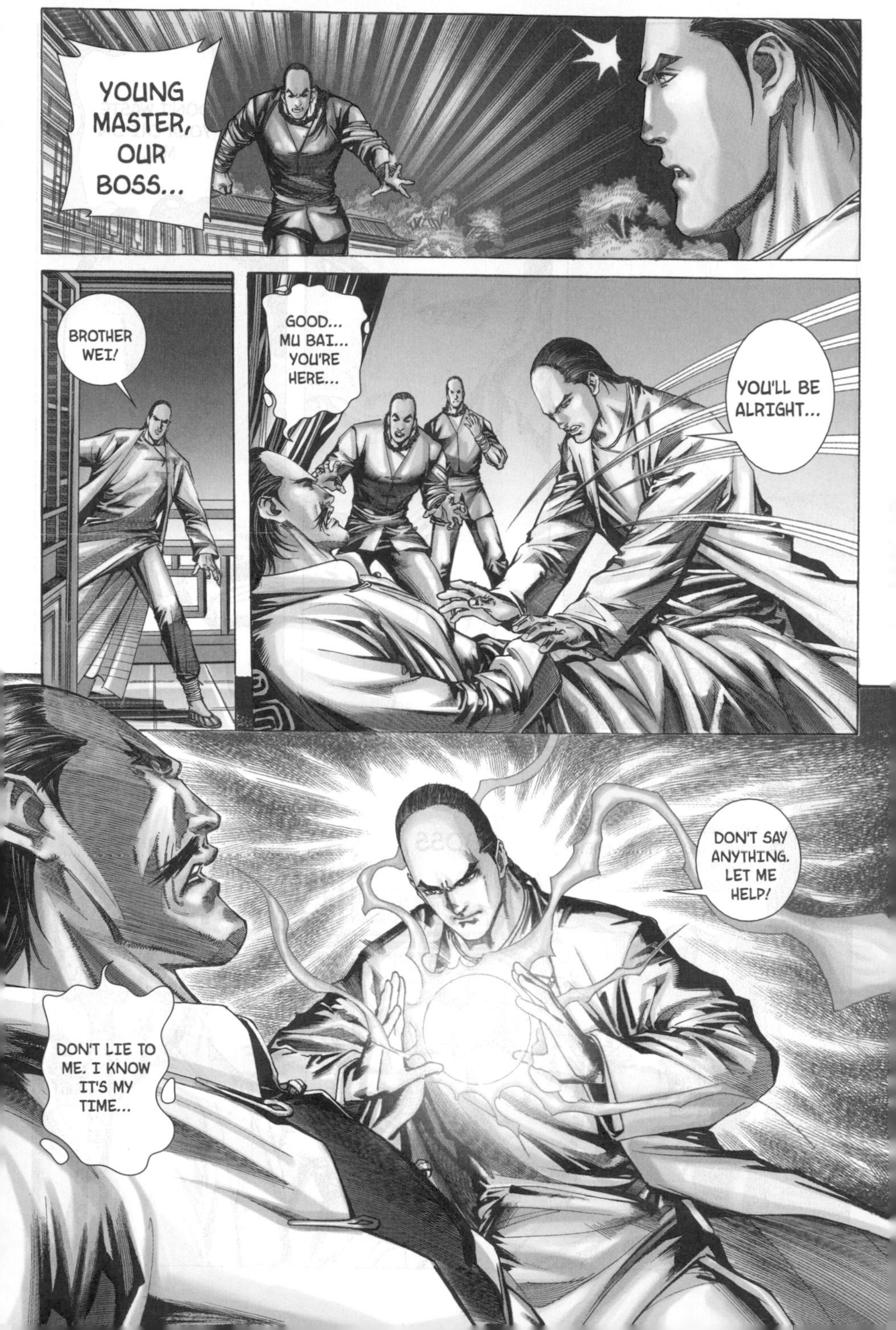
YOUNG MASTER, OUR BOSS...
BROTHER WEI!
GOOD... MU BAI... YOU'RE HERE...
YOU'LL BE ALRIGHT...
DON'T SAY ANYTHING. LET ME HELP!
DON'T LIE TO ME. I KNOW IT'S MY TIME...

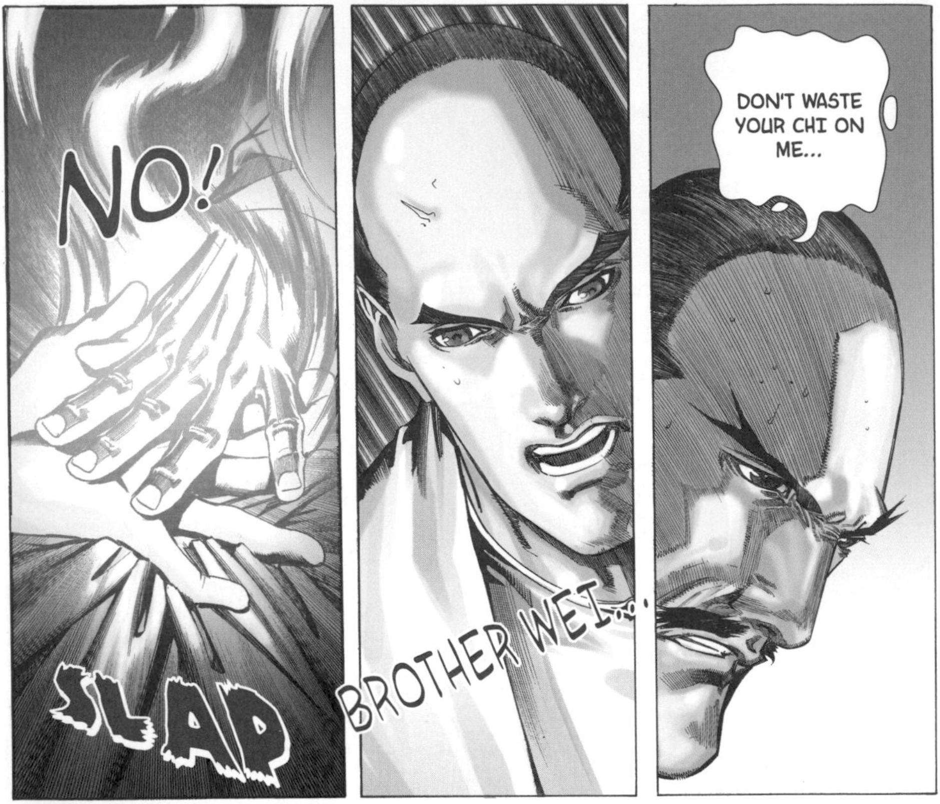
NO!
SLAP
BROTHER WEI...
DON'T WASTE YOUR CHI ON ME...

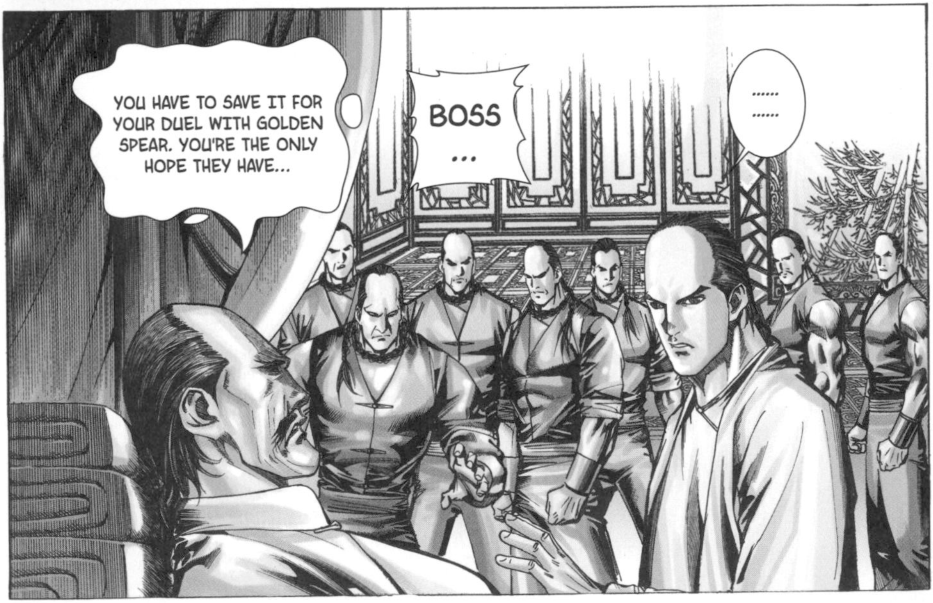
YOU HAVE TO SAVE IT FOR YOUR DUEL WITH GOLDEN SPEAR. YOU'RE THE ONLY HOPE THEY HAVE...
BOSS ...
......
......

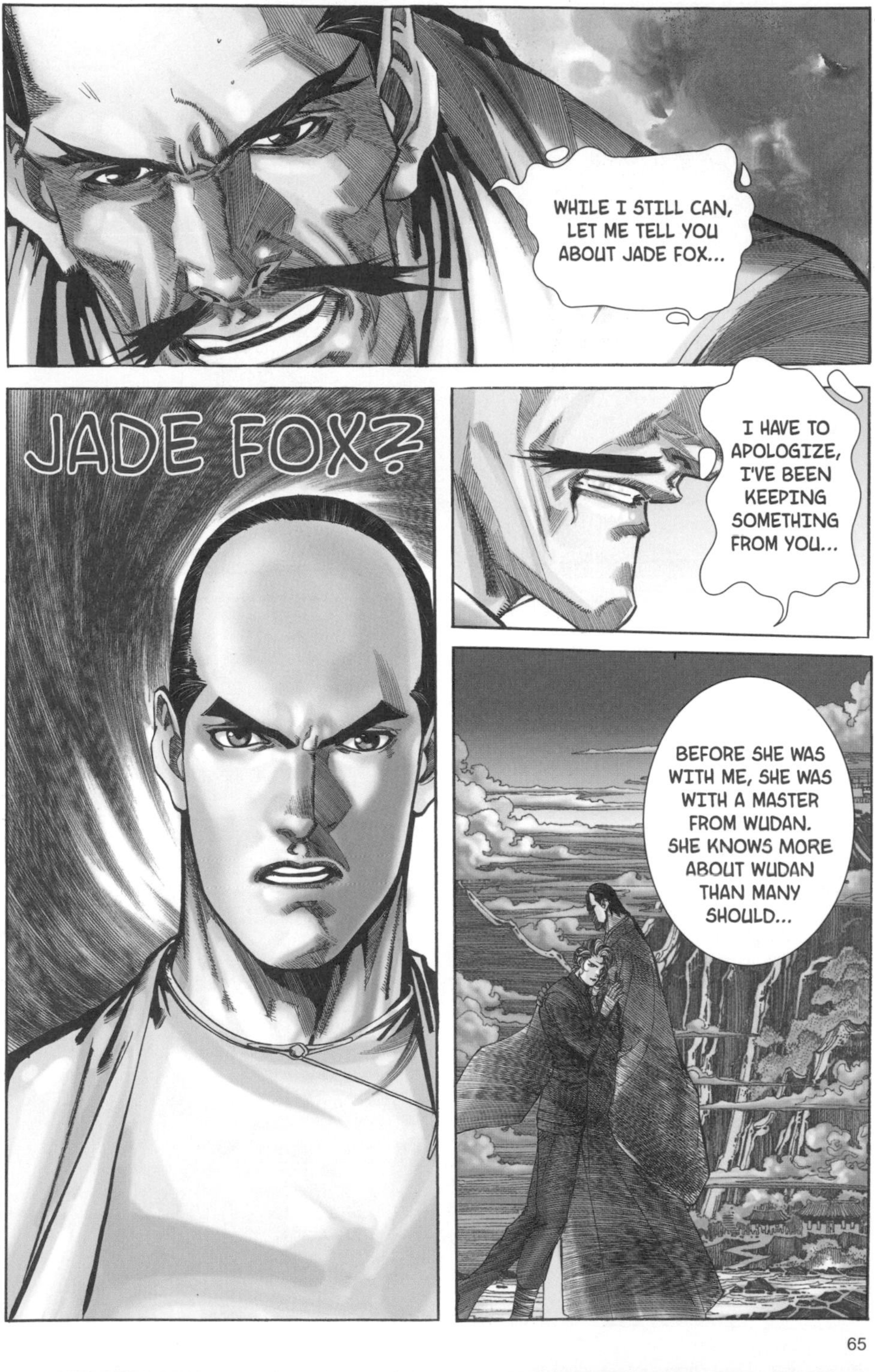
WHILE I STILL CAN, LET ME TELL YOU ABOUT JADE FOX...
JADE FOX?
I HAVE TO APOLOGIZE, I'VE BEEN KEEPING SOMETHING FROM YOU...
BEFORE SHE WAS WITH ME, SHE WAS WITH A MASTER FROM WUDAN. SHE KNOWS MORE ABOUT WUDAN THAN MANY SHOULD...

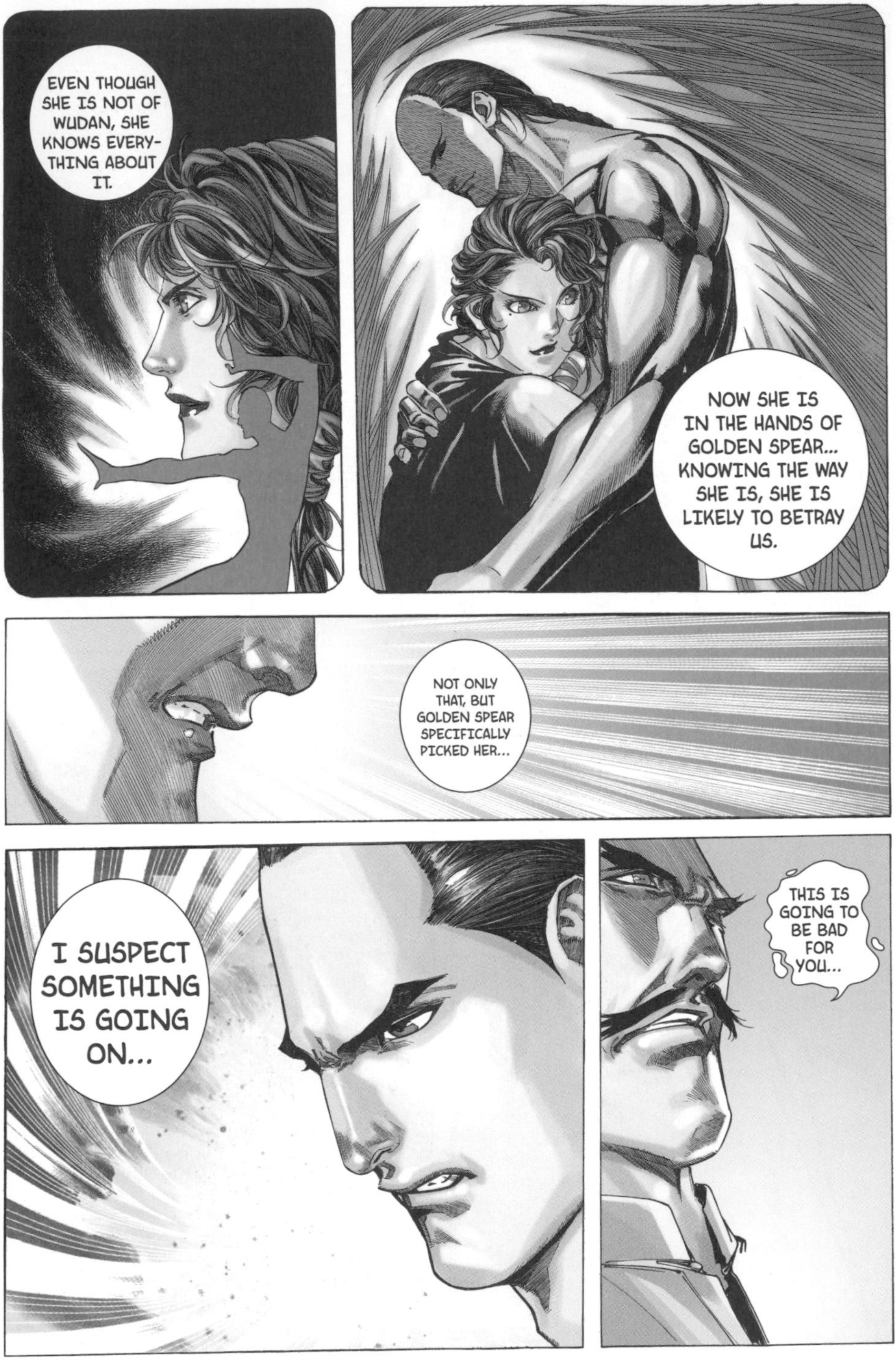
EVEN THOUGH SHE IS NOT OF WUDAN, SHE KNOWS EVERY-THING ABOUT IT.
NOW SHE IS IN THE HANDS OF GOLDEN SPEAR... KNOWING THE WAY SHE IS, SHE IS LIKELY TO BETRAY US.
NOT ONLY THAT, BUT GOLDEN SPEAR SPECIFICALLY PICKED HER...
I SUSPECT SOMETHING IS GOING ON...
THIS IS GOING TO BE BAD FOR YOU...

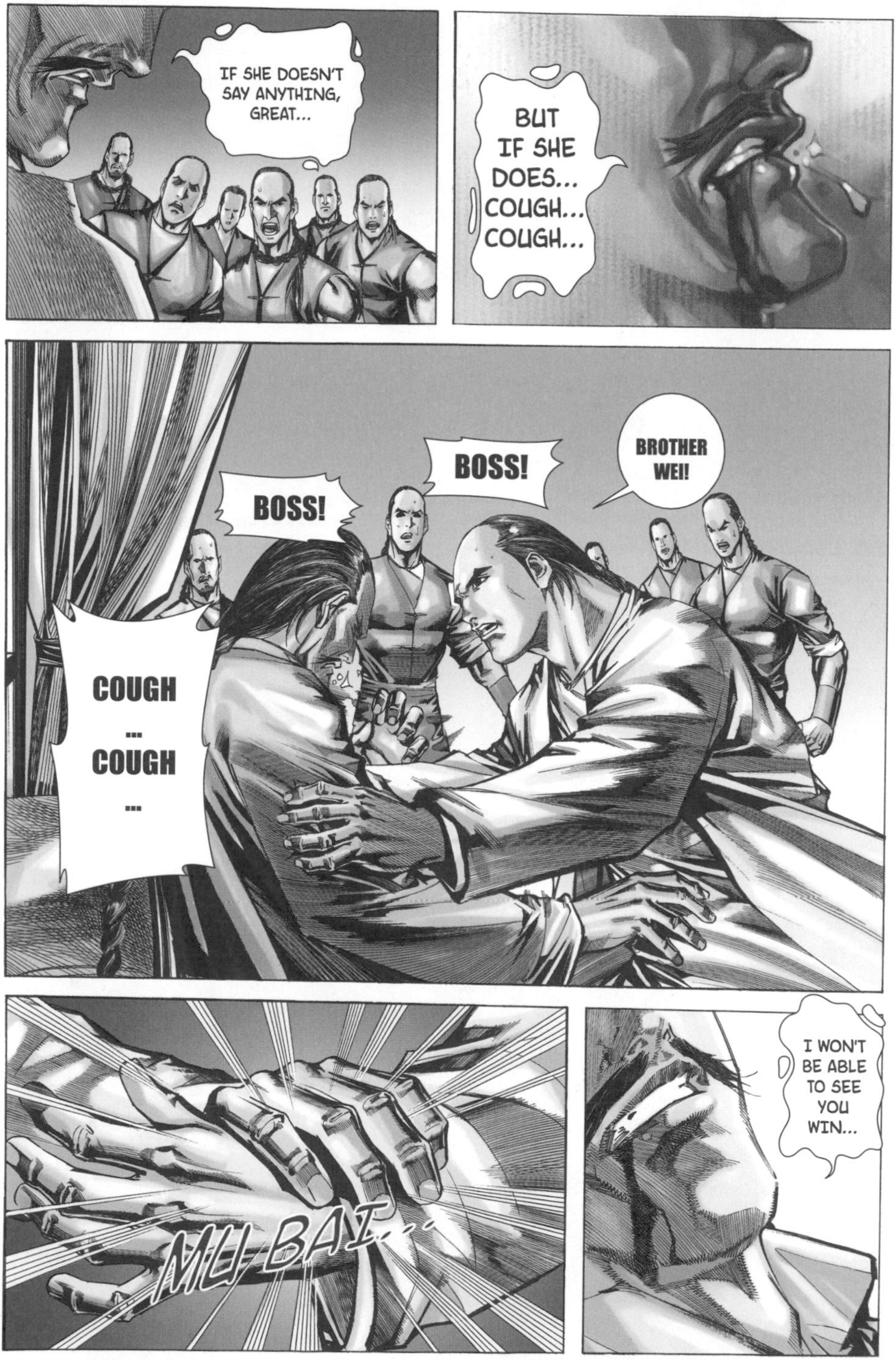
IF SHE DOESN'T SAY ANYTHING, GREAT...
BUT IF SHE DOES... COUGH... COUGH...
BOSS!
BOSS!
BROTHER WEI!
COUGH ... COUGH ...
MU BAI...
I WON'T BE ABLE TO SEE YOU WIN...

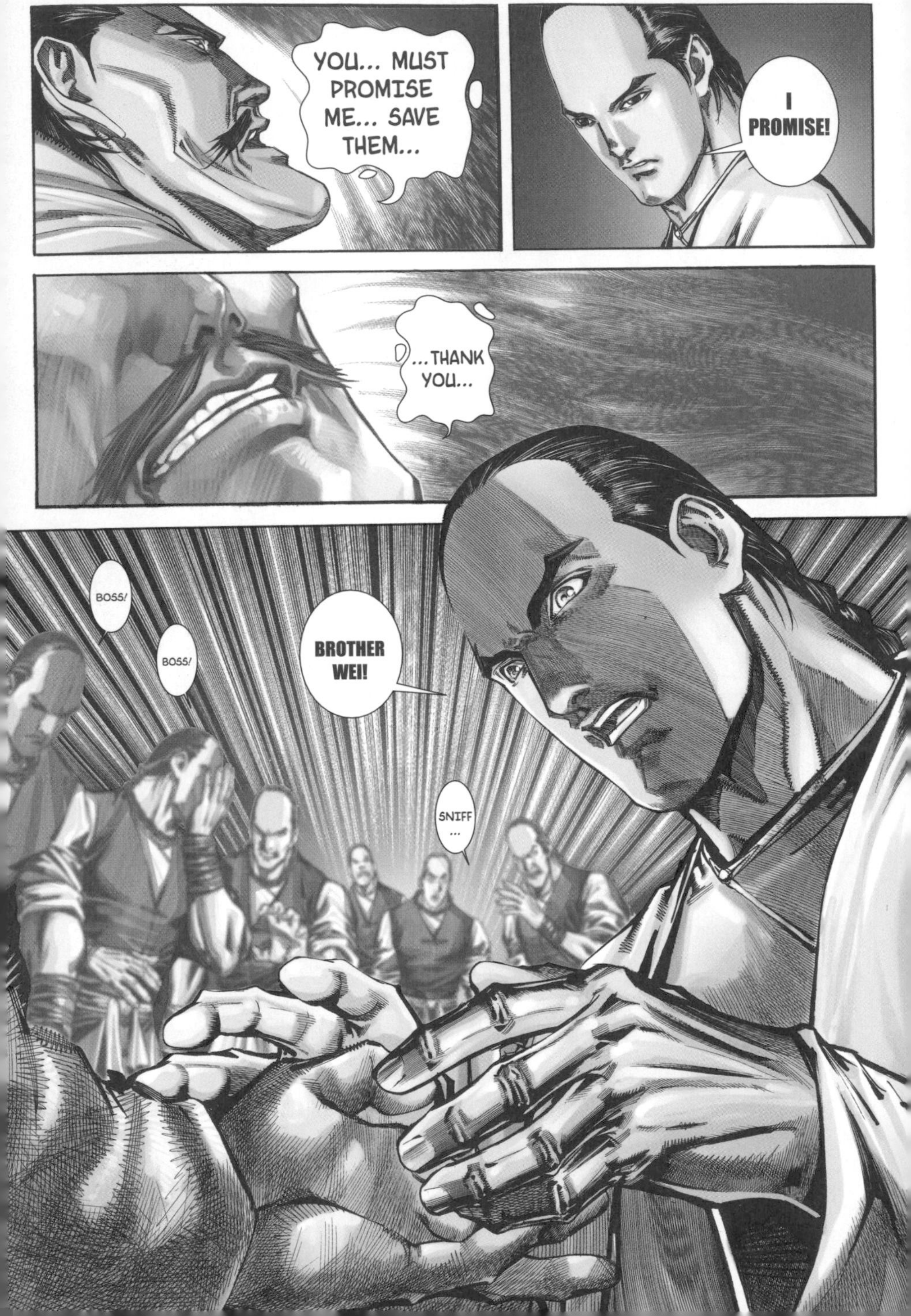

YOU... MUST PROMISE ME... SAVE THEM...
I PROMISE!
...THANK YOU...
BOSS!
BOSS!
BROTHER WEI!
SNIFF ...

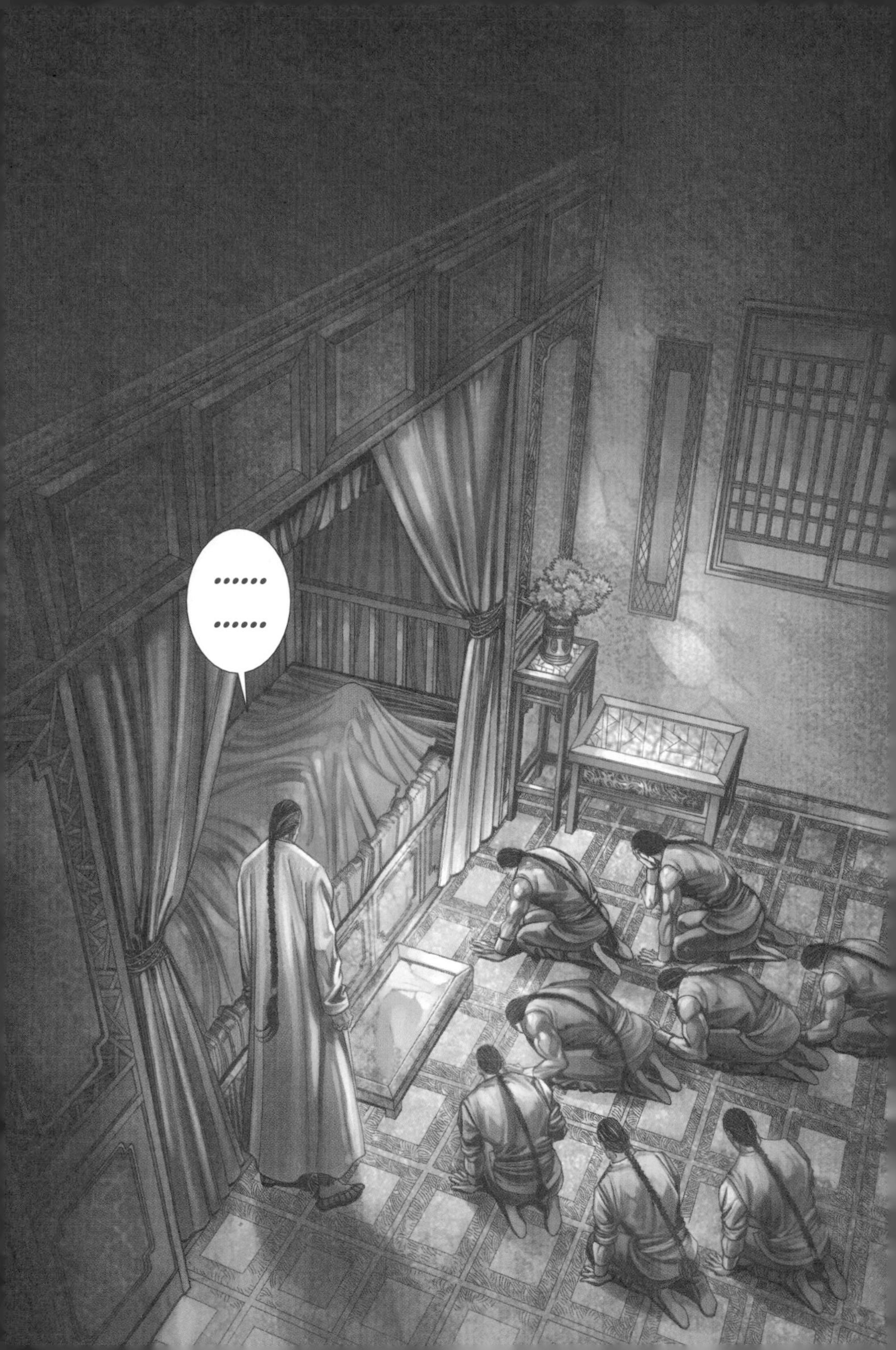
…… ……

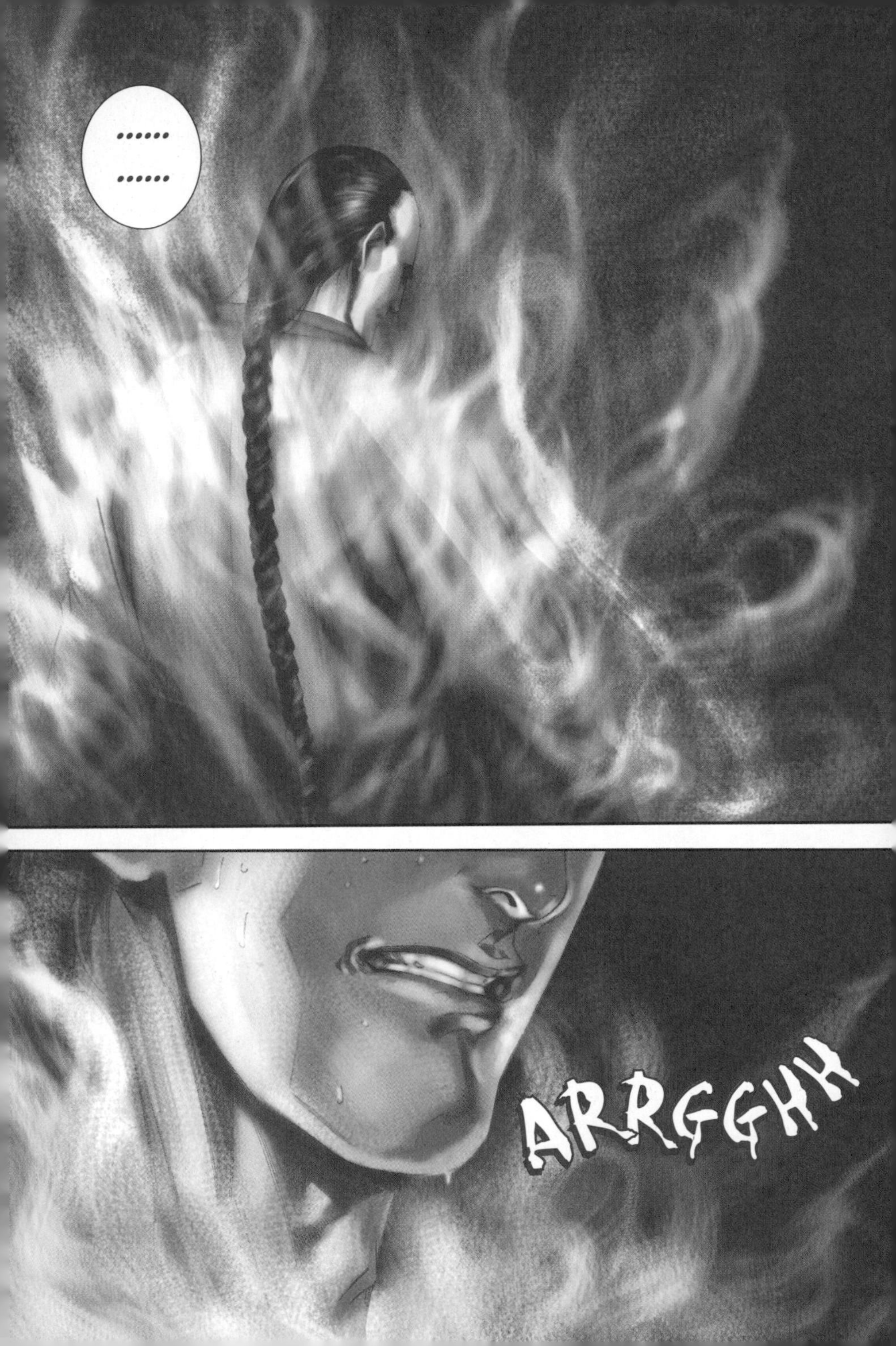

......
......
ARRGGHH

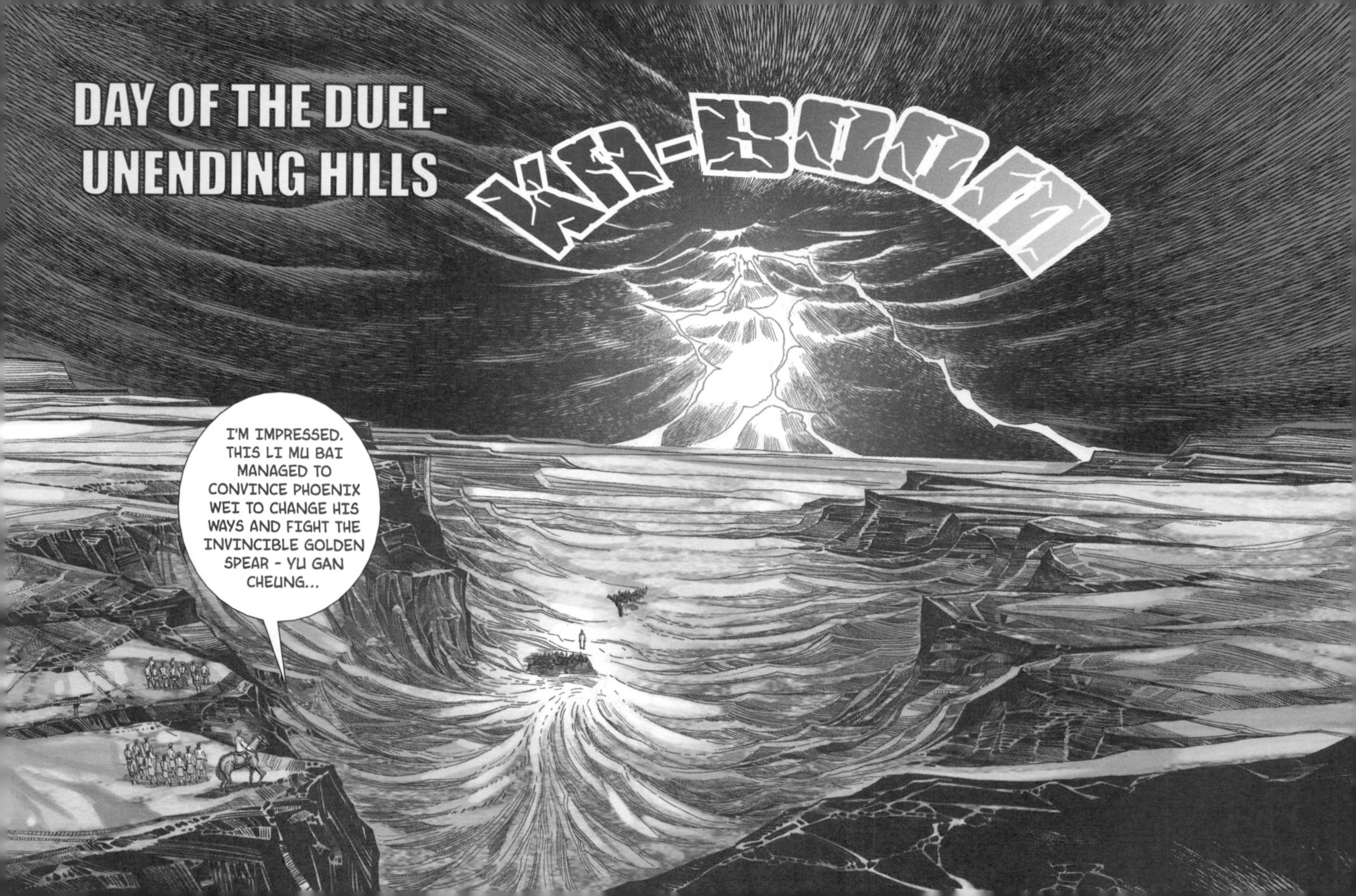
DAY OF THE DUEL- UNENDING HILLS
KA-BOOM
I'M IMPRESSED. THIS LI MU BAI MANAGED TO CONVINCE PHOENIX WEI TO CHANGE HIS WAYS AND FIGHT THE INVINCIBLE GOLDEN SPEAR - YU GAN CHEUNG...

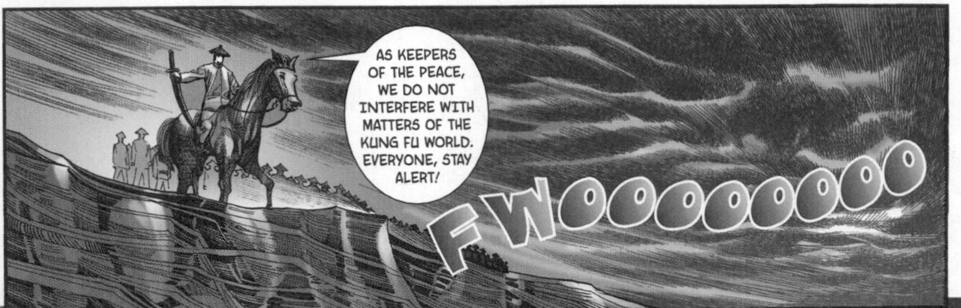
AS KEEPERS OF THE PEACE, WE DO NOT INTERFERE WITH MATTERS OF THE KUNG FU WORLD. EVERYONE, STAY ALERT!
FWOOOOOOOO

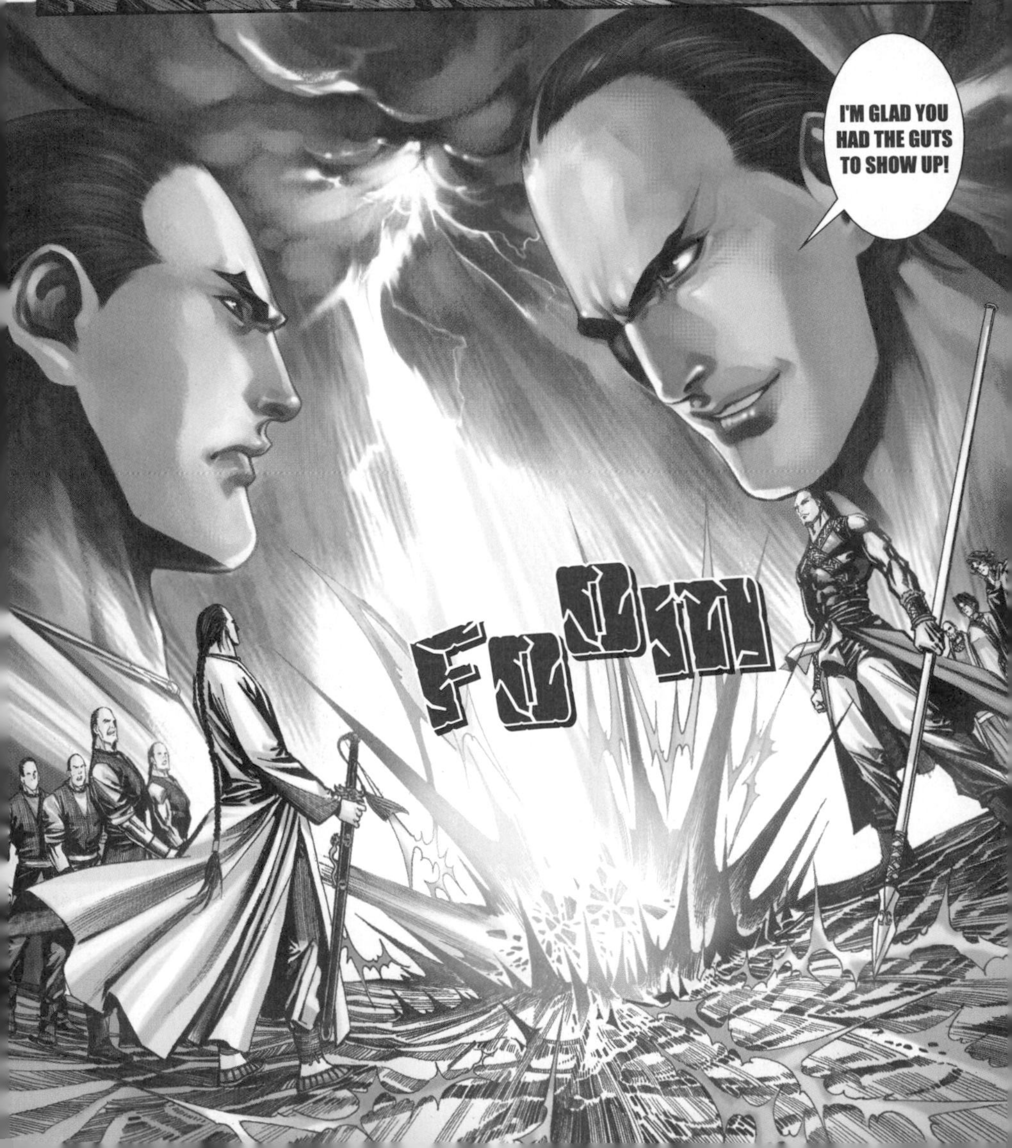
I'M GLAD YOU HAD THE GUTS TO SHOW UP!

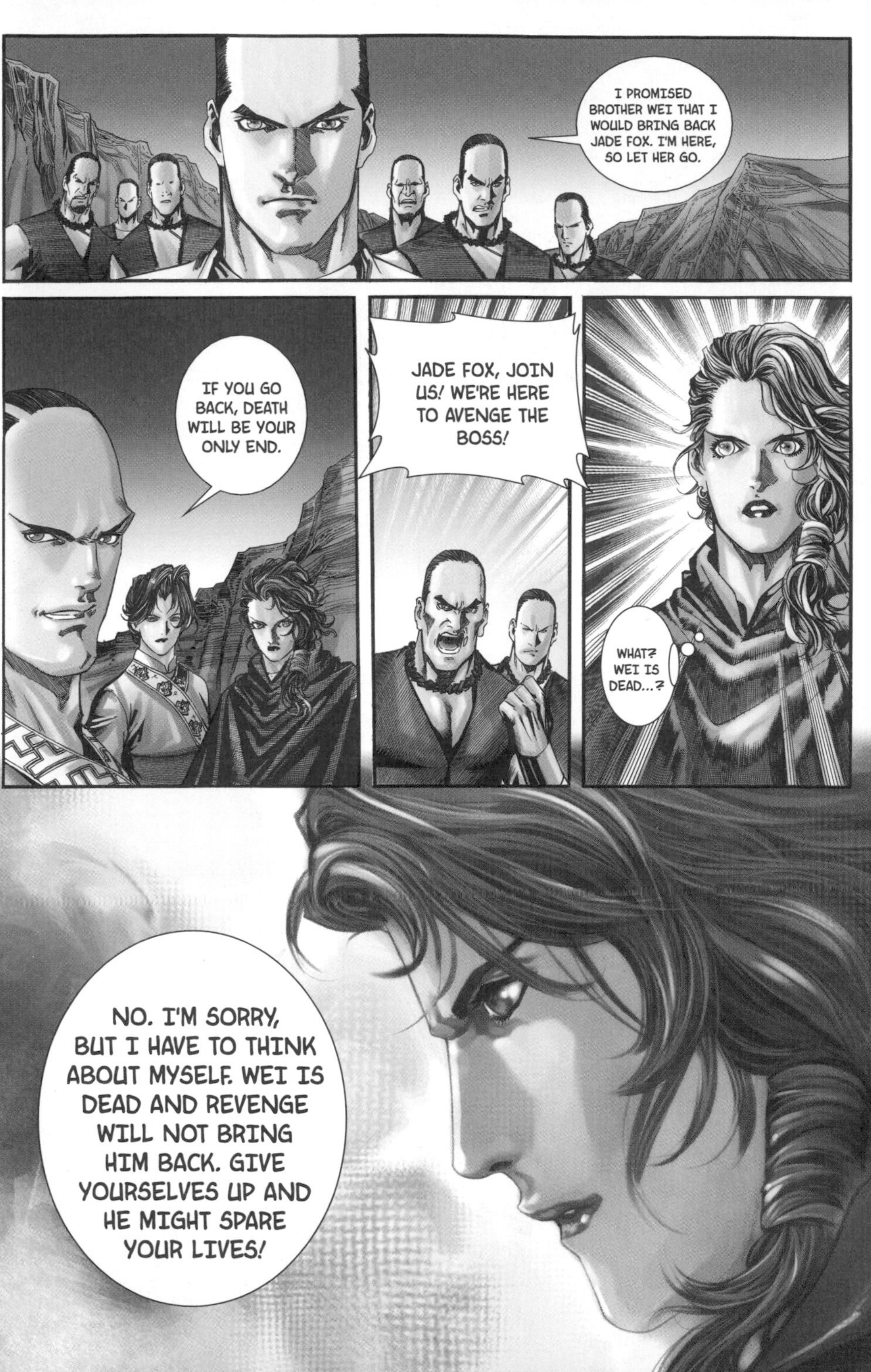
I PROMISED BROTHER WEI THAT I WOULD BRING BACK JADE FOX. I'M HERE, SO LET HER GO.
IF YOU GO BACK, DEATH WILL BE YOUR ONLY END.
JADE FOX, JOIN US! WE'RE HERE TO AVENGE THE BOSS!
WHAT? WEI IS DEAD...?
NO. I'M SORRY, BUT I HAVE TO THINK ABOUT MYSELF. WEI IS DEAD AND REVENGE WILL NOT BRING HIM BACK. GIVE YOURSELVES UP AND HE MIGHT SPARE YOUR LIVES!

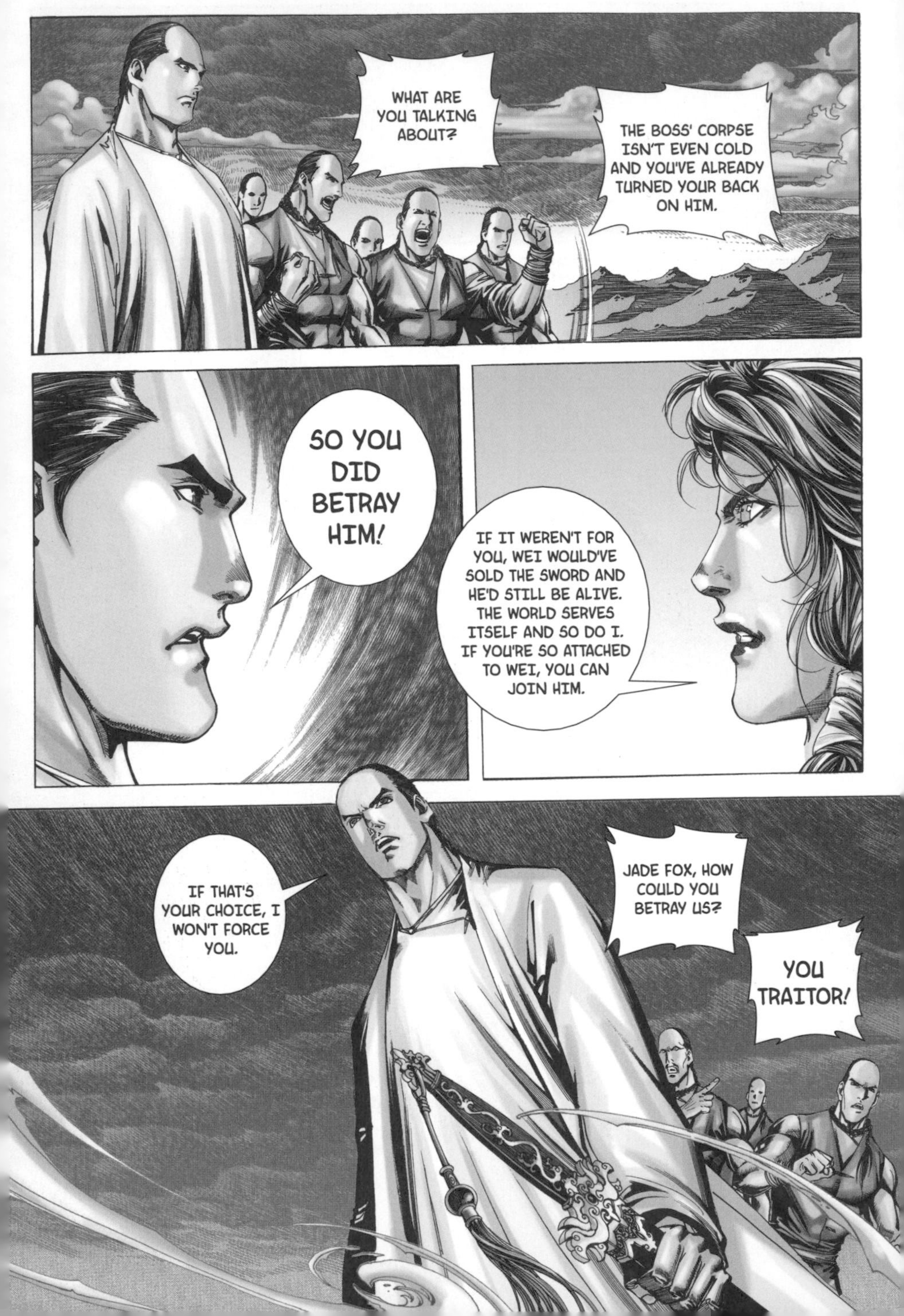
WHAT ARE YOU TALKING ABOUT?
THE BOSS' CORPSE ISN'T EVEN COLD AND YOU'VE ALREADY TURNED YOUR BACK ON HIM.
SO YOU DID BETRAY HIM!
IF IT WEREN'T FOR YOU, WEI WOULD'VE SOLD THE SWORD AND HE'D STILL BE ALIVE. THE WORLD SERVES ITSELF AND SO DO I. IF YOU'RE SO ATTACHED TO WEI, YOU CAN JOIN HIM.
IF THAT'S YOUR CHOICE, I WON'T FORCE YOU.
JADE FOX, HOW COULD YOU BETRAY US?
YOU TRAITOR!

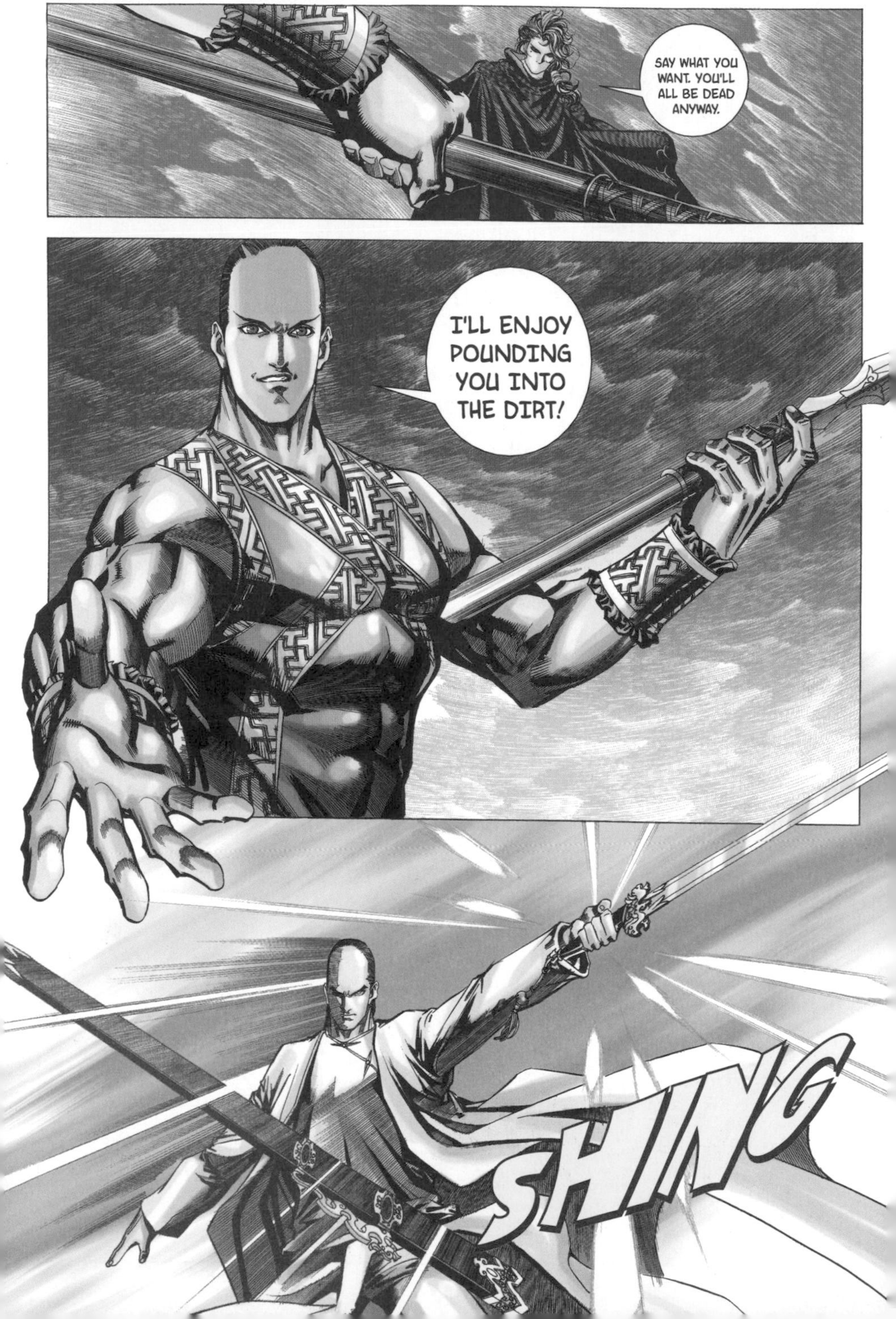
SAY WHAT YOU WANT. YOU'LL ALL BE DEAD ANYWAY.
I'LL ENJOY POUNDING YOU INTO THE DIRT!
SHING

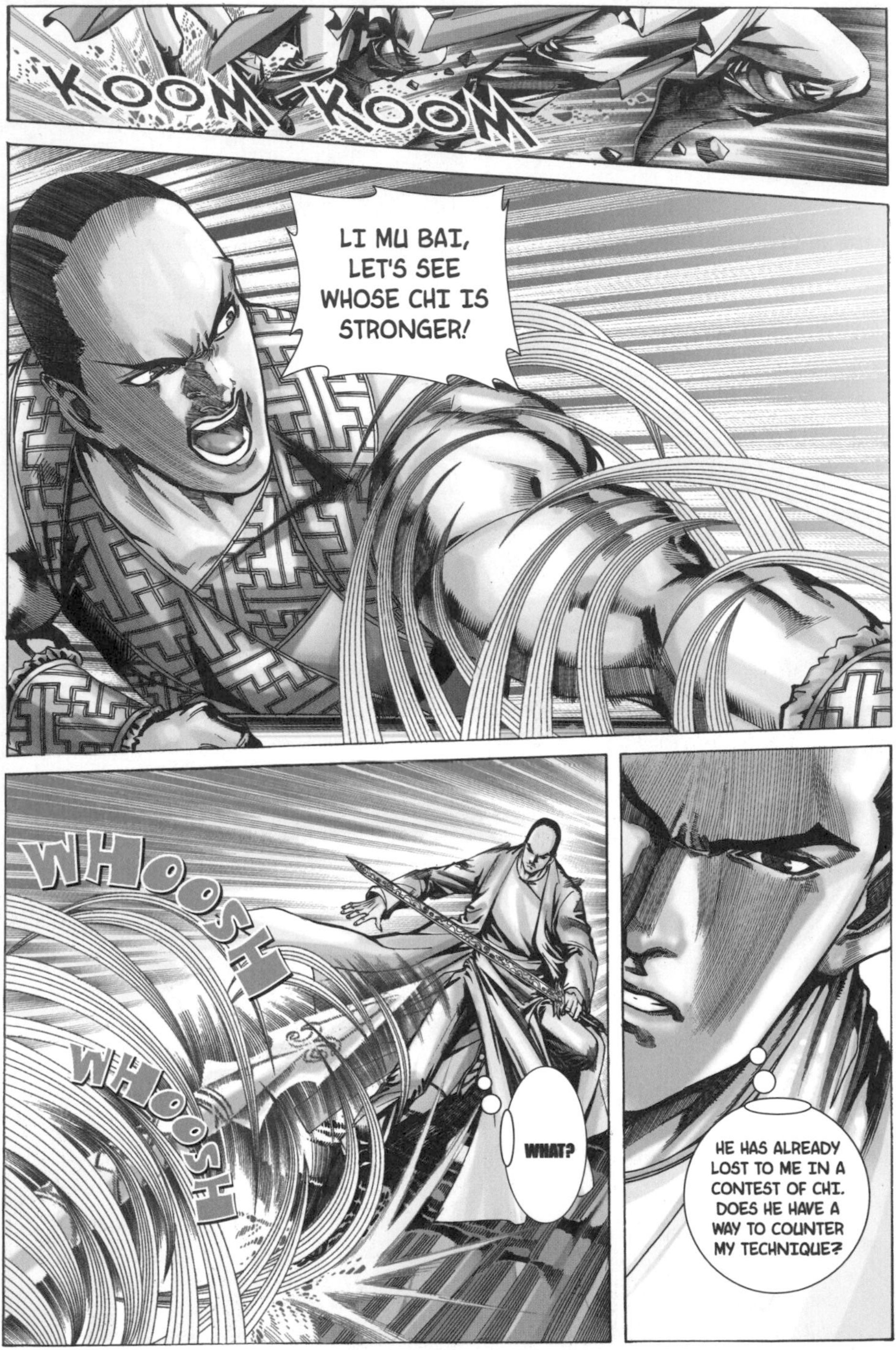
KOOM KOOM
LI MU BAI, LET'S SEE WHOSE CHI IS STRONGER!
WHOOSH
WHOOSH
WHAT?
HE HAS ALREADY LOST TO ME IN A CONTEST OF CHI. DOES HE HAVE A WAY TO COUNTER MY TECHNIQUE?

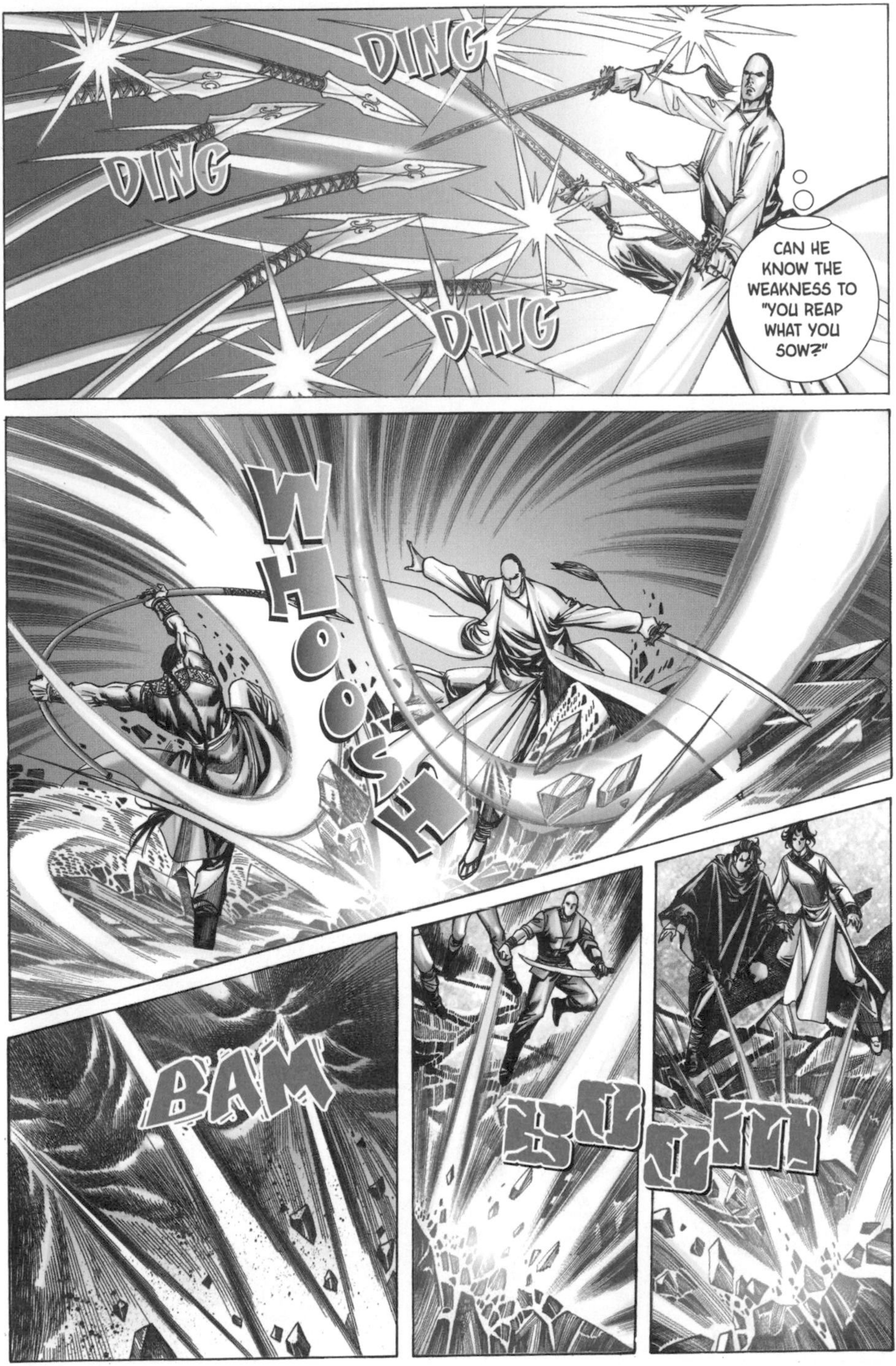
DING
DING
DING
CAN HE KNOW THE WEAKNESS TO "YOU REAP WHAT YOU SOW?"
WHOOSH
BAM

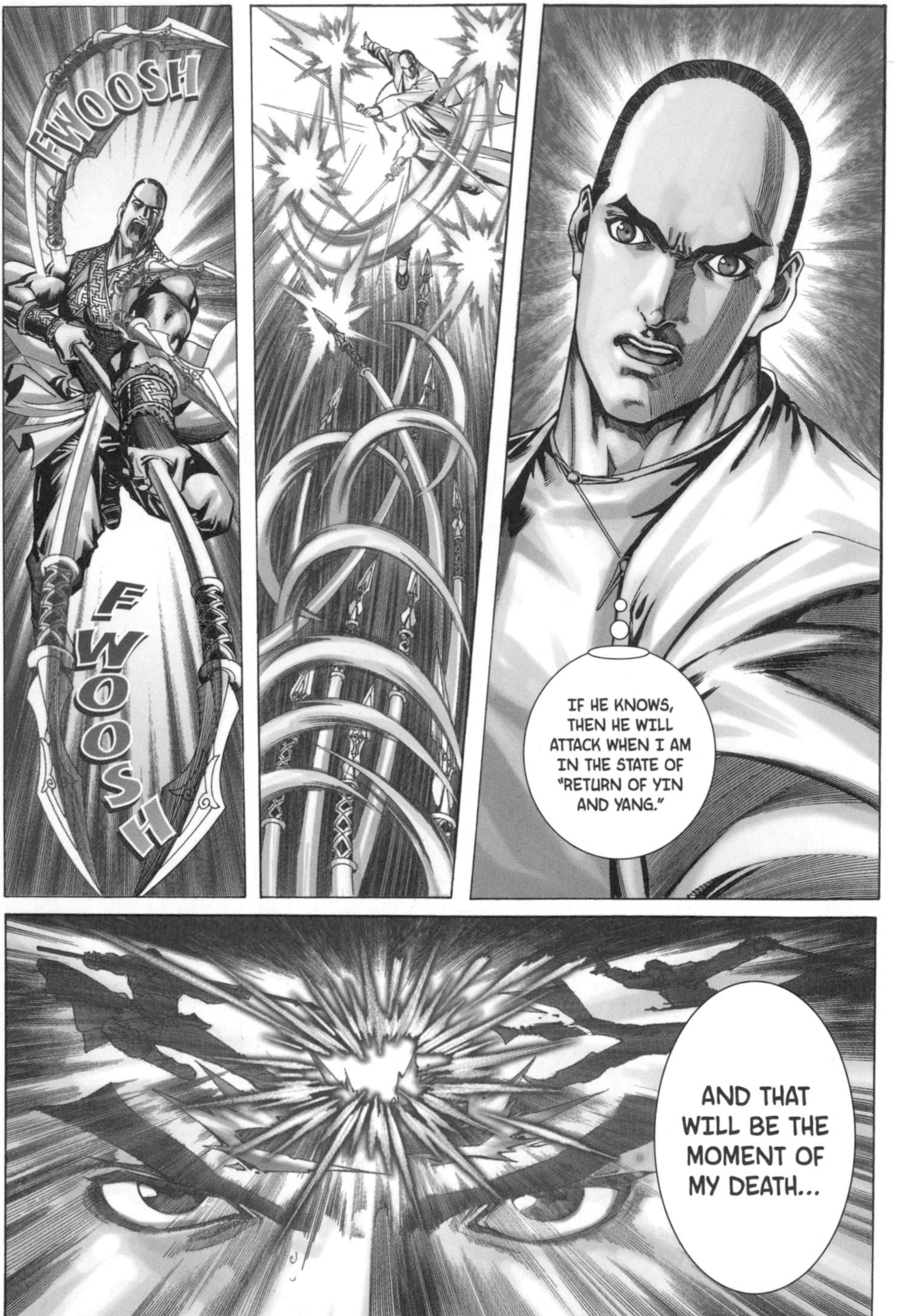
FWOOSH
FWOOSH
IF HE KNOWS, THEN HE WILL ATTACK WHEN I AM IN THE STATE OF "RETURN OF YIN AND YANG."
AND THAT WILL BE THE MOMENT OF MY DEATH...

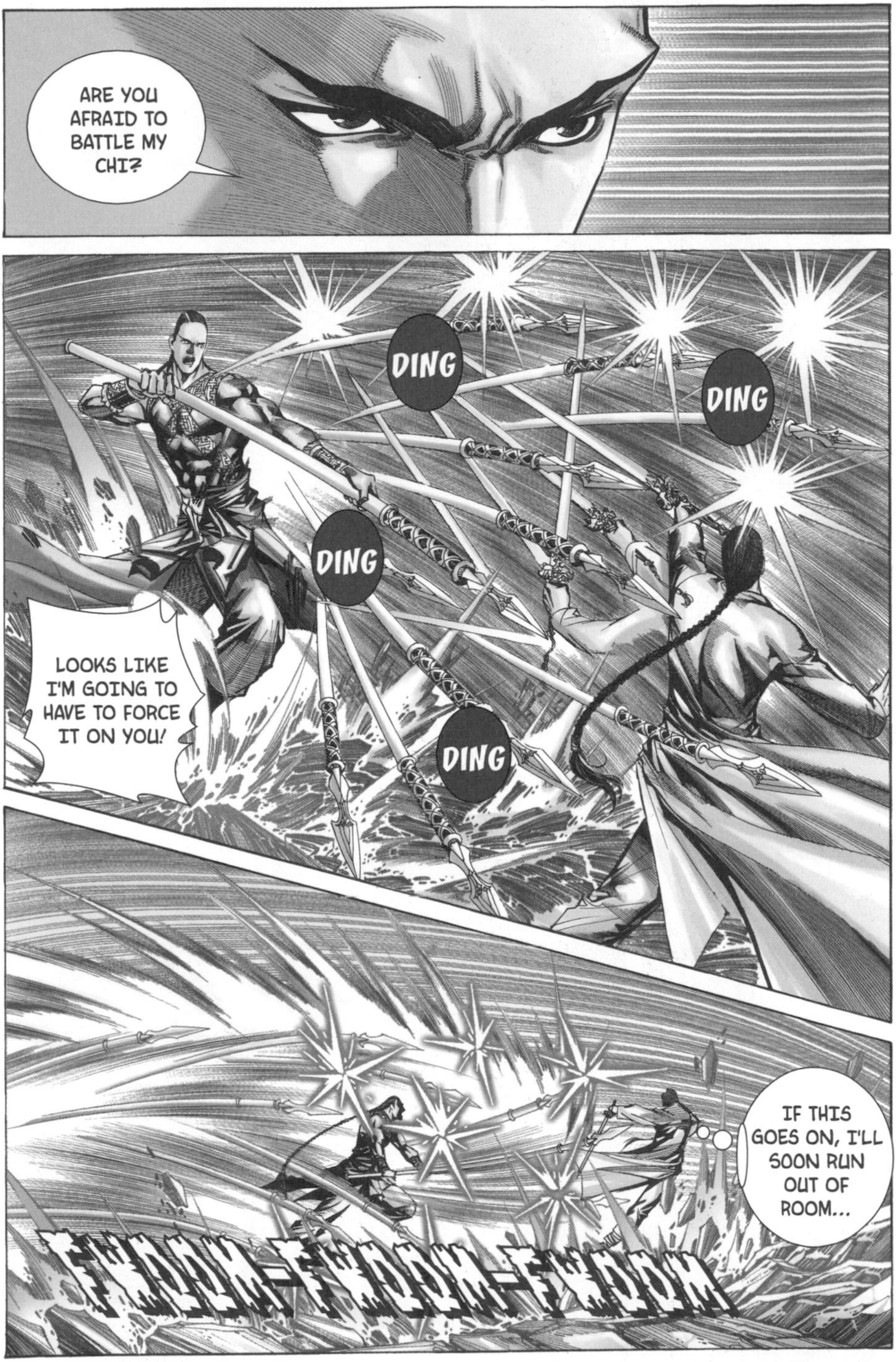
ARE YOU AFRAID TO BATTLE MY CHI?
DING
DING
DING
DING
LOOKS LIKE I'M GOING TO HAVE TO FORCE IT ON YOU!
IF THIS GOES ON, I'LL SOON RUN OUT OF ROOM...
FWOOM-FWOOM-FWOOM

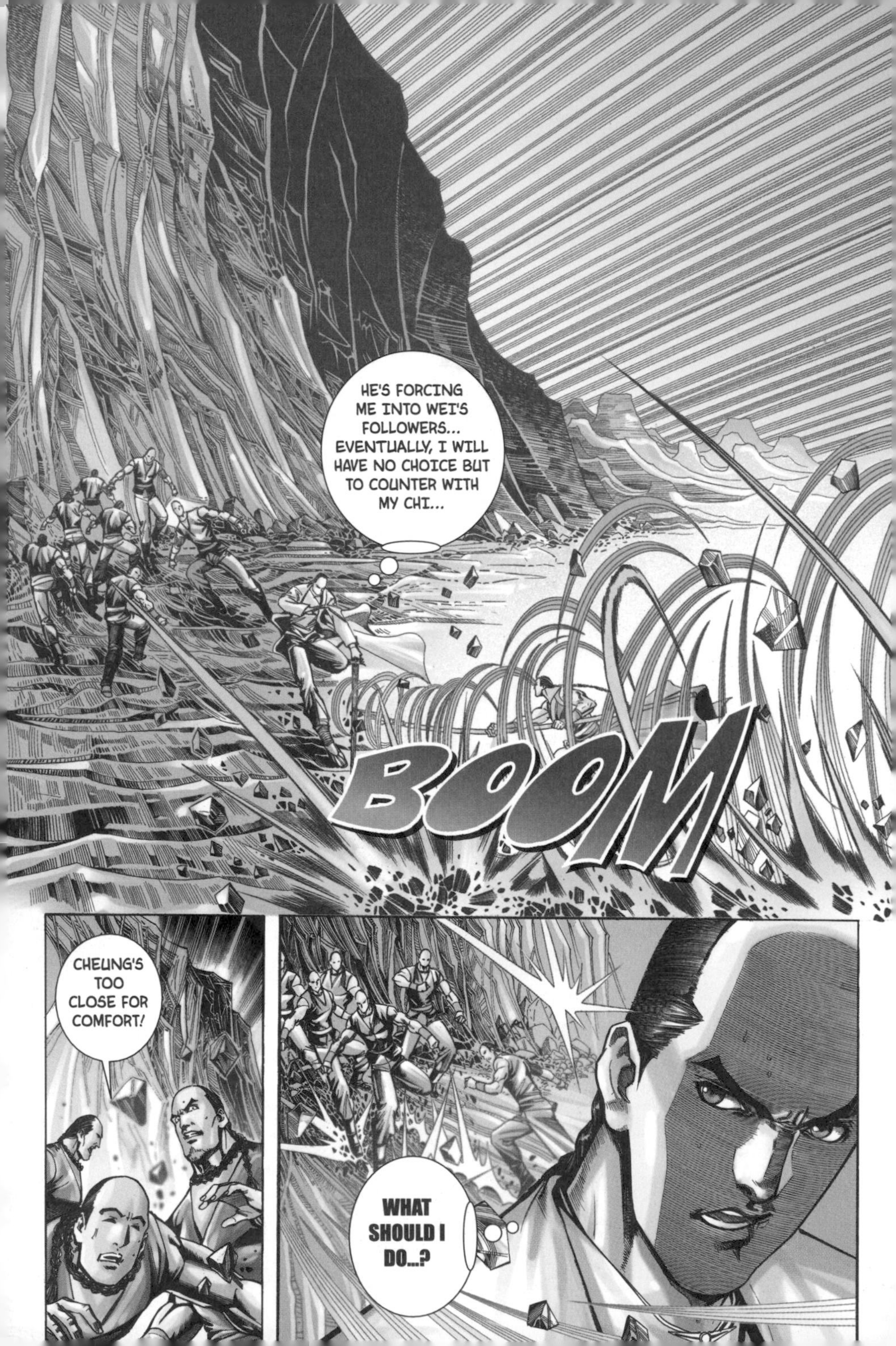
HE'S FORCING ME INTO WEI'S FOLLOWERS... EVENTUALLY, I WILL HAVE NO CHOICE BUT TO COUNTER WITH MY CHI...
BOOM
CHEUNG'S TOO CLOSE FOR COMFORT!
WHAT SHOULD I DO...?

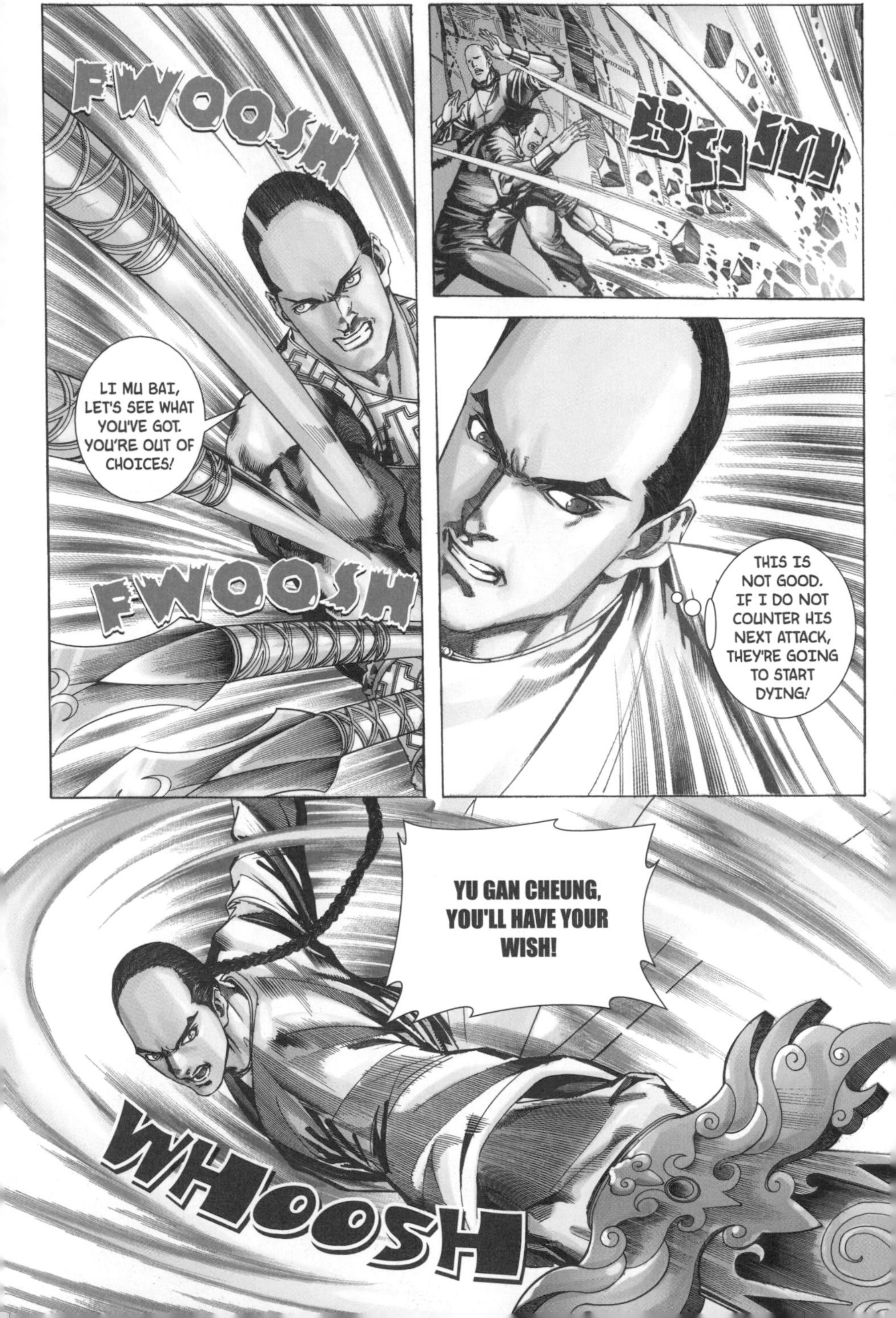
FWOOSH
LI MU BAI, LET'S SEE WHAT YOU'VE GOT. YOU'RE OUT OF CHOICES!
FWOOSH
THIS IS NOT GOOD. IF I DO NOT COUNTER HIS NEXT ATTACK, THEY'RE GOING TO START DYING!
YU GAN CHEUNG, YOU'LL HAVE YOUR WISH!
WHOOSH

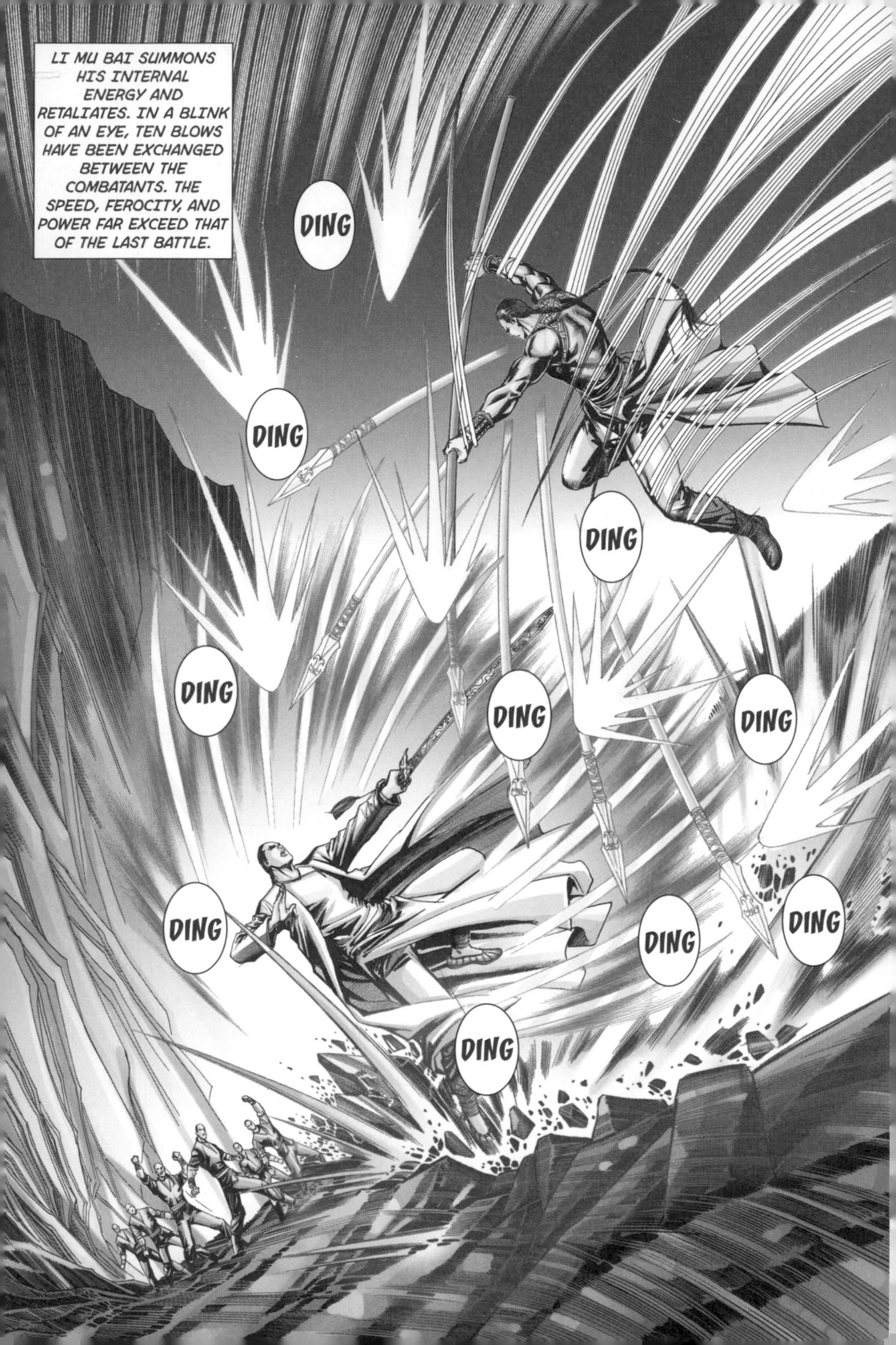
LI MU BAI SUMMONS HIS INTERNAL ENERGY AND RETALIATES. IN A BLINK OF AN EYE, TEN BLOWS HAVE BEEN EXCHANGED BETWEEN THE COMBATANTS. THE SPEED, FEROCITY, AND POWER FAR EXCEED THAT OF THE LAST BATTLE.
DING
DING
DING
DING
DING
DING
DING
DING
DING
DING

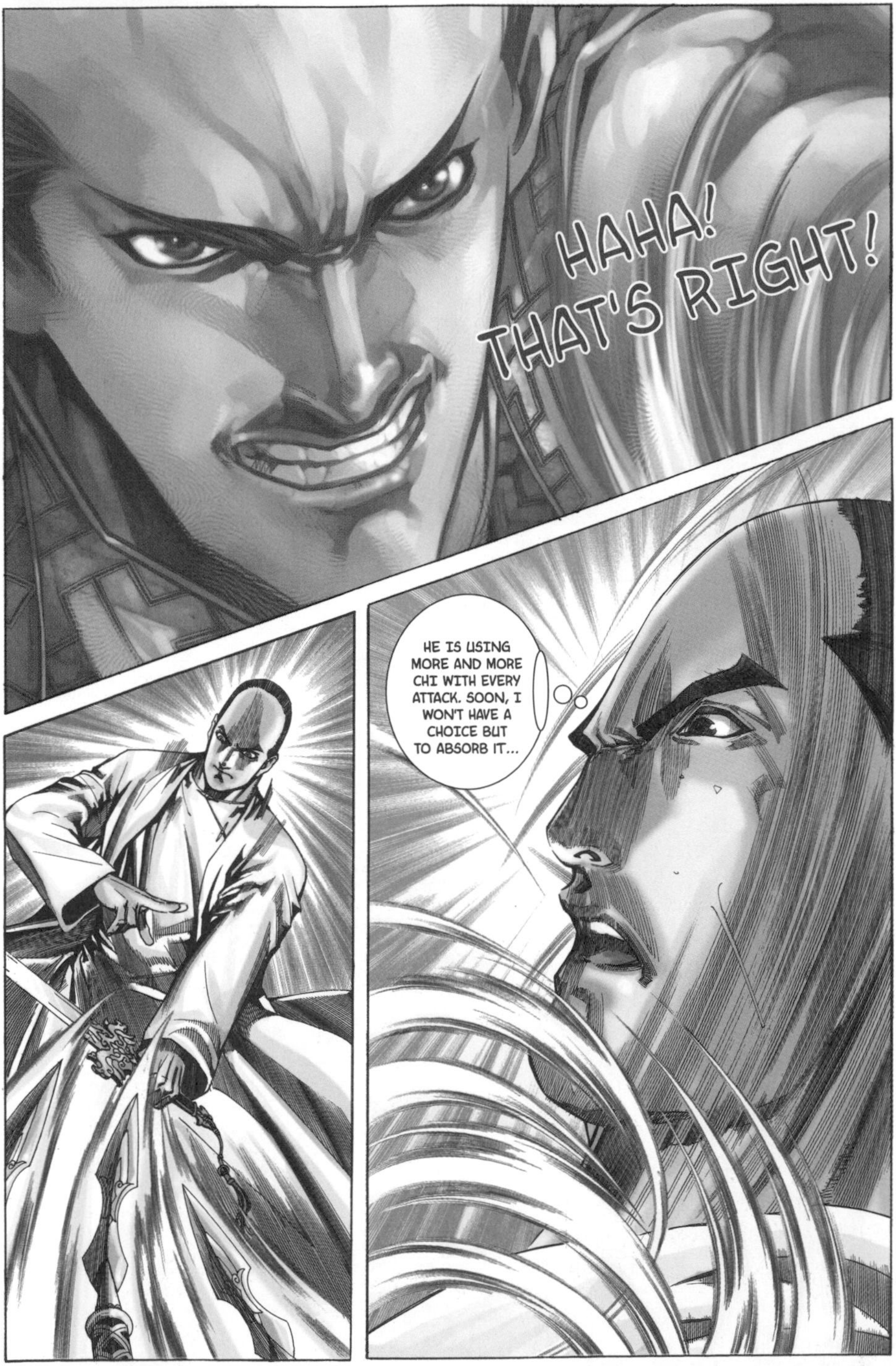
HAHA! THAT'S RIGHT!
HE IS USING MORE AND MORE CHI WITH EVERY ATTACK. SOON, I WON'T HAVE A CHOICE BUT TO ABSORB IT...

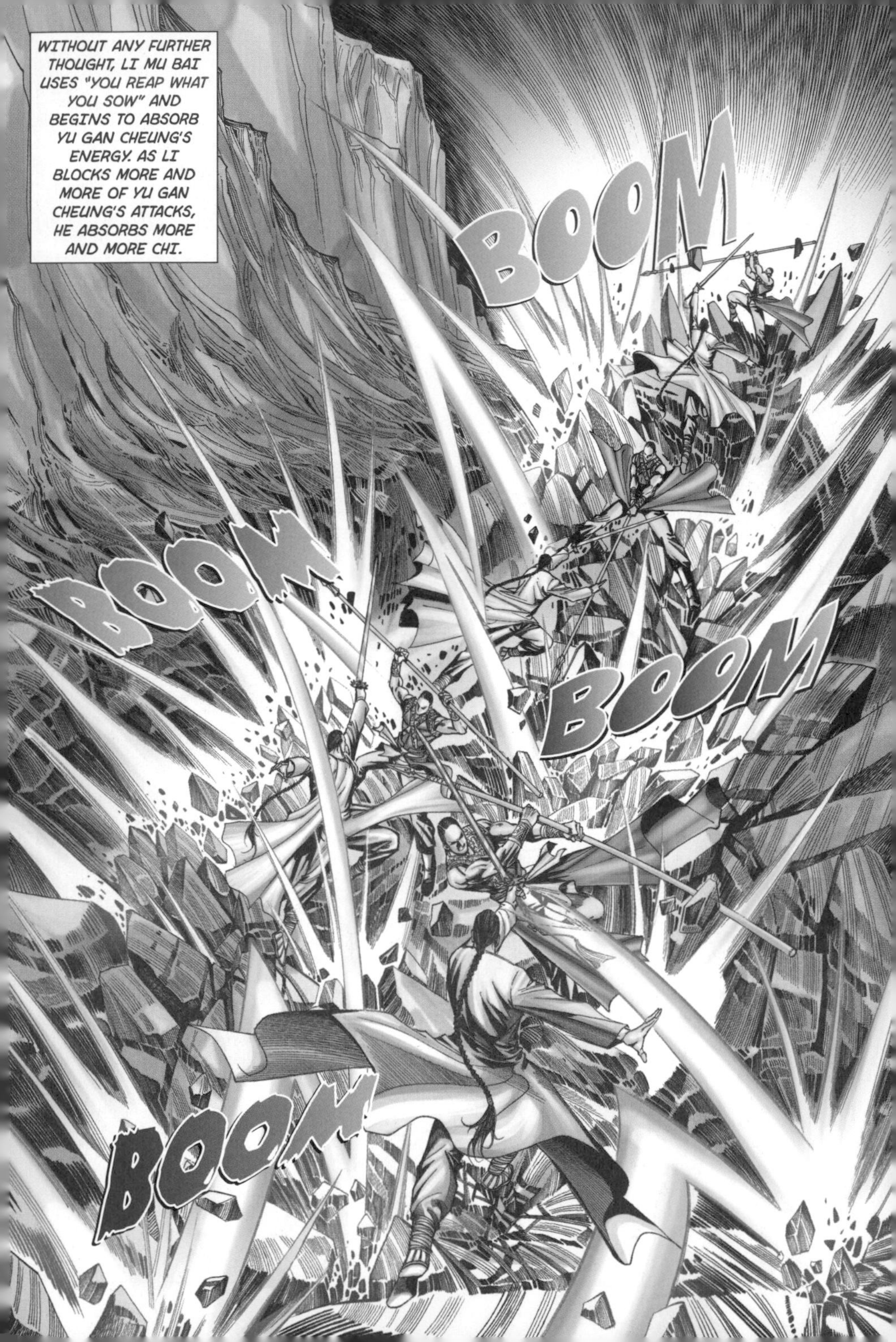
WITHOUT ANY FURTHER THOUGHT, LI MU BAI USES "YOU REAP WHAT YOU SOW" AND BEGINS TO ABSORB YU GAN CHEUNG'S ENERGY. AS LI BLOCKS MORE AND MORE OF YU GAN CHEUNG'S ATTACKS, HE ABSORBS MORE AND MORE CHI.
BOOM
BOOM
BOOM
BOOM

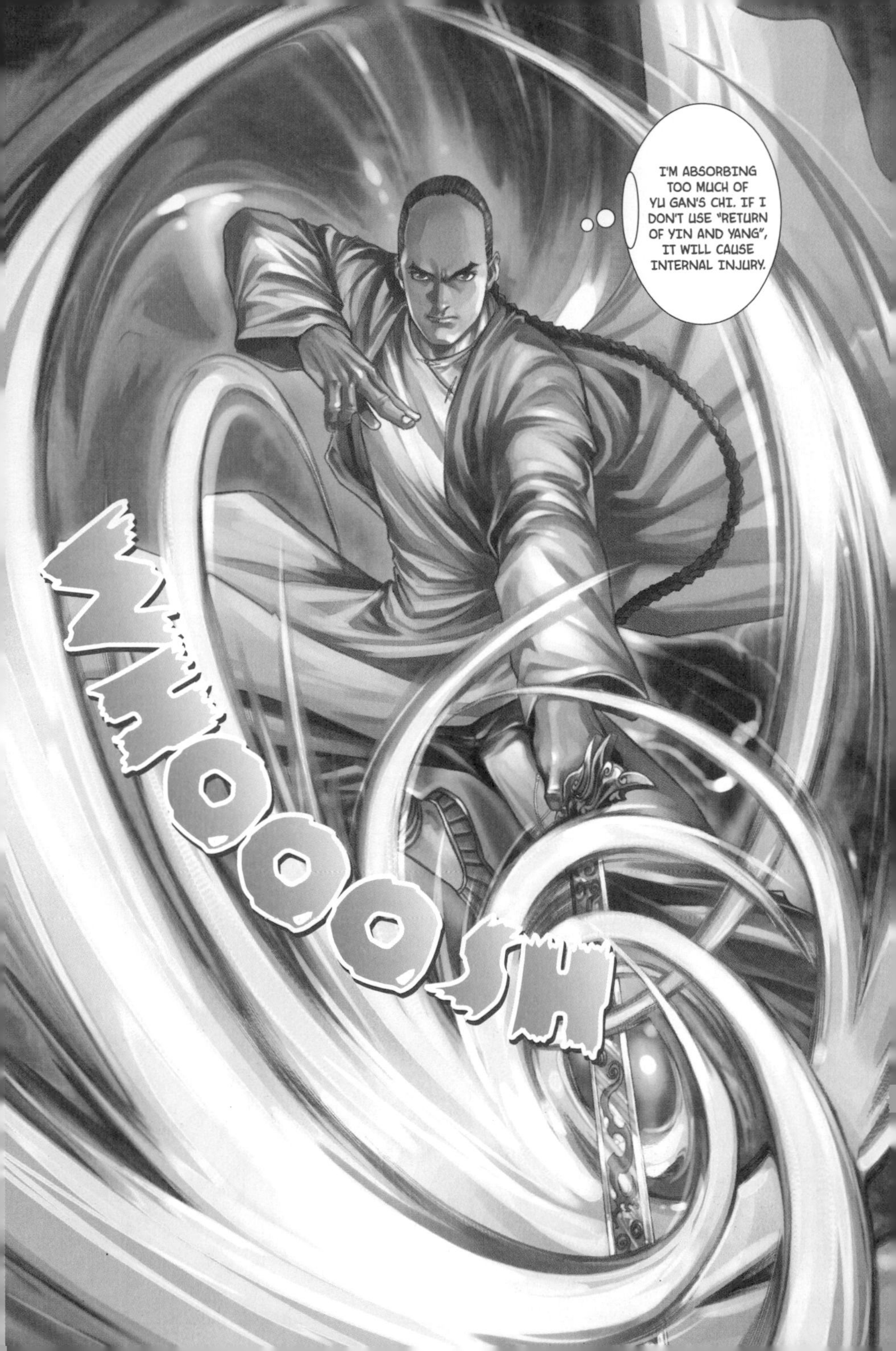
I'M ABSORBING TOO MUCH OF YU GAN'S CHI. IF I DON'T USE "RETURN OF YIN AND YANG", IT WILL CAUSE INTERNAL INJURY.
WHOOOOSH

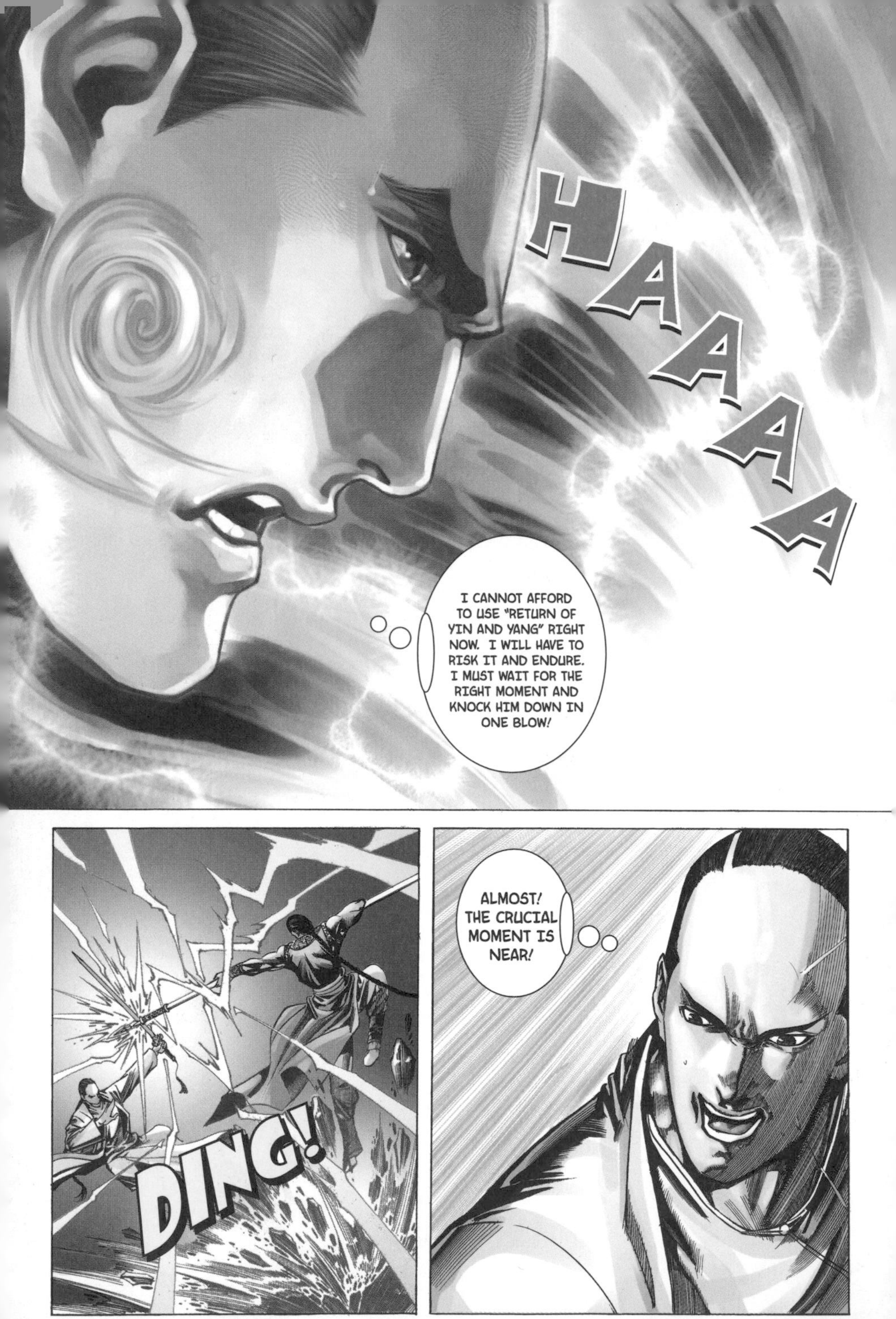
HAAAAA
I CANNOT AFFORD TO USE "RETURN OF YIN AND YANG" RIGHT NOW. I WILL HAVE TO RISK IT AND ENDURE. I MUST WAIT FOR THE RIGHT MOMENT AND KNOCK HIM DOWN IN ONE BLOW!
DING!
ALMOST! THE CRUCIAL MOMENT IS NEAR!

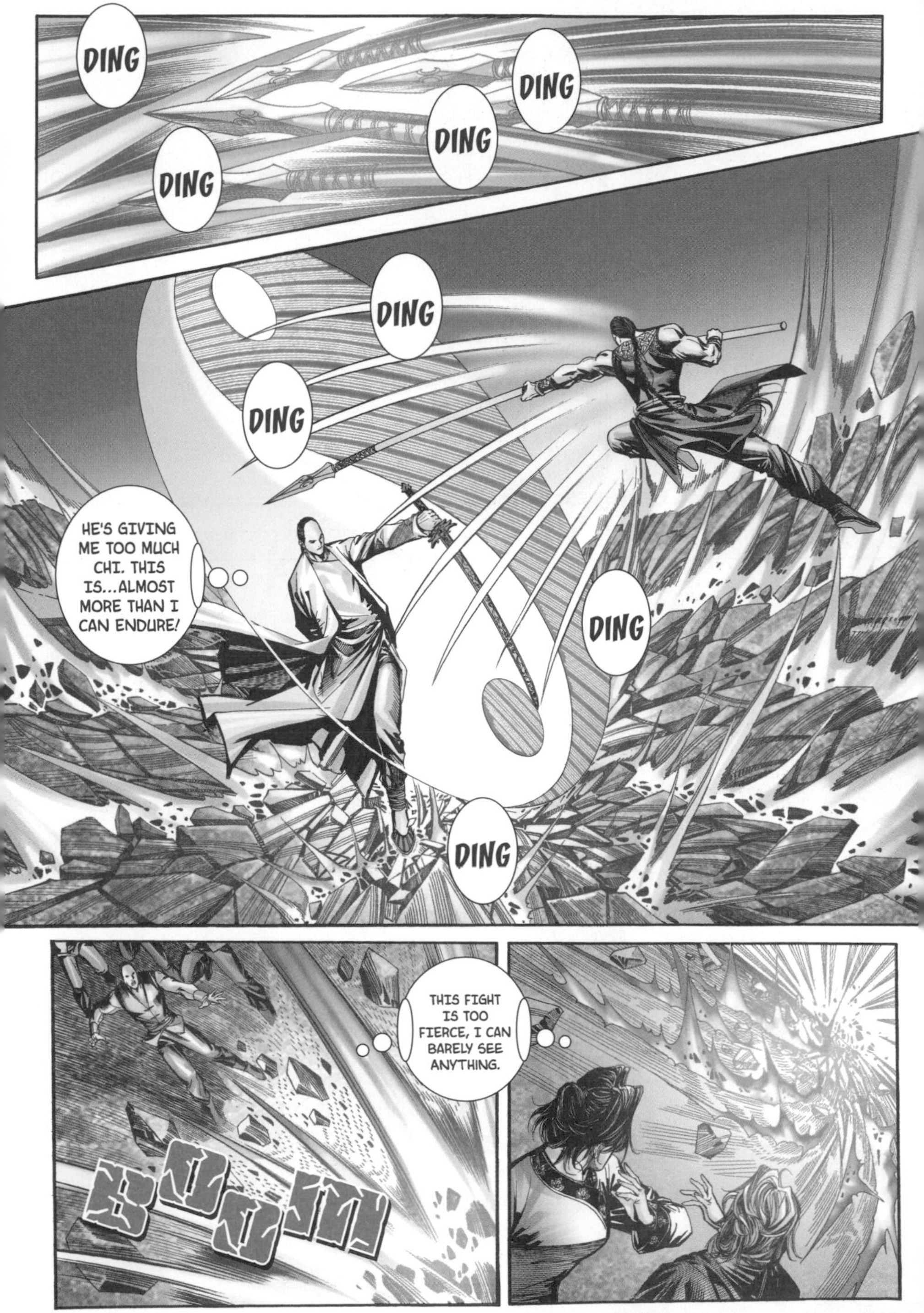
DING
DING
DING
DING
DING
DING
HE'S GIVING ME TOO MUCH CHI. THIS IS...ALMOST MORE THAN I CAN ENDURE!
DING
DING
THIS FIGHT IS TOO FIERCE, I CAN BARELY SEE ANYTHING.

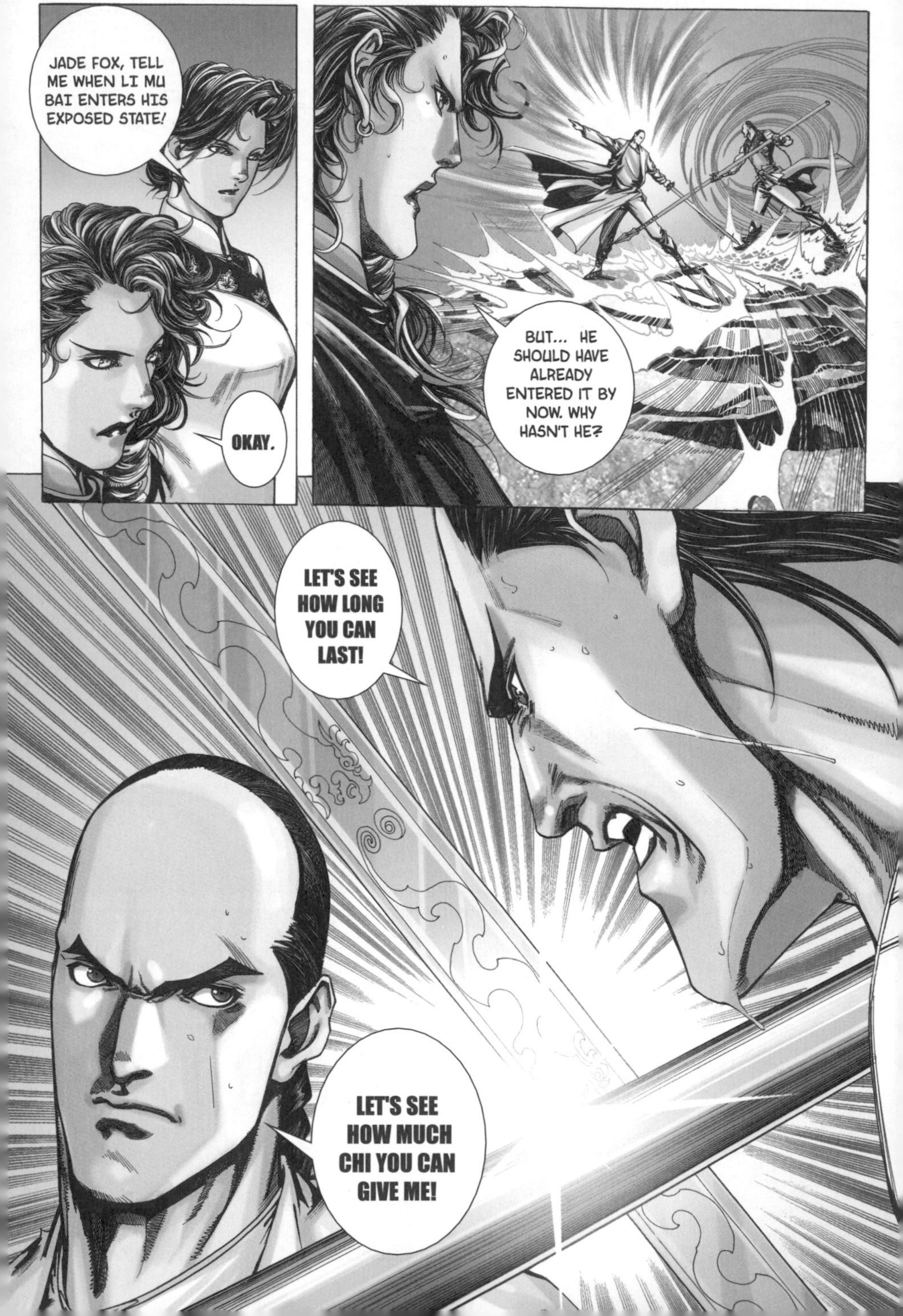
JADE FOX, TELL ME WHEN LI MU BAI ENTERS HIS EXPOSED STATE!
OKAY.
BUT... HE SHOULD HAVE ALREADY ENTERED IT BY NOW. WHY HASN'T HE?
LET'S SEE HOW LONG YOU CAN LAST!
LET'S SEE HOW MUCH CHI YOU CAN GIVE ME!

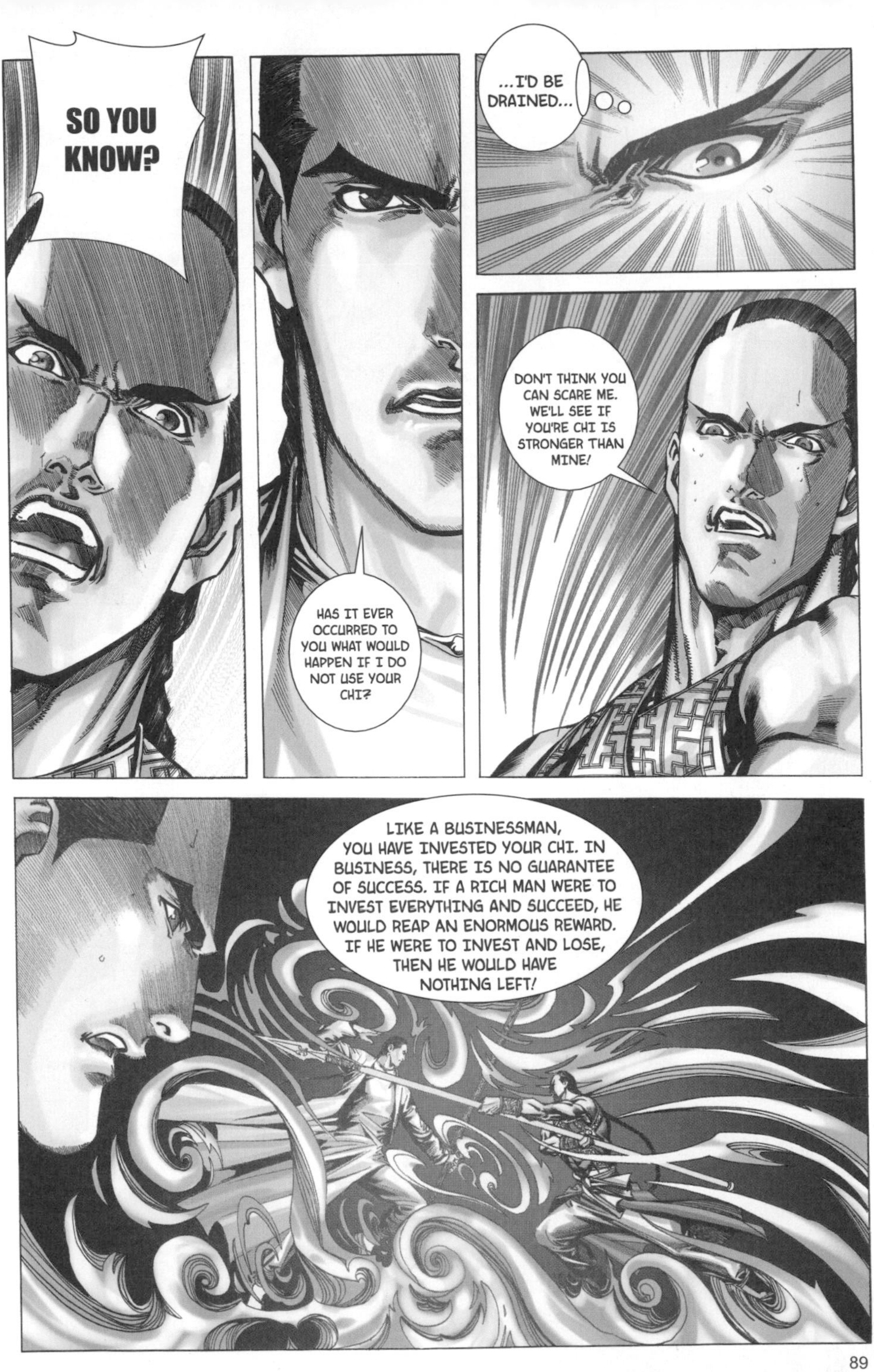
SO YOU KNOW?
...I'D BE DRAINED...
HAS IT EVER OCCURRED TO YOU WHAT WOULD HAPPEN IF I DO NOT USE YOUR CHI?
DON'T THINK YOU CAN SCARE ME. WE'LL SEE IF YOU'RE CHI IS STRONGER THAN MINE!
LIKE A BUSINESSMAN, YOU HAVE INVESTED YOUR CHI. IN BUSINESS, THERE IS NO GUARANTEE OF SUCCESS. IF A RICH MAN WERE TO INVEST EVERYTHING AND SUCCEED, HE WOULD REAP AN ENORMOUS REWARD. IF HE WERE TO INVEST AND LOSE, THEN HE WOULD HAVE NOTHING LEFT!

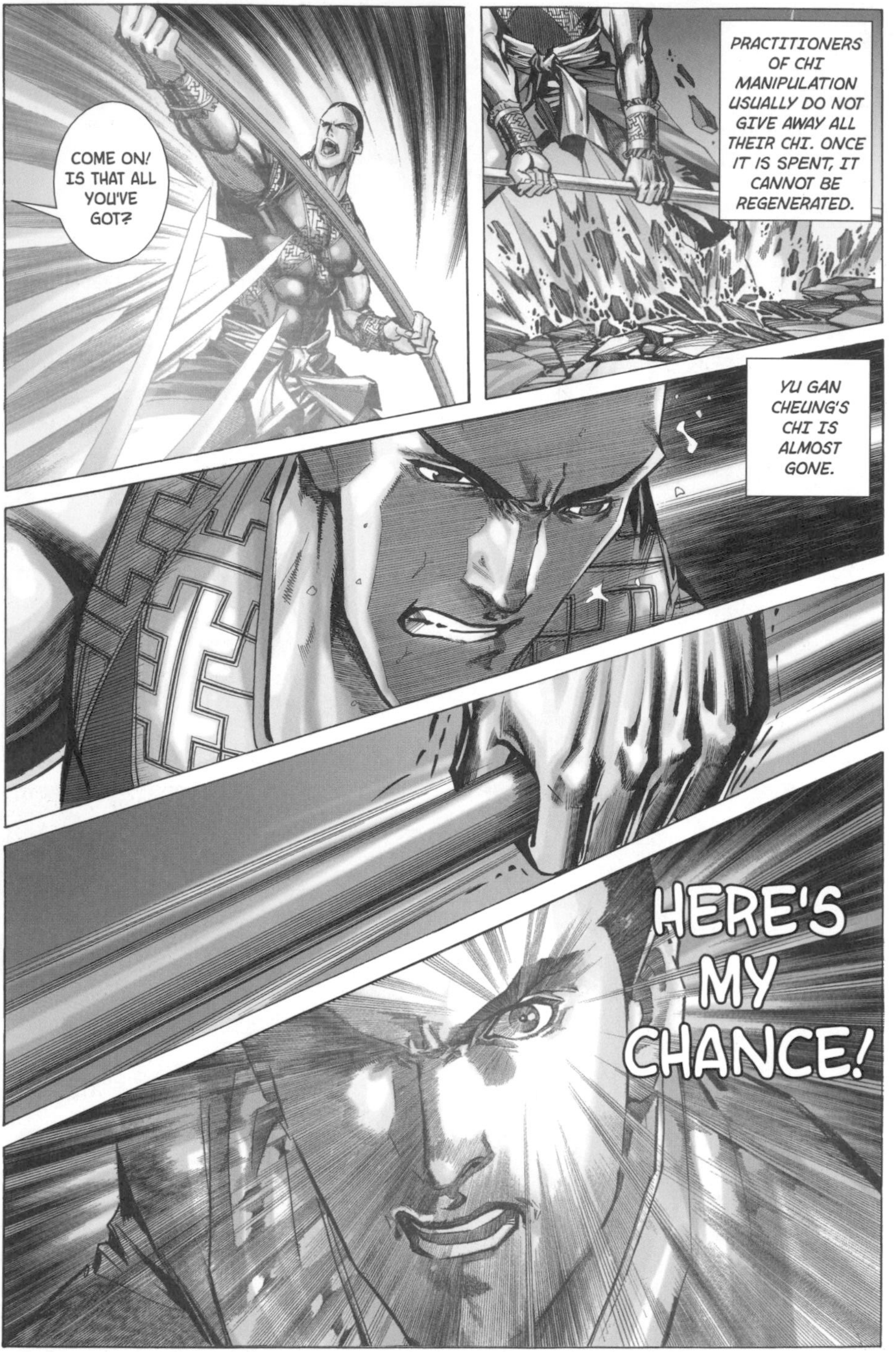
COME ON! IS THAT ALL YOU'VE GOT?
PRACTITIONERS OF CHI MANIPULATION USUALLY DO NOT GIVE AWAY ALL THEIR CHI. ONCE IT IS SPENT, IT CANNOT BE REGENERATED.
YU GAN CHEUNG'S CHI IS ALMOST GONE.
HERE'S MY CHANCE!

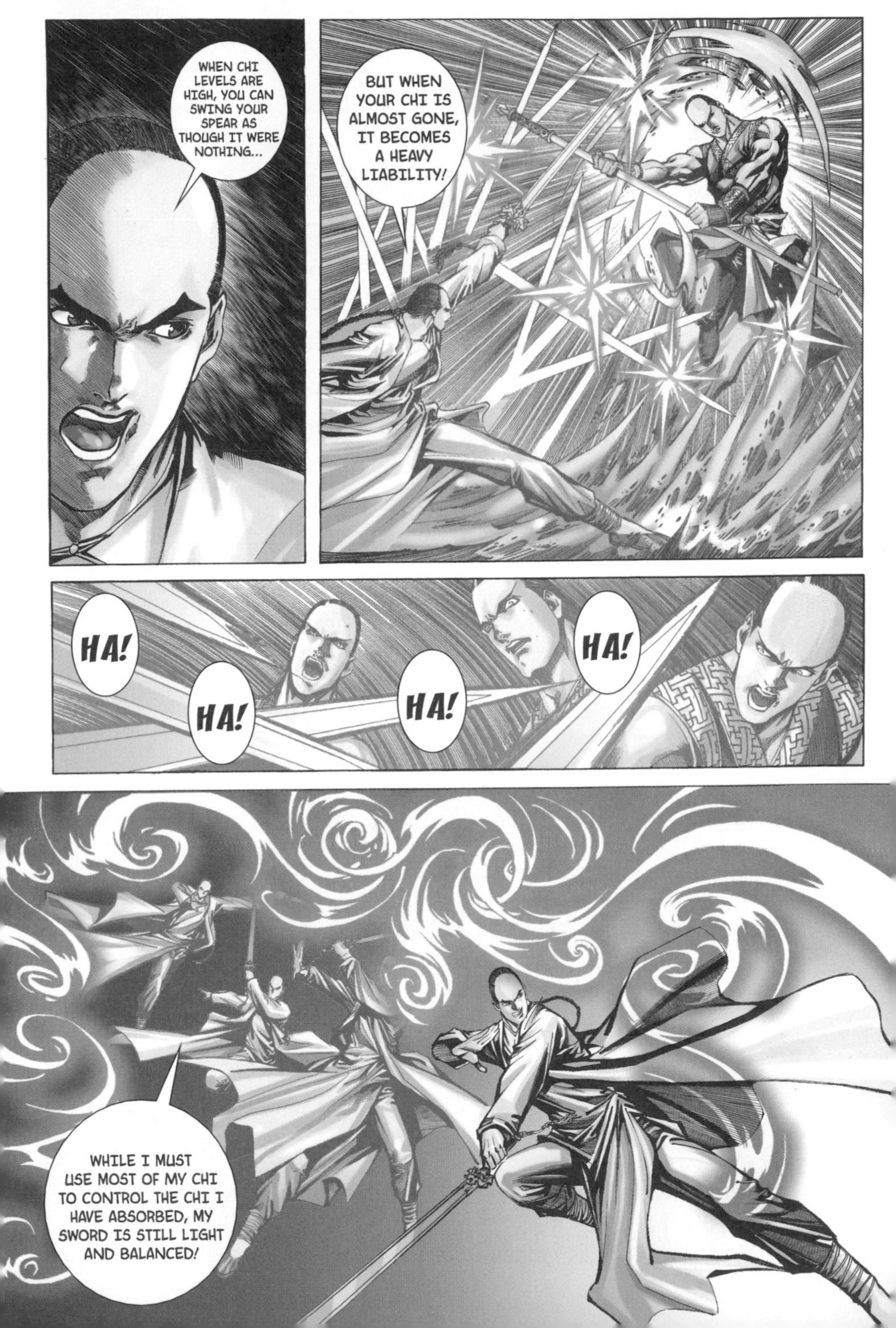
WHEN CHI LEVELS ARE HIGH, YOU CAN SWING YOUR SPEAR AS THOUGH IT WERE NOTHING...
BUT WHEN YOUR CHI IS ALMOST GONE, IT BECOMES A HEAVY LIABILITY!
HA!
HA!
HA!
HA!
WHILE I MUST USE MOST OF MY CHI TO CONTROL THE CHI I HAVE ABSORBED, MY SWORD IS STILL LIGHT AND BALANCED!

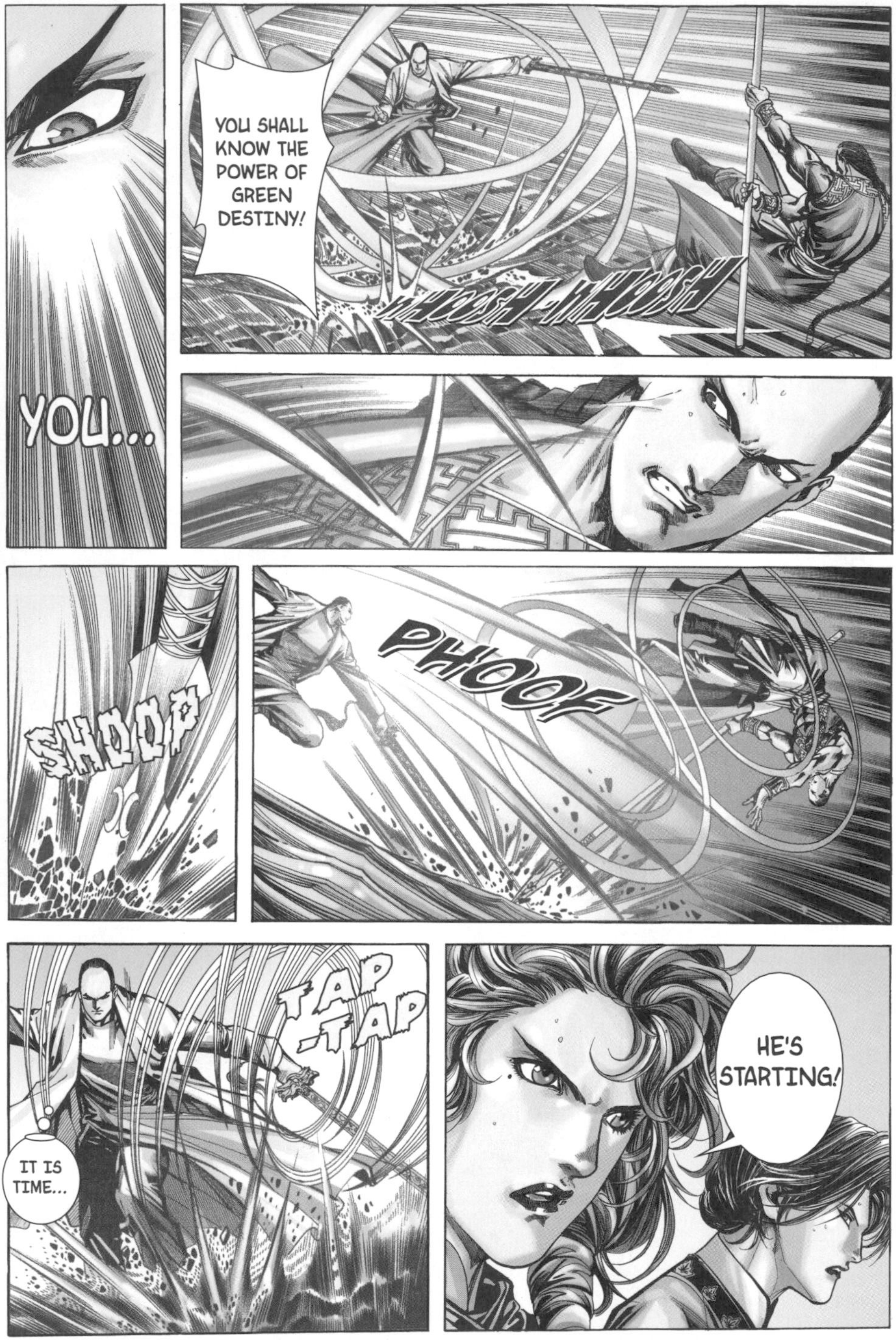
YOU SHALL KNOW THE POWER OF GREEN DESTINY!
YOU...
SHOOP
PHOOF
TAP-TAP
IT IS TIME...
HE'S STARTING!

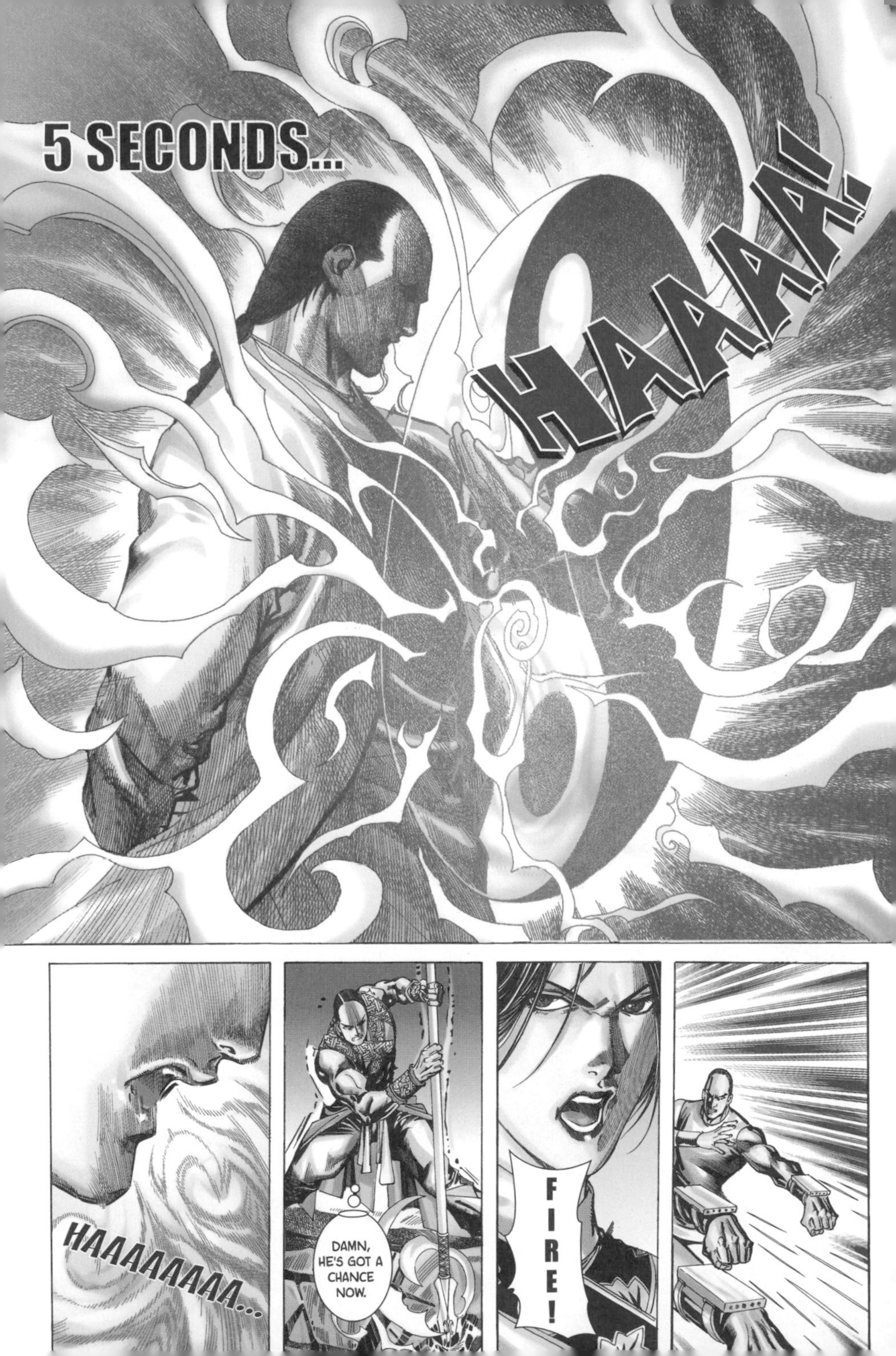
5 SECONDS...
HAAAA!
HAAAAAAAAA...
DAMN, HE'S GOT A CHANCE NOW.
FIRE!

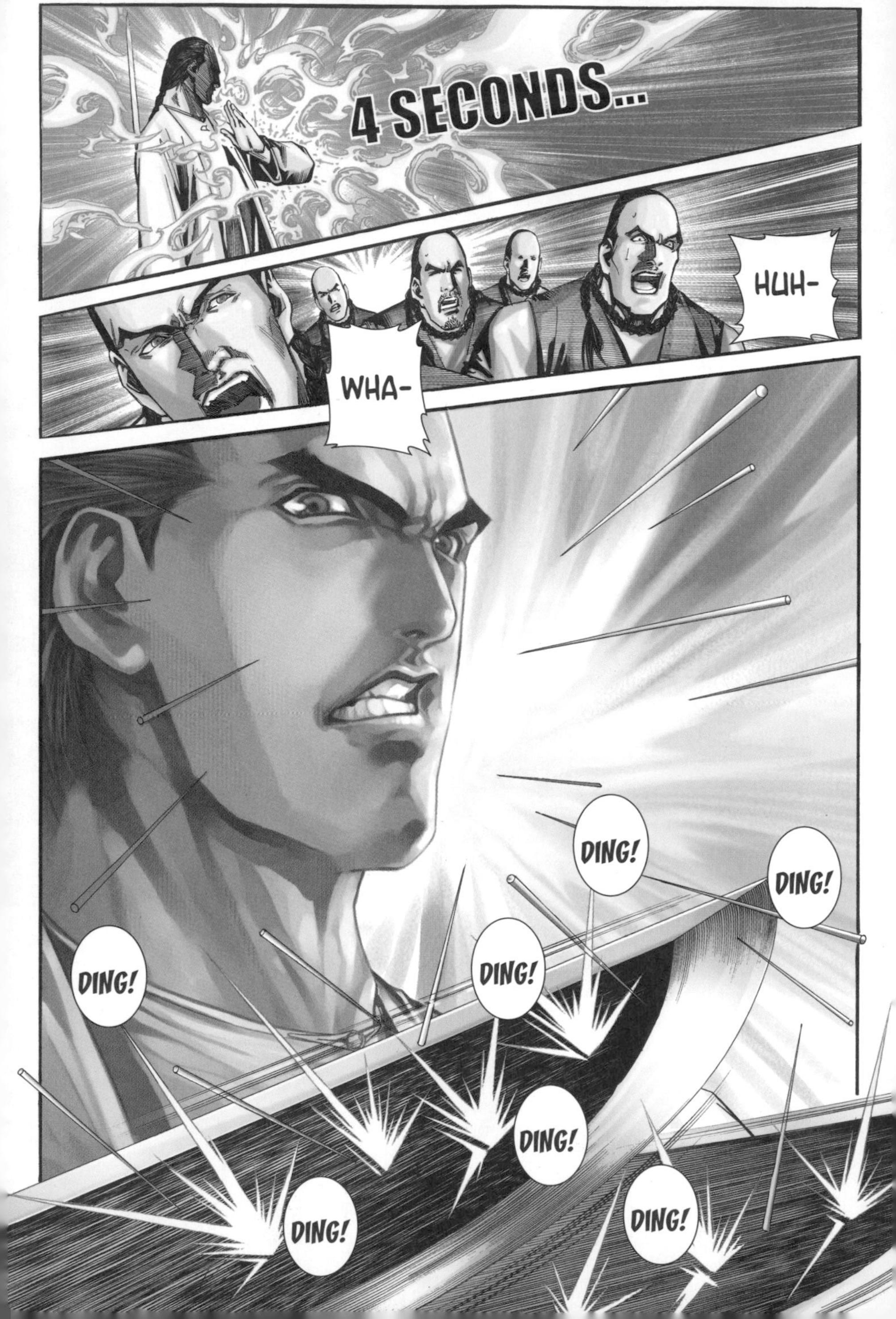
4 SECONDS...
HUH-
WHA-
DING!
DING!
DING!
DING!
DING!
DING!
DING!

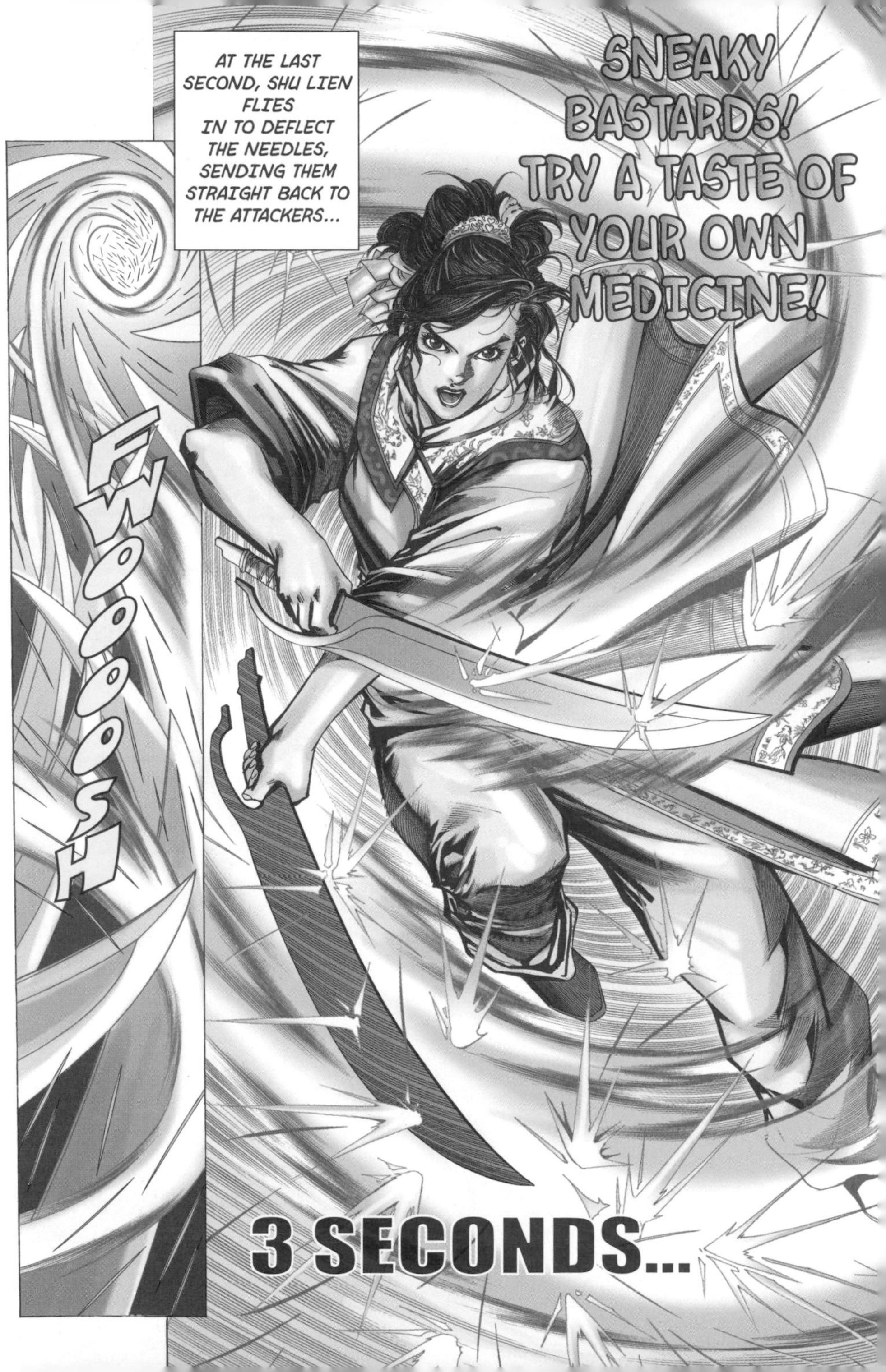

AT THE LAST SECOND, SHU LIEN FLIES IN TO DEFLECT THE NEEDLES, SENDING THEM STRAIGHT BACK TO THE ATTACKERS...
SNEAKY BASTARDS! TRY A TASTE OF YOUR OWN MEDICINE!
FWOOOOOSH
3 SECONDS...

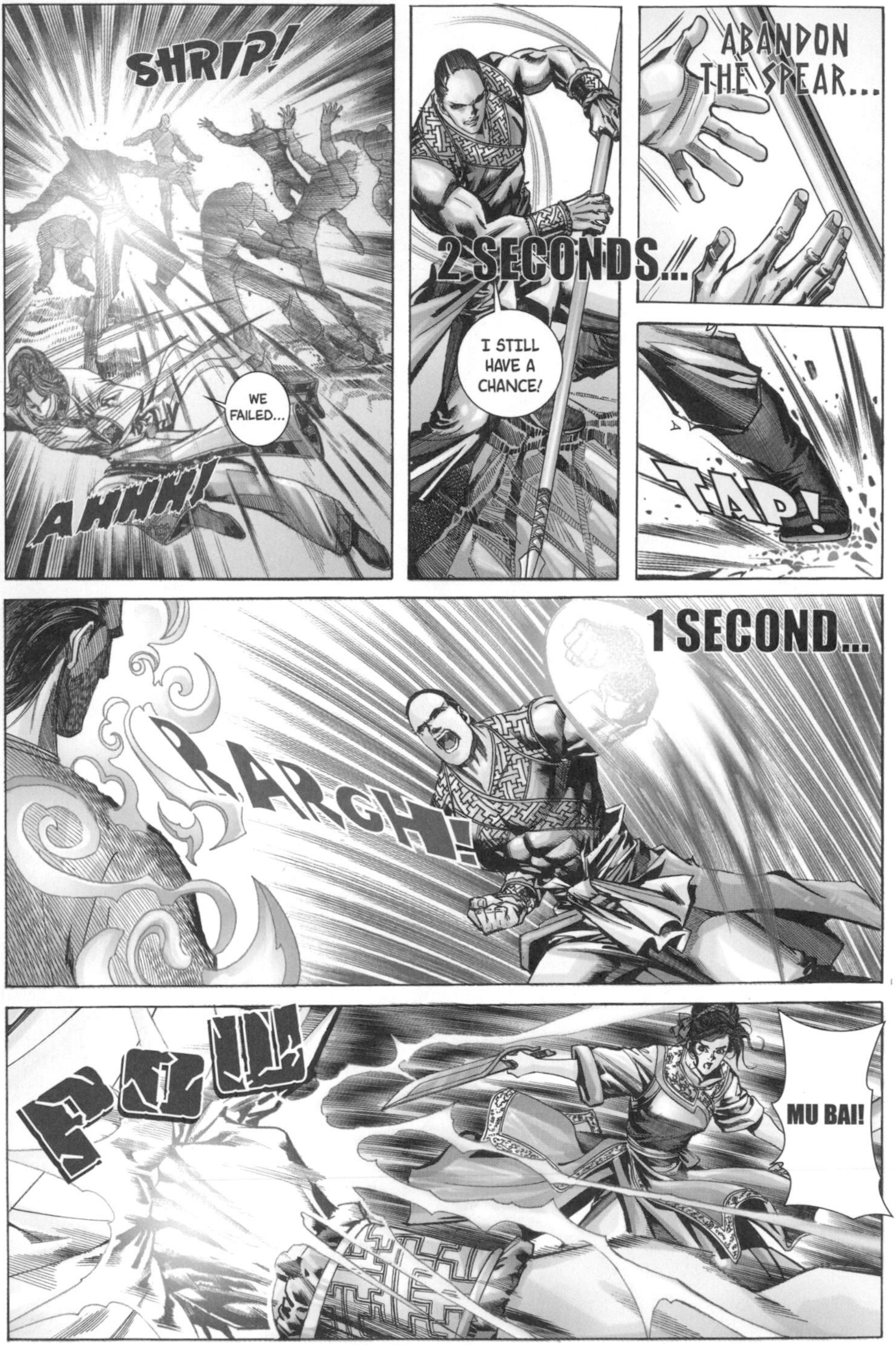
SHRIP!
WE FAILED...
AHHH!
2 SECONDS...
I STILL HAVE A CHANCE!
ABANDON THE SPEAR...
TAP!
1 SECOND...
RARGH!
MU BAI!

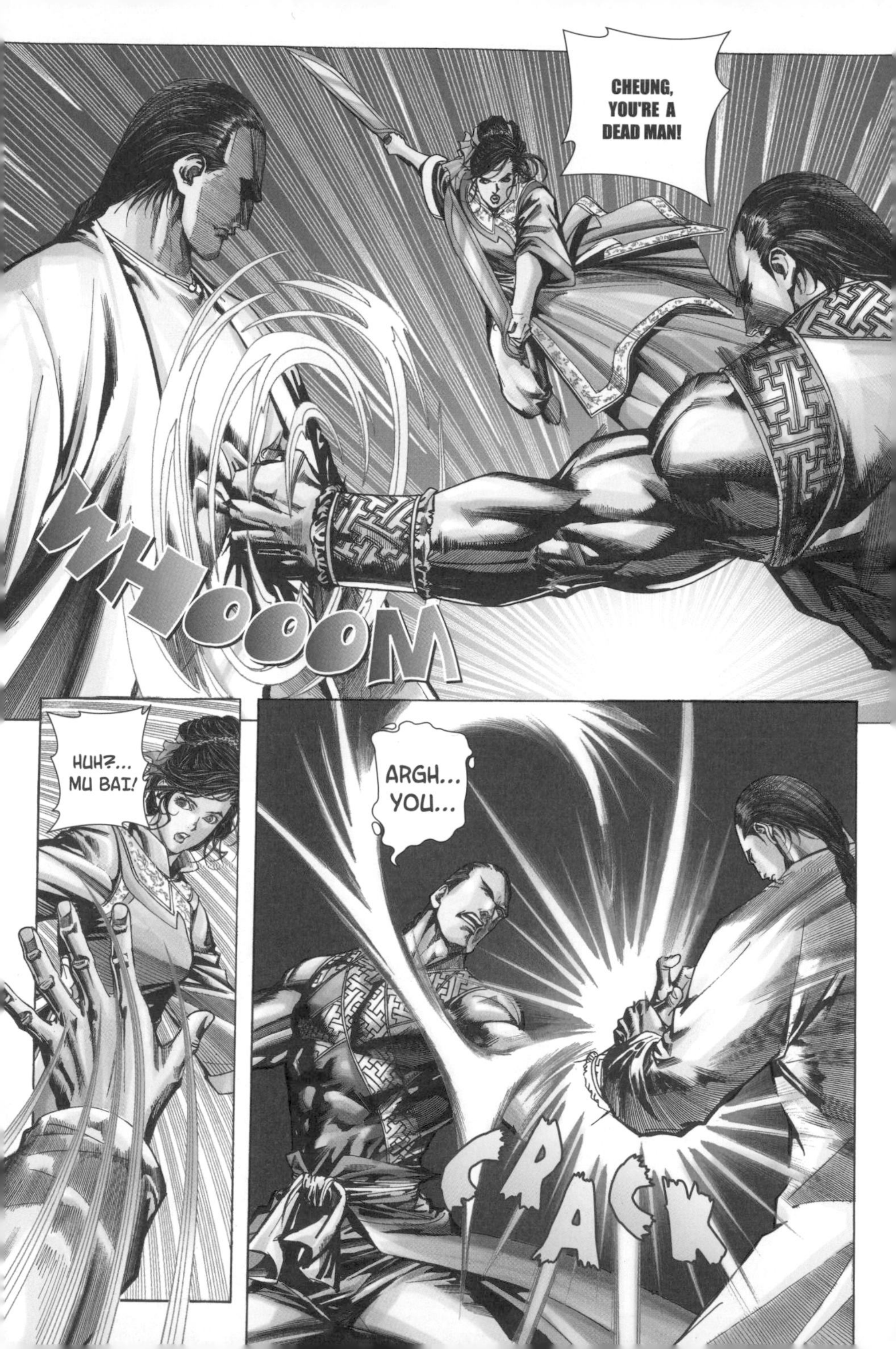
CHEUNG, YOU'RE A DEAD MAN!
WHOOOOM
HUH?... MU BAI!
ARGH... YOU...
CRACK

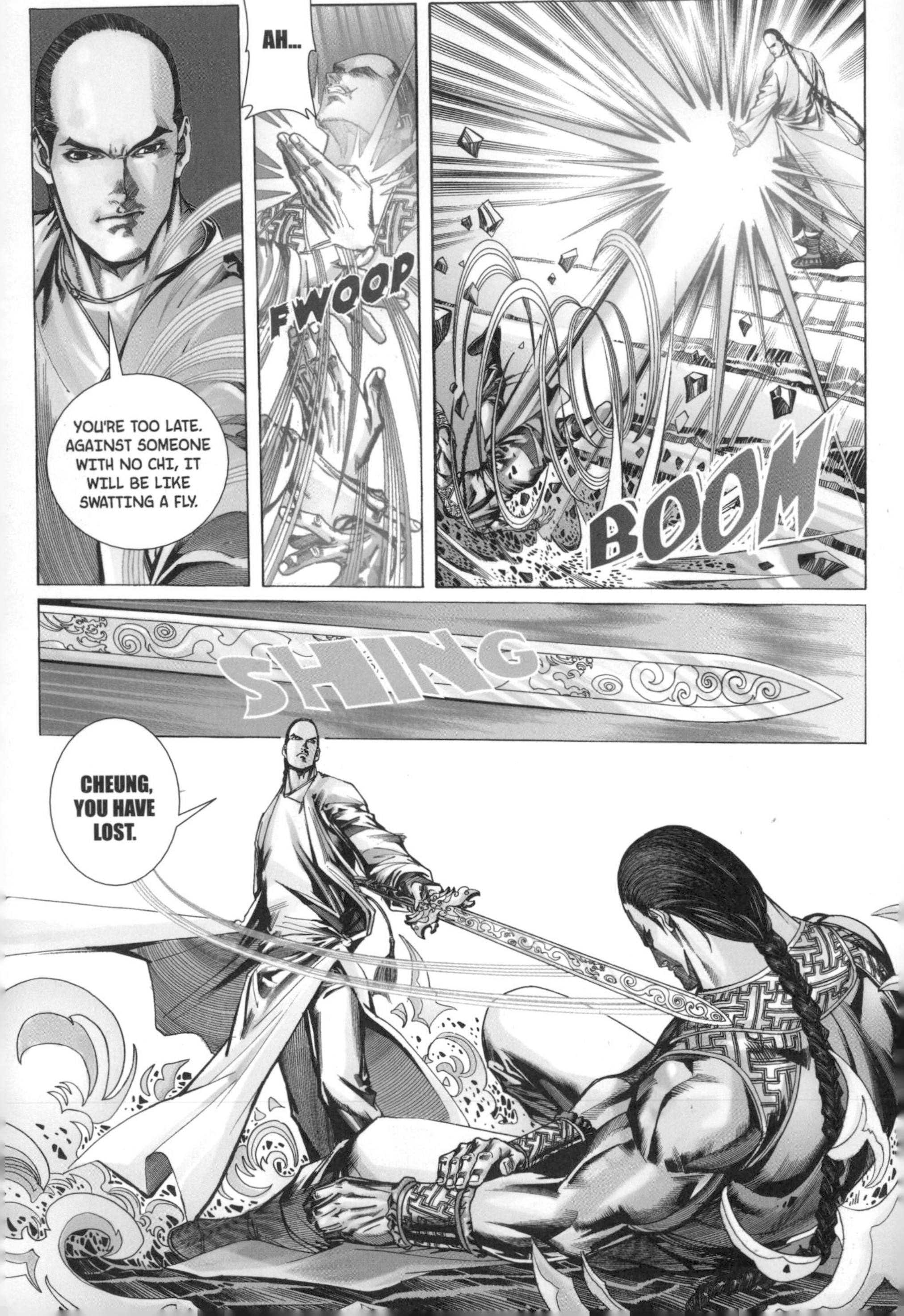
YOU'RE TOO LATE. AGAINST SOMEONE WITH NO CHI, IT WILL BE LIKE SWATTING A FLY.
AH...
FWOOP
BOOM
SHING
CHEUNG, YOU HAVE LOST.

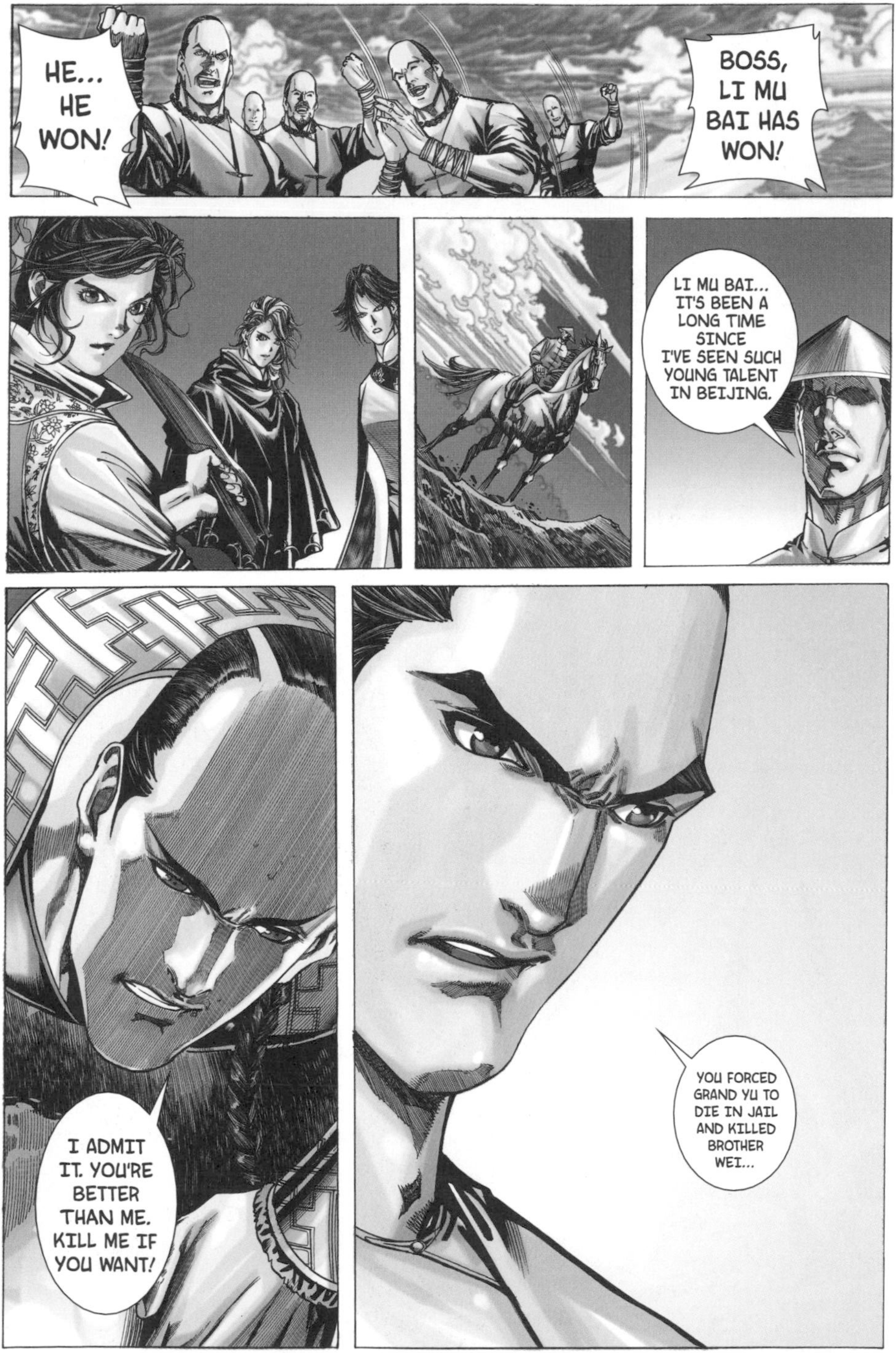
HE... HE WON!
BOSS, LI MU BAI HAS WON!
LI MU BAI... IT'S BEEN A LONG TIME SINCE I'VE SEEN SUCH YOUNG TALENT IN BEIJING.
I ADMIT IT. YOU'RE BETTER THAN ME. KILL ME IF YOU WANT!
YOU FORCED GRAND YU TO DIE IN JAIL AND KILLED BROTHER WEI...

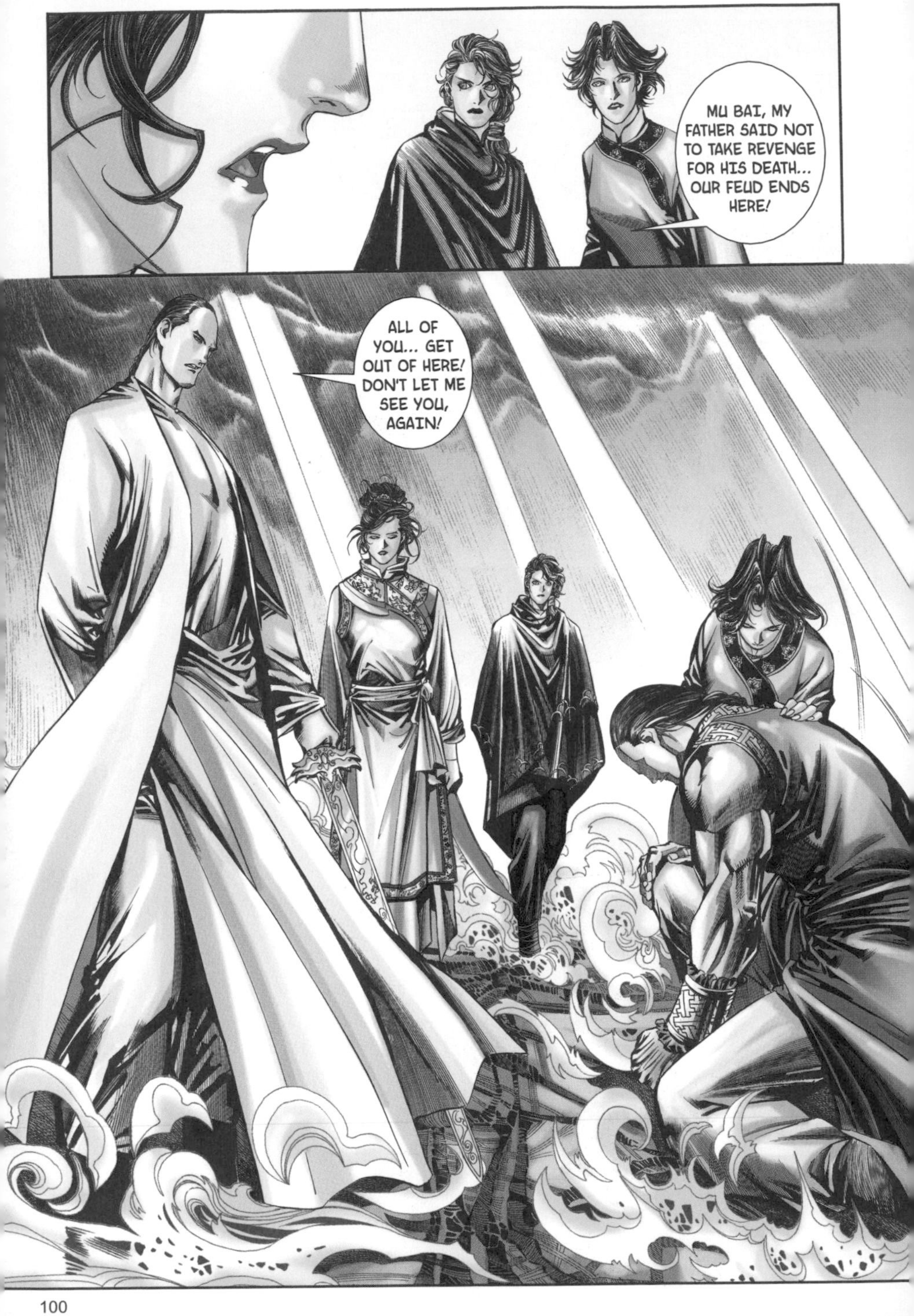
MU BAI, MY FATHER SAID NOT TO TAKE REVENGE FOR HIS DEATH... OUR FEUD ENDS HERE!
ALL OF YOU... GET OUT OF HERE! DON'T LET ME SEE YOU, AGAIN!

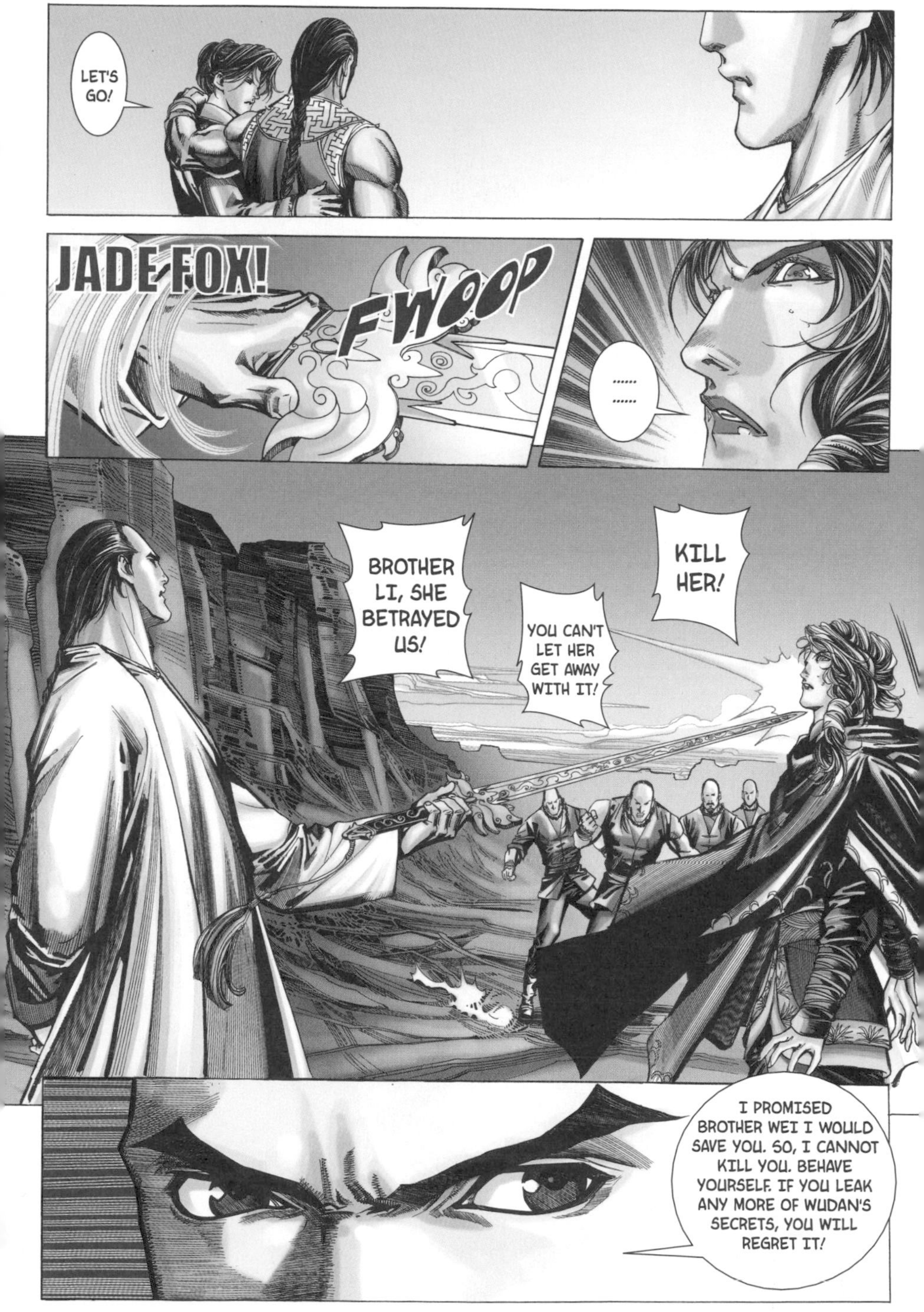
LET'S GO!
JADE FOX!
FWOOP
......
......
BROTHER LI, SHE BETRAYED US!
KILL HER!
YOU CAN'T LET HER GET AWAY WITH IT!
I PROMISED BROTHER WEI I WOULD SAVE YOU. SO, I CANNOT KILL YOU. BEHAVE YOURSELF. IF YOU LEAK ANY MORE OF WUDAN'S SECRETS, YOU WILL REGRET IT!

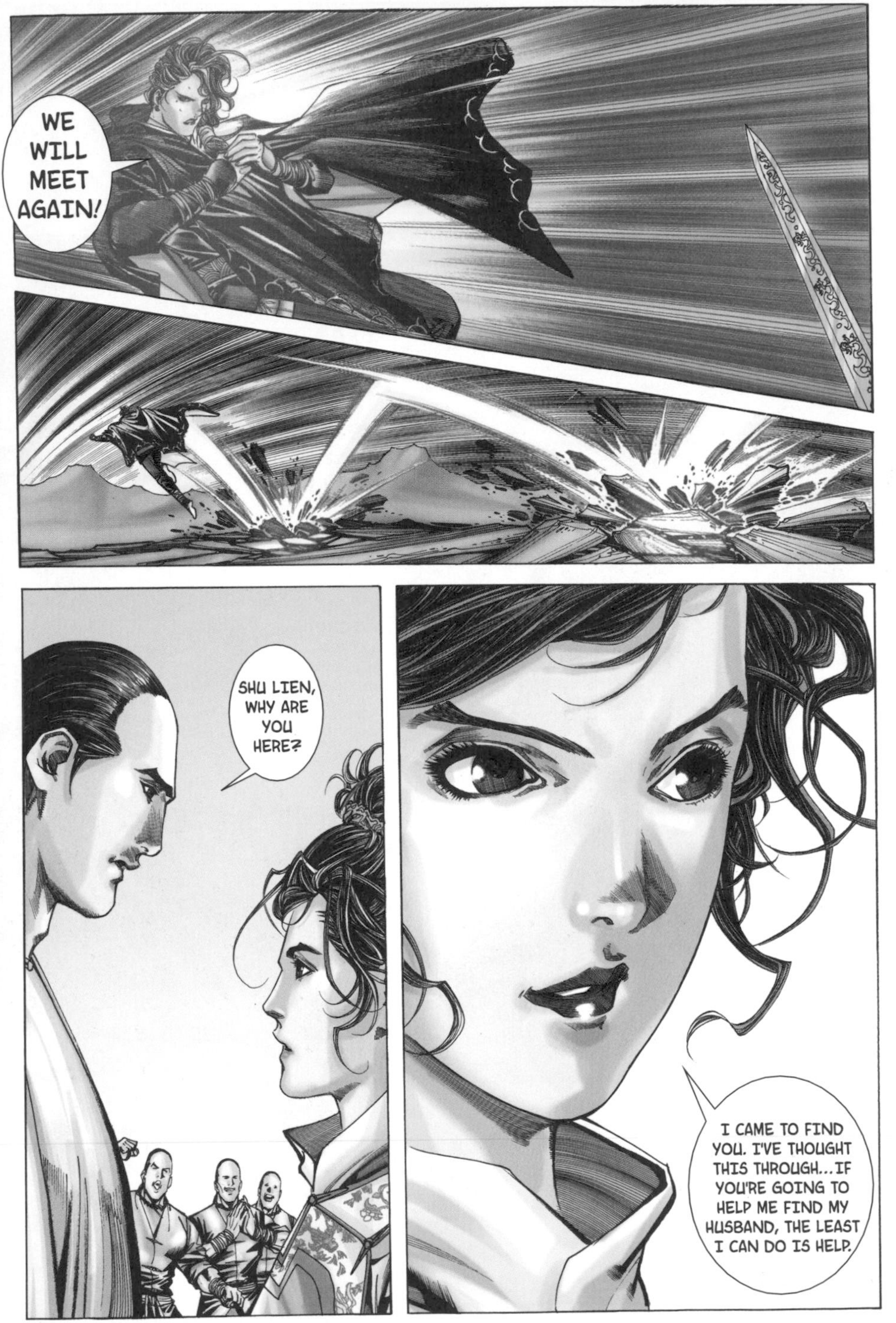
WE WILL MEET AGAIN!
SHU LIEN, WHY ARE YOU HERE?
I CAME TO FIND YOU. I'VE THOUGHT THIS THROUGH...IF YOU'RE GOING TO HELP ME FIND MY HUSBAND, THE LEAST I CAN DO IS HELP.

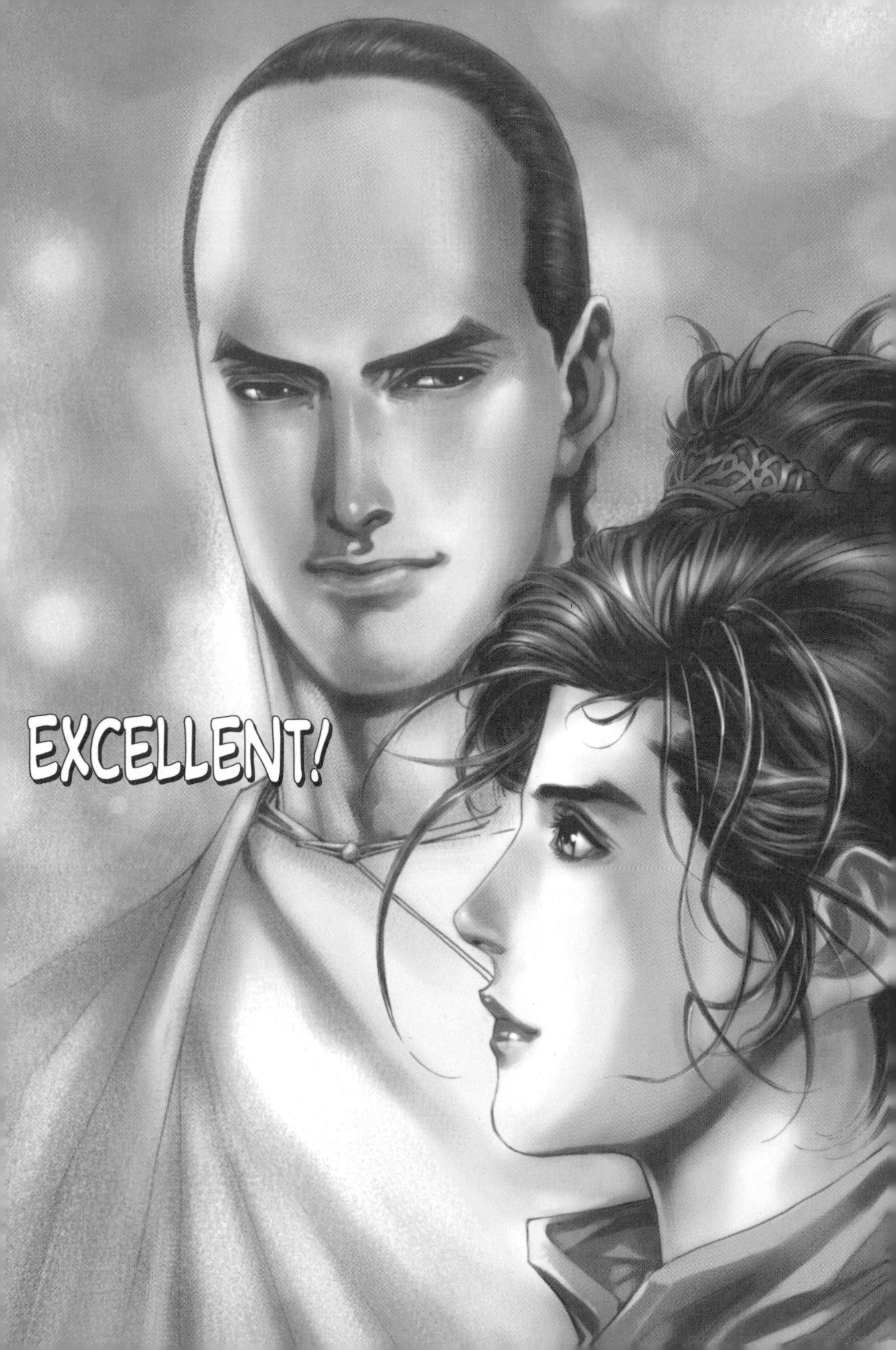
EXCELLENT!

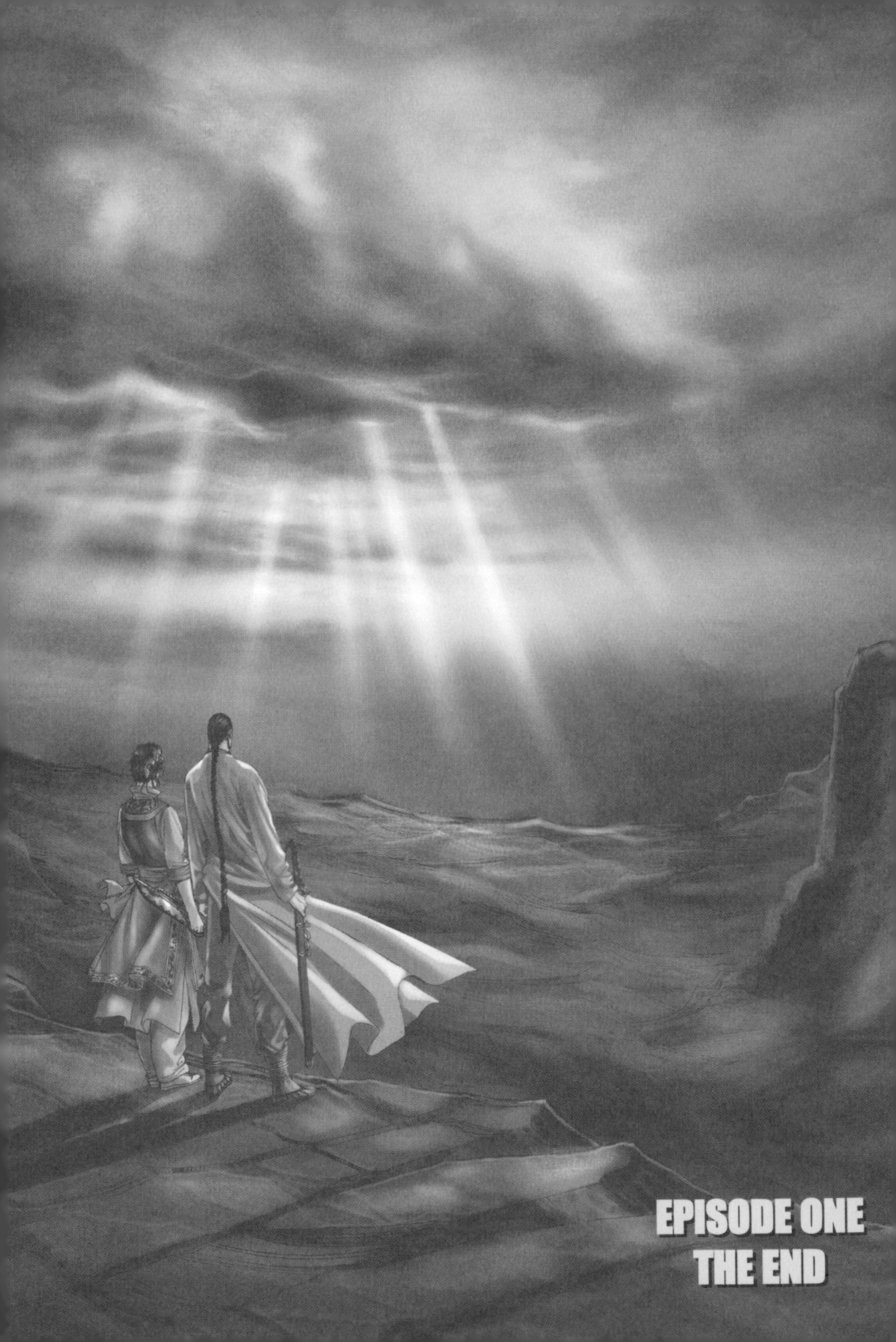
EPISODE ONE
THE END

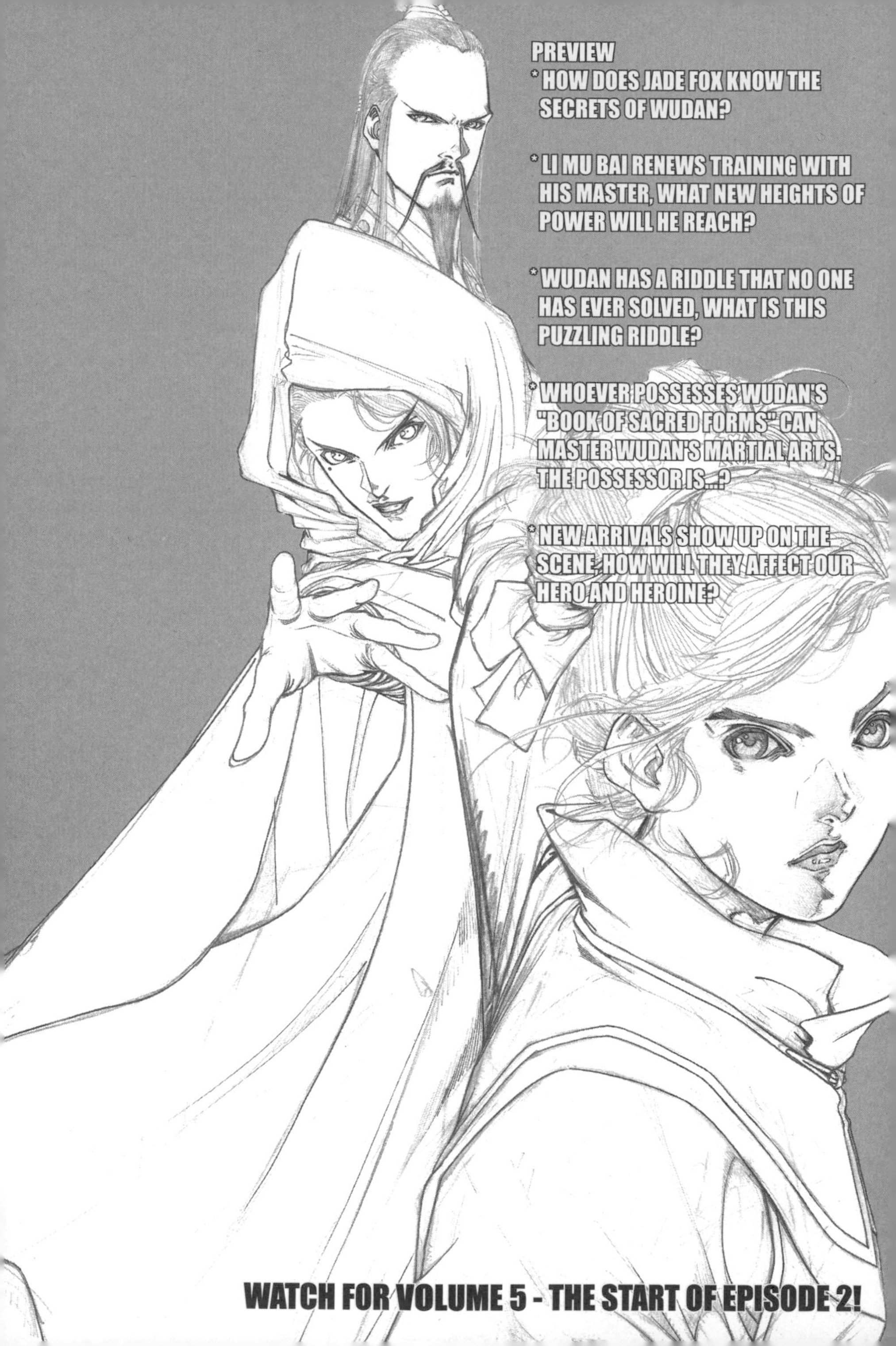
PREVIEW
* HOW DOES JADE FOX KNOW THE SECRETS OF WUDAN?
* LI MU BAI RENEWS TRAINING WITH HIS MASTER, WHAT NEW HEIGHTS OF POWER WILL HE REACH?
* WUDAN HAS A RIDDLE THAT NO ONE HAS EVER SOLVED, WHAT IS THIS PUZZLING RIDDLE?
* WHOEVER POSSESSES WUDAN'S "BOOK OF SACRED FORMS" CAN MASTER WUDAN'S MARTIAL ARTS. THE POSSESSOR IS...?
* NEW ARRIVALS SHOW UP ON THE SCENE, HOW WILL THEY AFFECT OUR HERO AND HEROINE?
WATCH FOR VOLUME 5 - THE START OF EPISODE 2!

ANDY'S DIARY

THIS VOLUME IS LATE AND OVER-BUDGET. I'D LIKE TO APOLOGIZE TO ALL MY READERS FOR THE DELAY.

THESE PAST FEW YEARS, THE SCRIPTS HAVE BEEN ON TIME. SCRIPTS FOR SAINT LEGEND, KING OF FIGHTERS, AND OTHER COMICS I'VE WORKED ON WERE SELDOM LATE. CROUCHING TIGER HAS PLENTY OF EXISTING MATERIAL TO WORK WITH, BUT THINGS CAN HAPPEN AND THEY DID. SINCE OUR COMPANY IS FOCUSED ON PUBLISHING WEEKLY COMICS, WHICH IS THE PACE WE ARE ACCUSTOMED TO. IT'S BEEN DIFFICULT TO FIND OUR PACE SINCE CROUCHING TIGER IS A NEW FORMAT AND WE'RE TRYING NEW THINGS ALL THE TIME.

TO ACCOMMODATE THE NEW FORMAT, WE WERE FORCED TO MODIFY OUR RELEASE SCHEDULE.

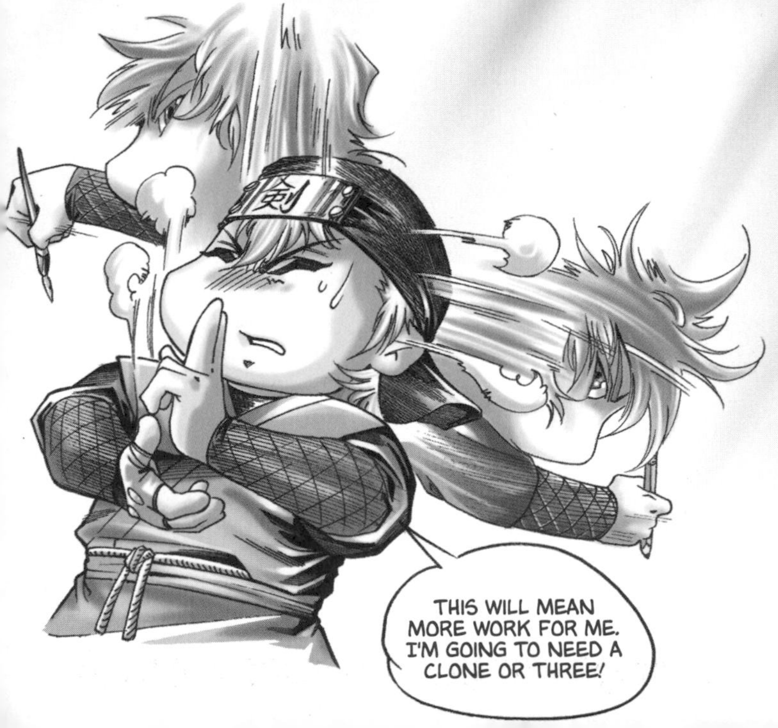
THIS WILL MEAN MORE WORK FOR ME. I'M GOING TO NEED A CLONE OR THREE!

ANDY'S DIARY

THE SECOND EPISODE WILL HAVE MORE DIALOGUE. HOPEFULLY THIS WILL BE COMFORTABLE WITH HONG KONG AND WESTERN READERS. THE FACT IS, WE TOOK OUT A LOT OF DIALOGUE IN THE FIRST FOUR VOLUMES OF CROUCHING TIGER. I REGRET TAKING THEM OUT AND AM TEMPTED TO RESTORE THEM. THAT WAY, I COULD HAVE A COMPLETE VERSION OF THE COMIC, WHICH WILL SURELY PLEASE MY HONG KONG READERS AS WELL AS SOME OF MY WESTERN ONES. IN FUTURE VOLUMES, I WILL INCLUDE 10-15 EXTRA PAGES AS A GIFT TO MY READERS. I HOPE ALL OF YOU WILL LIKE IT.

ANDY SETO

STORY OF THE TAO

King Lee instructs the younger of two sons (Prince Lee) to seek the path of Buddha and all it's wonderful powers. Soon after, the King and his closest heir die suspiciously, and the ambitious Queen is suspected of treason. The Queen is powerful and well protected by many skilled Kung Fu masters. Now earthly representatives of four religious sects, Taoism, Buddhism, Mysticism and Shinto rally together to teach and protect young Prince Lee from his malevolent stepmother and her many denizens. Little do they know it will take their combined efforts to defeat a foe that threatens spirituality as they know it.

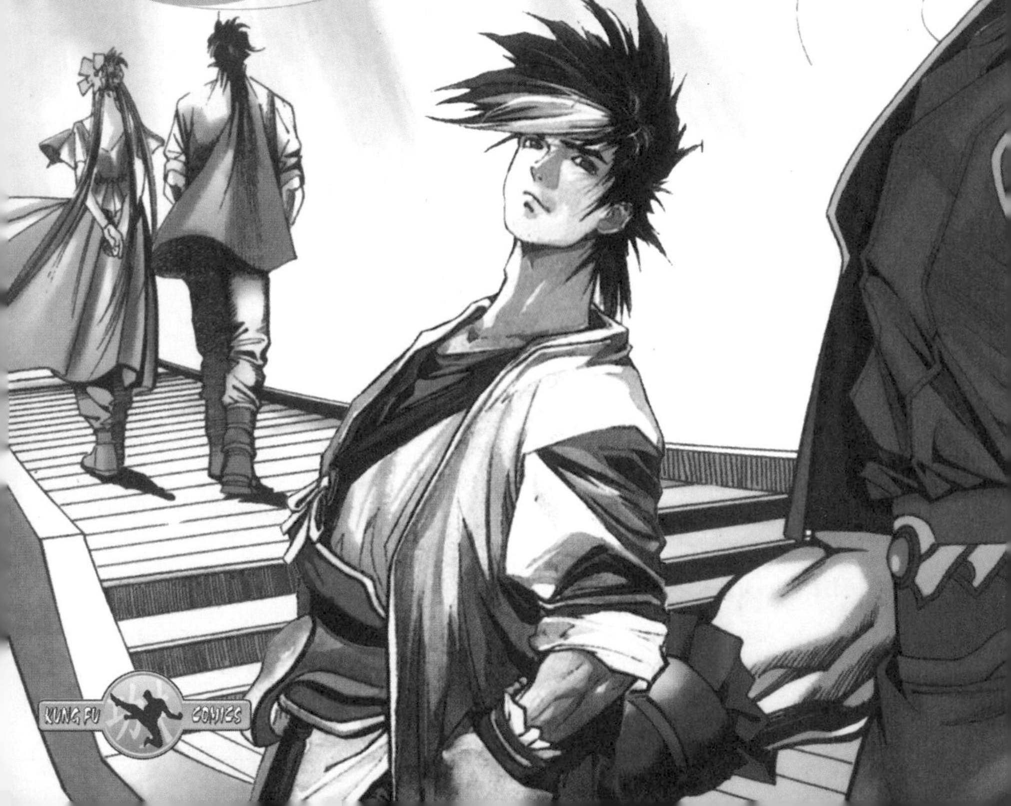
KUNG FU COMICS

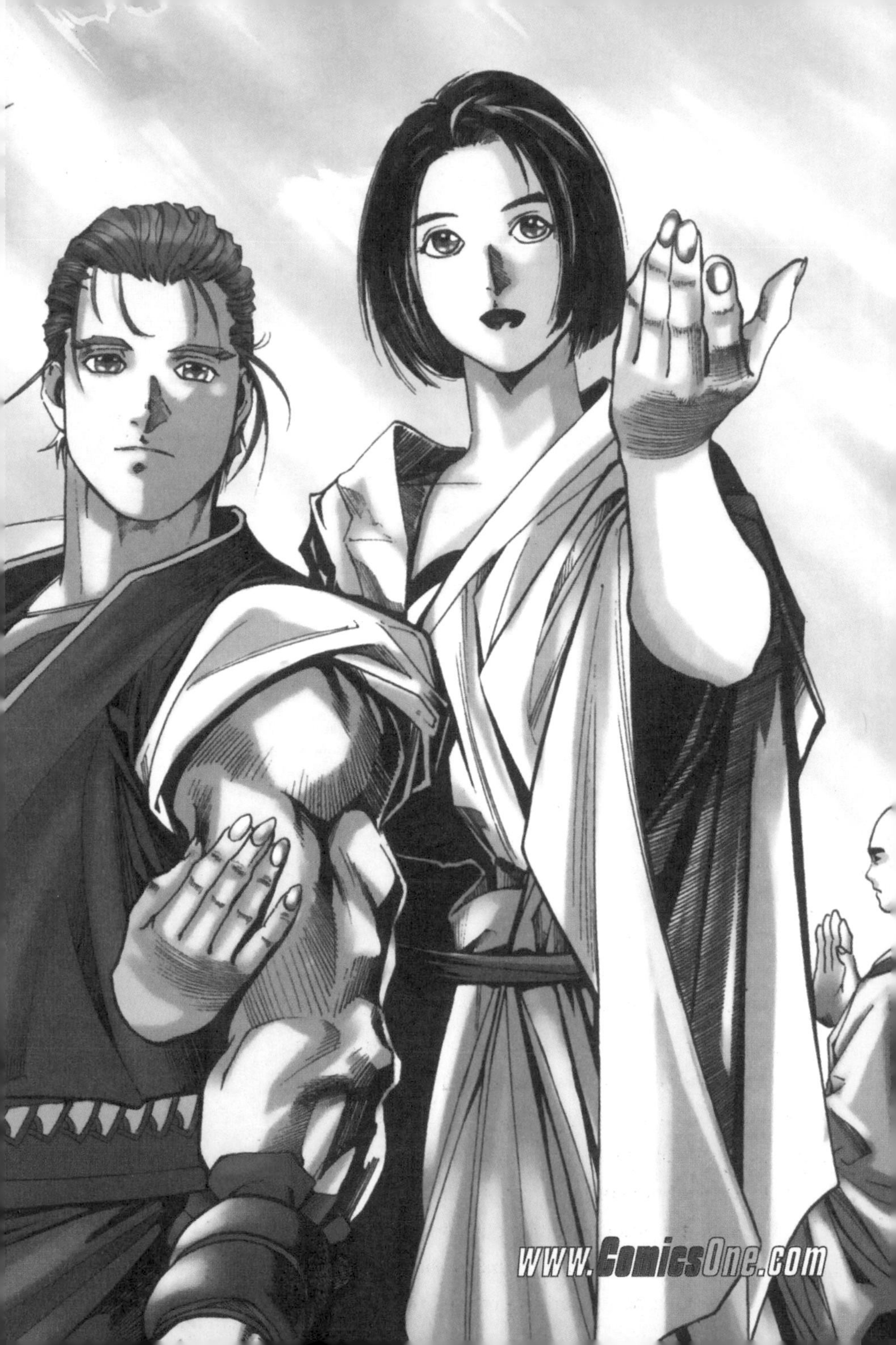
www.ComicsOne.com

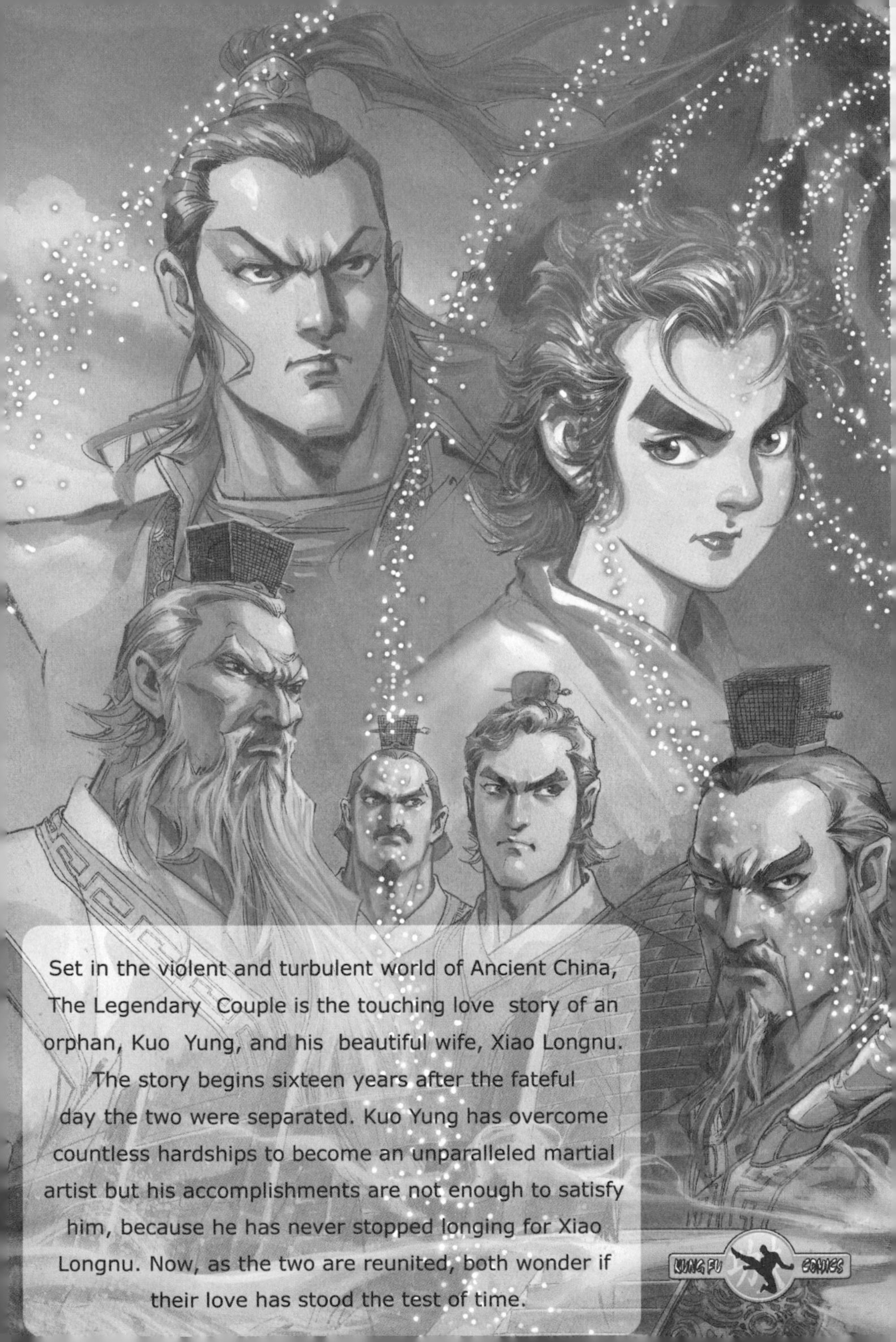

Set in the violent and turbulent world of Ancient China, The Legendary Couple is the touching love story of an orphan, Kuo Yung, and his beautiful wife, Xiao Longnu. The story begins sixteen years after the fateful day the two were separated. Kuo Yung has overcome countless hardships to become an unparalleled martial artist but his accomplishments are not enough to satisfy him, because he has never stopped longing for Xiao Longnu. Now, as the two are reunited, both wonder if their love has stood the test of time.

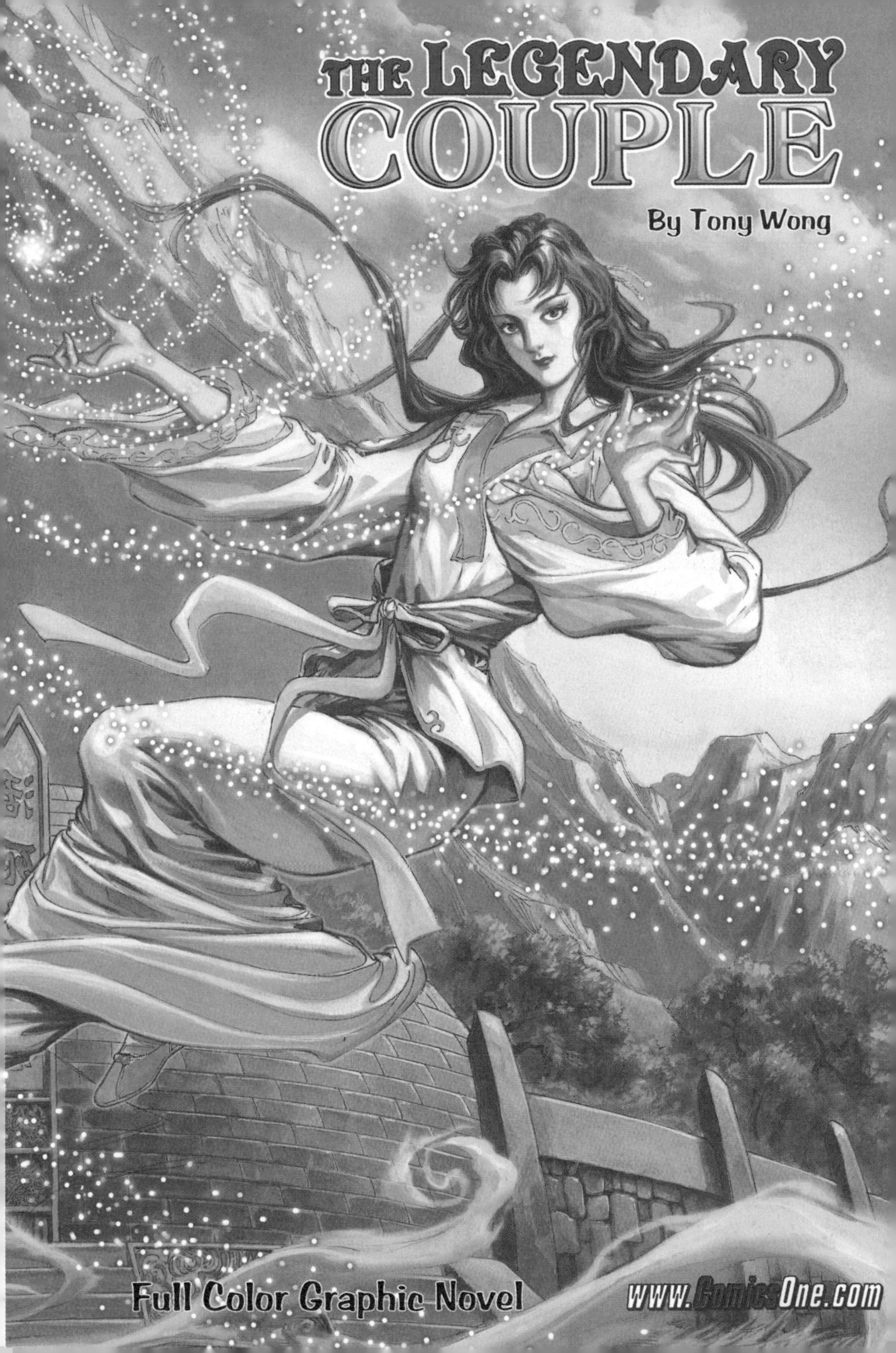
THE LEGENDARY COUPLE
By Tony Wong
Full Color Graphic Novel
www.ComicsOne.com

THE LEGENDARY COUPLE SAMPLE PAGE

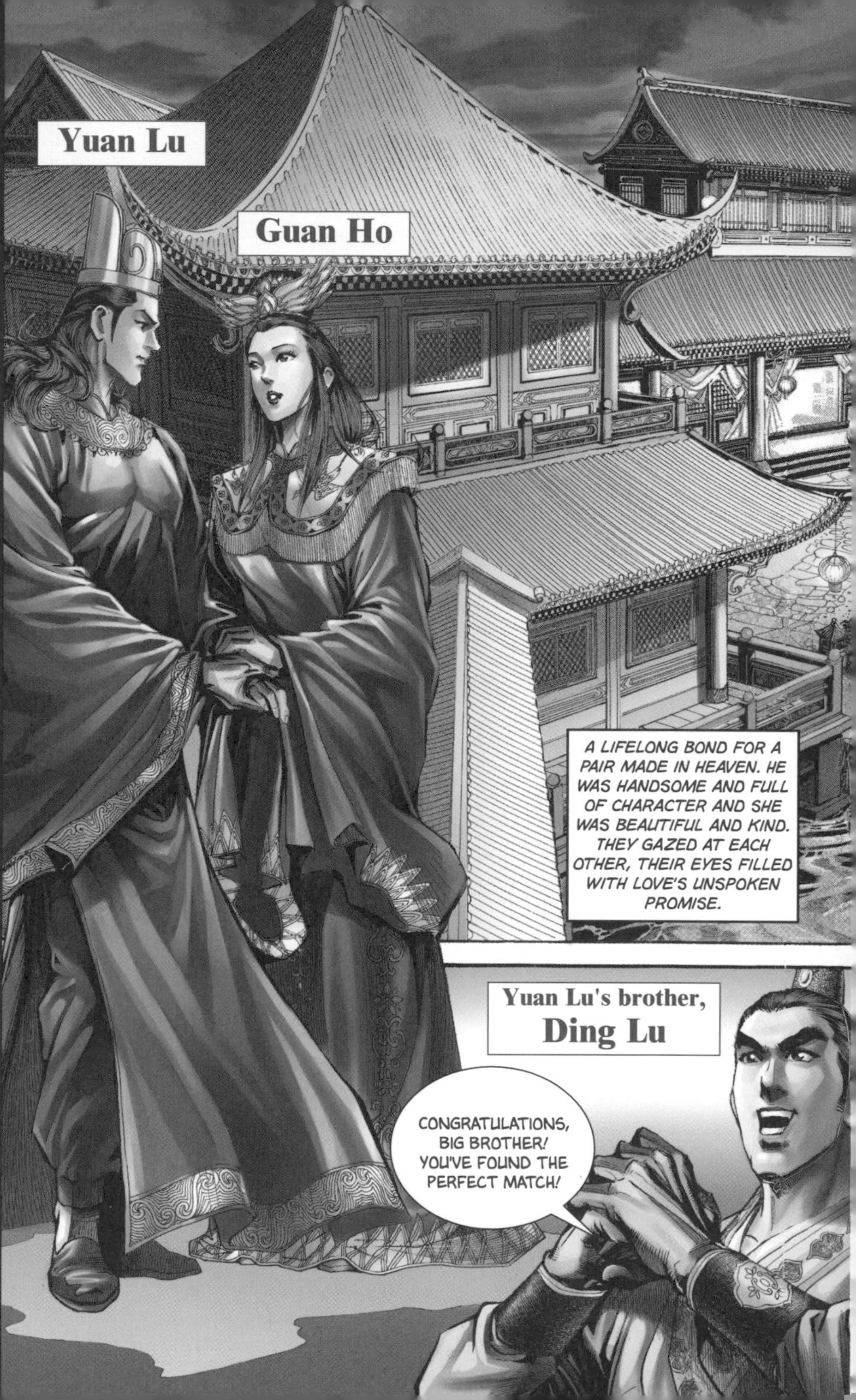
Yuan Lu
Guan Ho
A LIFELONG BOND FOR A PAIR MADE IN HEAVEN. HE WAS HANDSOME AND FULL OF CHARACTER AND SHE WAS BEAUTIFUL AND KIND. THEY GAZED AT EACH OTHER, THEIR EYES FILLED WITH LOVE'S UNSPOKEN PROMISE.
Yuan Lu's brother, Ding Lu
CONGRATULATIONS, BIG BROTHER! YOU'VE FOUND THE PERFECT MATCH!

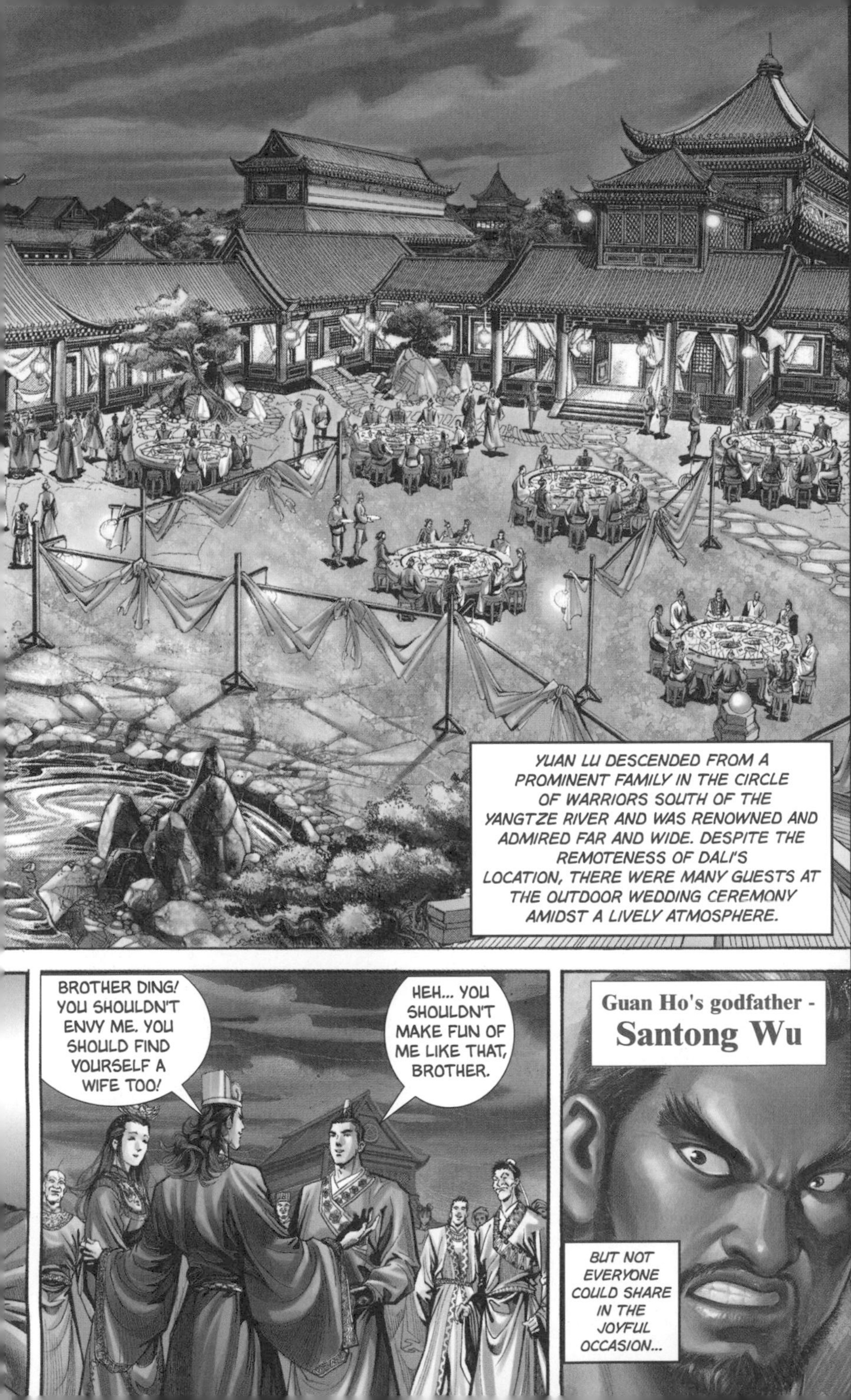
YUAN LU DESCENDED FROM A PROMINENT FAMILY IN THE CIRCLE OF WARRIORS SOUTH OF THE YANGTZE RIVER AND WAS RENOWNED AND ADMIRED FAR AND WIDE. DESPITE THE REMOTENESS OF DALI'S LOCATION, THERE WERE MANY GUESTS AT THE OUTDOOR WEDDING CEREMONY AMIDST A LIVELY ATMOSPHERE.
BROTHER DING! YOU SHOULDN'T ENVY ME. YOU SHOULD FIND YOURSELF A WIFE TOO!
HEH... YOU SHOULDN'T MAKE FUN OF ME LIKE THAT, BROTHER.
Guan Ho's godfather - Santong Wu
BUT NOT EVERYONE COULD SHARE IN THE JOYFUL OCCASION...

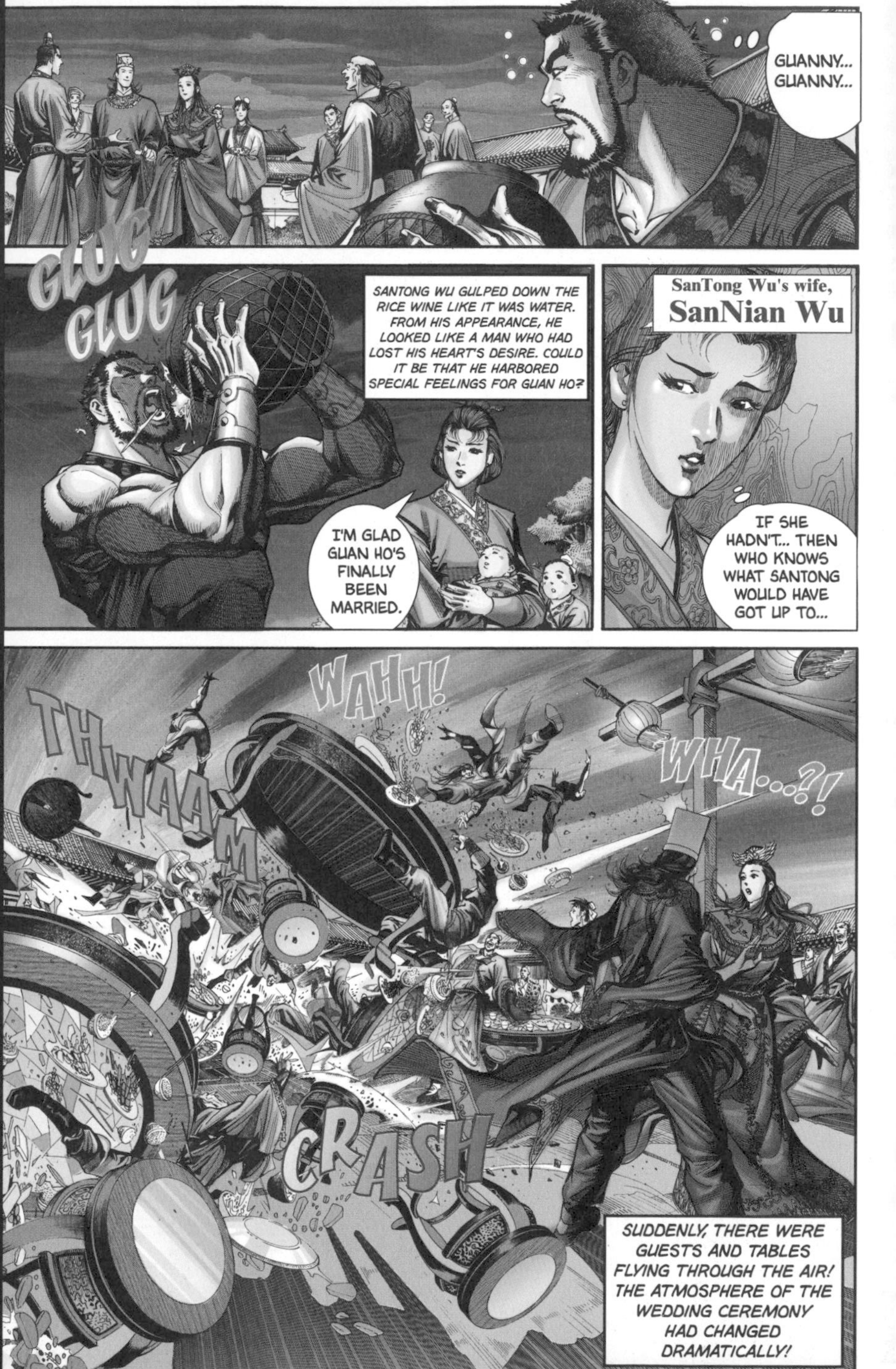
GUANNY... GUANNY...
GLUG GLUG
SANTONG WU GULPED DOWN THE RICE WINE LIKE IT WAS WATER. FROM HIS APPEARANCE, HE LOOKED LIKE A MAN WHO HAD LOST HIS HEART'S DESIRE. COULD IT BE THAT HE HARBORED SPECIAL FEELINGS FOR GUAN HO?
I'M GLAD GUAN HO'S FINALLY BEEN MARRIED.
SanTong Wu's wife, SanNian Wu
IF SHE HADN'T... THEN WHO KNOWS WHAT SANTONG WOULD HAVE GOT UP TO...
THWAAAM
WAHH!
WHA...?!
CRASH
SUDDENLY, THERE WERE GUESTS AND TABLES FLYING THROUGH THE AIR! THE ATMOSPHERE OF THE WEDDING CEREMONY HAD CHANGED DRAMATICALLY!

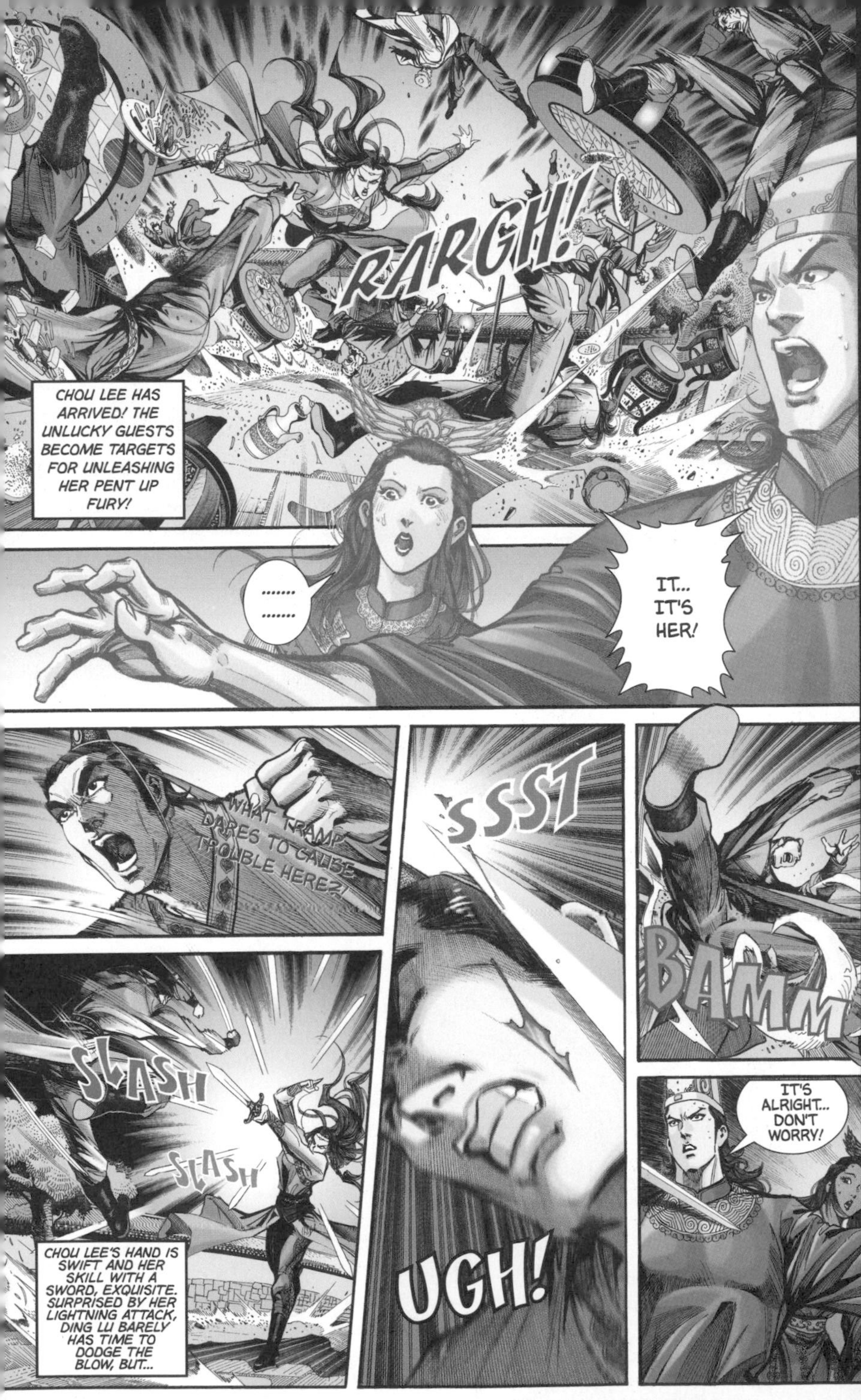
RARGH!
CHOU LEE HAS ARRIVED! THE UNLUCKY GUESTS BECOME TARGETS FOR UNLEASHING HER PENT UP FURY!
....
....
IT... IT'S HER!
WHAT TRAMP DARES TO CAUSE TROUBLE HERE?!
SSST
BAMM
SLASH
SLASH
CHOU LEE'S HAND IS SWIFT AND HER SKILL WITH A SWORD, EXQUISITE. SURPRISED BY HER LIGHTNING ATTACK, DING LU BARELY HAS TIME TO DODGE THE BLOW, BUT...
UGH!
IT'S ALRIGHT... DON'T WORRY!

CHOU, WHY ARE YOU TAKING THIS SO HARD? THE LOVE BETWEEN A MAN AND A WOMAN CAN'T BE FORCED!
I ADMIT I WAS ATTRACTED TO YOU BEFORE. BUT ONCE WE GOT TO KNOW EACH OTHER, WE BOTH KNEW THAT OUR PERSONALITIES DIDN'T MATCH. IT WOULD HAVE ONLY BEEN WORSE FOR BOTH OF US IF WE CARRIED ON. DON'T MAKE THINGS WORSE NOW BY GOING TOO FAR!
HUMPH! IN OTHER WORDS, YOU WERE TIRED OF ME AND WANTED SOMEONE NEW!

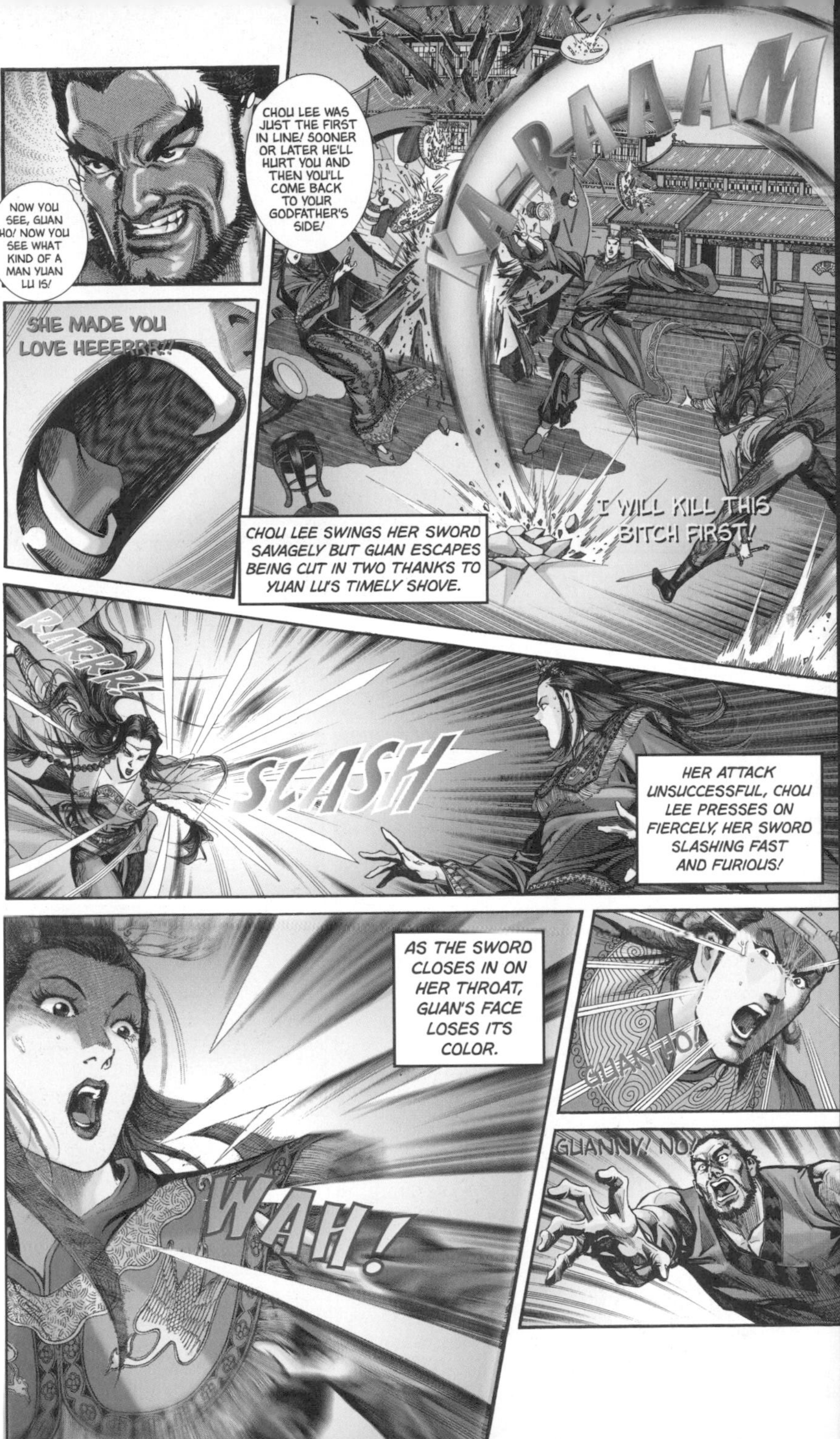
NOW YOU SEE, GUAN HO! NOW YOU SEE WHAT KIND OF A MAN YUAN LU IS!
CHOU LEE WAS JUST THE FIRST IN LINE! SOONER OR LATER HE'LL HURT YOU AND THEN YOU'LL COME BACK TO YOUR GODFATHER'S SIDE!
KA-RAAAM
SHE MADE YOU LOVE HEEERRR!!
I WILL KILL THIS BITCH FIRST!
CHOU LEE SWINGS HER SWORD SAVAGELY BUT GUAN ESCAPES BEING CUT IN TWO THANKS TO YUAN LU'S TIMELY SHOVE.
RARRR!
SLASH
HER ATTACK UNSUCCESSFUL, CHOU LEE PRESSES ON FIERCELY, HER SWORD SLASHING FAST AND FURIOUS!
AS THE SWORD CLOSES IN ON HER THROAT, GUAN'S FACE LOSES ITS COLOR.
WAH!
GUAN HO!
GUANN! NO!

THE LEGENDARY COUPLE SAMPLE PAGE

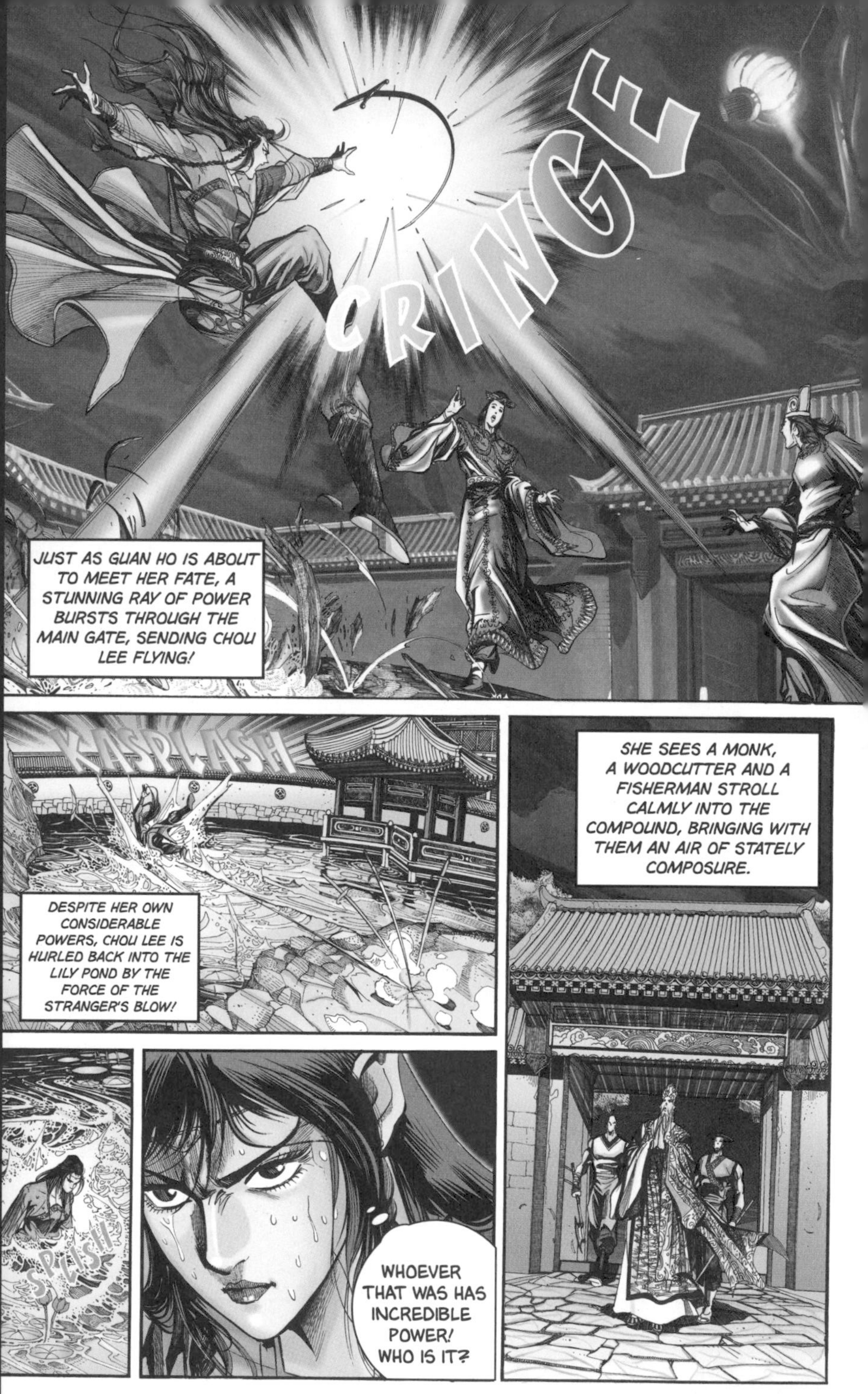
CRINGE
JUST AS GUAN HO IS ABOUT TO MEET HER FATE, A STUNNING RAY OF POWER BURSTS THROUGH THE MAIN GATE, SENDING CHOU LEE FLYING!
KASPLASH
DESPITE HER OWN CONSIDERABLE POWERS, CHOU LEE IS HURLED BACK INTO THE LILY POND BY THE FORCE OF THE STRANGER'S BLOW!
SPLISH
WHOEVER THAT WAS HAS INCREDIBLE POWER! WHO IS IT?
SHE SEES A MONK, A WOODCUTTER AND A FISHERMAN STROLL CALMLY INTO THE COMPOUND, BRINGING WITH THEM AN AIR OF STATELY COMPOSURE.

THE LEGENDARY COUPLE SAMPLE PAGE

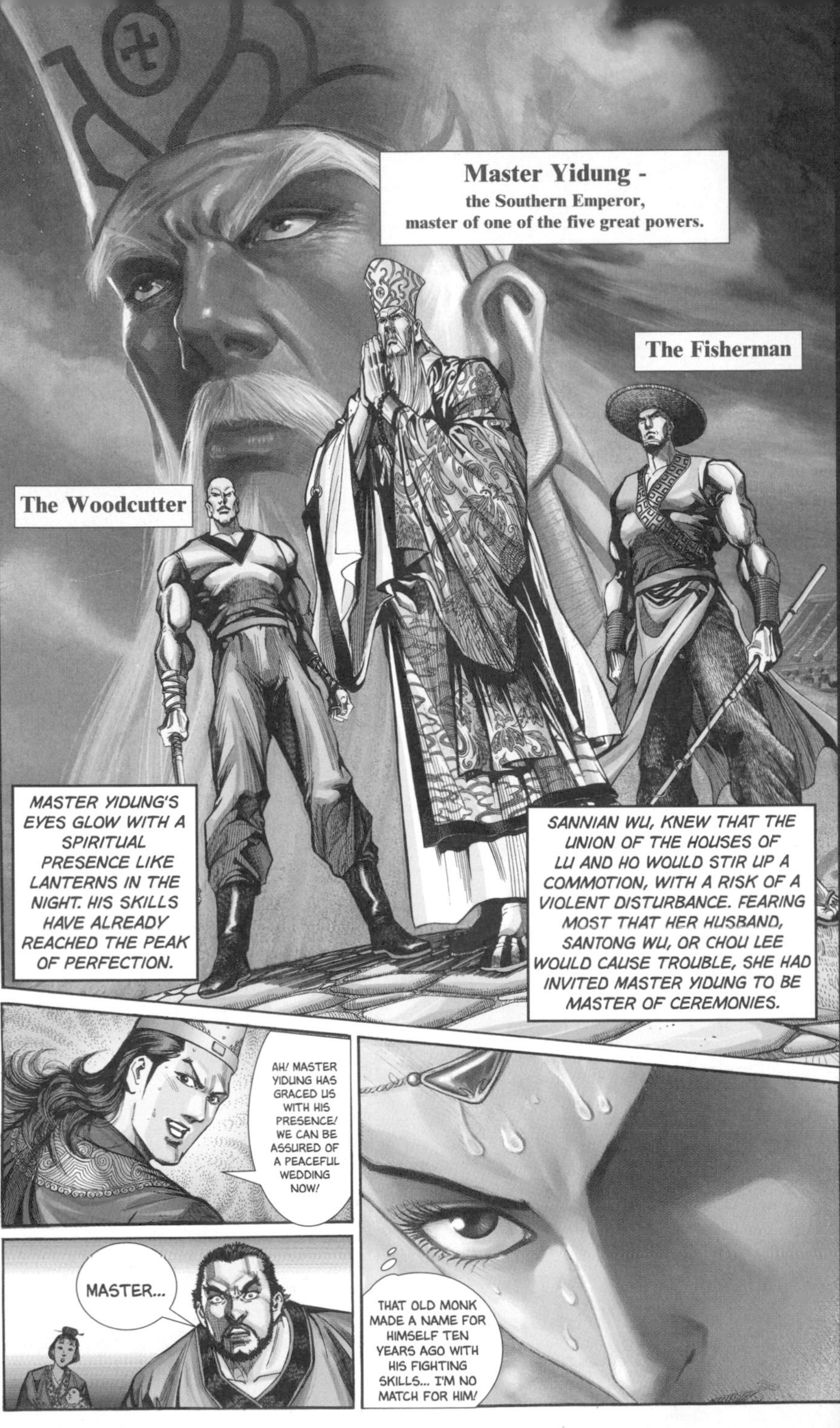

Master Yidung -
the Southern Emperor,
master of one of the five great powers.
The Fisherman
The Woodcutter
MASTER YIDUNG'S EYES GLOW WITH A SPIRITUAL PRESENCE LIKE LANTERNS IN THE NIGHT. HIS SKILLS HAVE ALREADY REACHED THE PEAK OF PERFECTION.
SANNIAN WU, KNEW THAT THE UNION OF THE HOUSES OF LU AND HO WOULD STIR UP A COMMOTION, WITH A RISK OF A VIOLENT DISTURBANCE. FEARING MOST THAT HER HUSBAND, SANTONG WU, OR CHOU LEE WOULD CAUSE TROUBLE, SHE HAD INVITED MASTER YIDUNG TO BE MASTER OF CEREMONIES.
AH! MASTER YIDUNG HAS GRACED US WITH HIS PRESENCE! WE CAN BE ASSURED OF A PEACEFUL WEDDING NOW!
MASTER...
THAT OLD MONK MADE A NAME FOR HIMSELF TEN YEARS AGO WITH HIS FIGHTING SKILLS... I'M NO MATCH FOR HIM!

THE LEGENDARY COUPLE SAMPLE PAGE

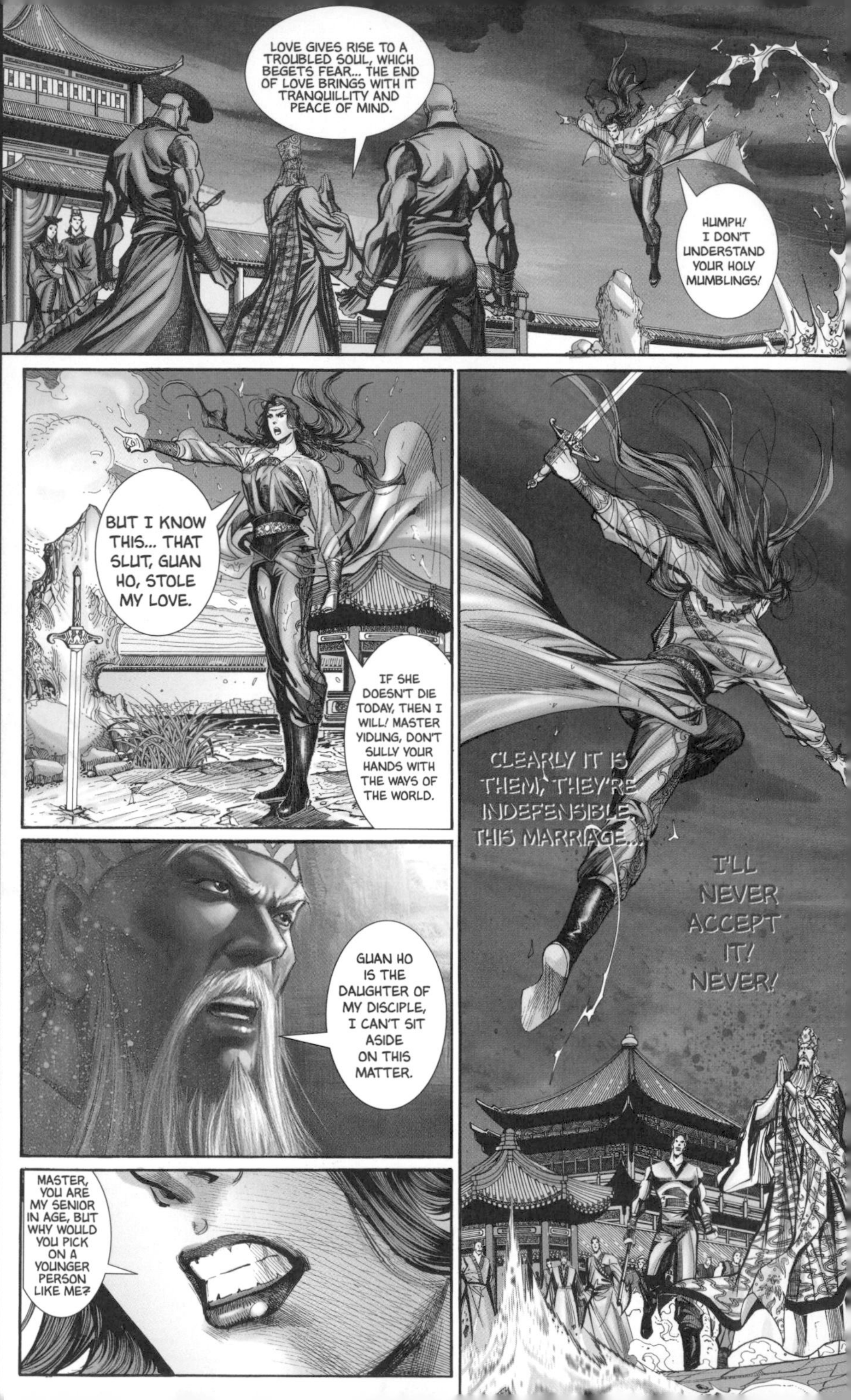
LOVE GIVES RISE TO A TROUBLED SOUL, WHICH BEGETS FEAR... THE END OF LOVE BRINGS WITH IT TRANQUILLITY AND PEACE OF MIND.
HUMPH! I DON'T UNDERSTAND YOUR HOLY MUMBLINGS!
BUT I KNOW THIS... THAT SLUT, GUAN HO, STOLE MY LOVE.
IF SHE DOESN'T DIE TODAY, THEN I WILL! MASTER YIDUNG, DON'T SULLY YOUR HANDS WITH THE WAYS OF THE WORLD.
GUAN HO IS THE DAUGHTER OF MY DISCIPLE, I CAN'T SIT ASIDE ON THIS MATTER.
MASTER, YOU ARE MY SENIOR IN AGE, BUT WHY WOULD YOU PICK ON A YOUNGER PERSON LIKE ME?
CLEARLY IT IS THEM, THEY'RE INDEFENSIBLE, THIS MARRIAGE...
I'LL NEVER ACCEPT IT! NEVER!

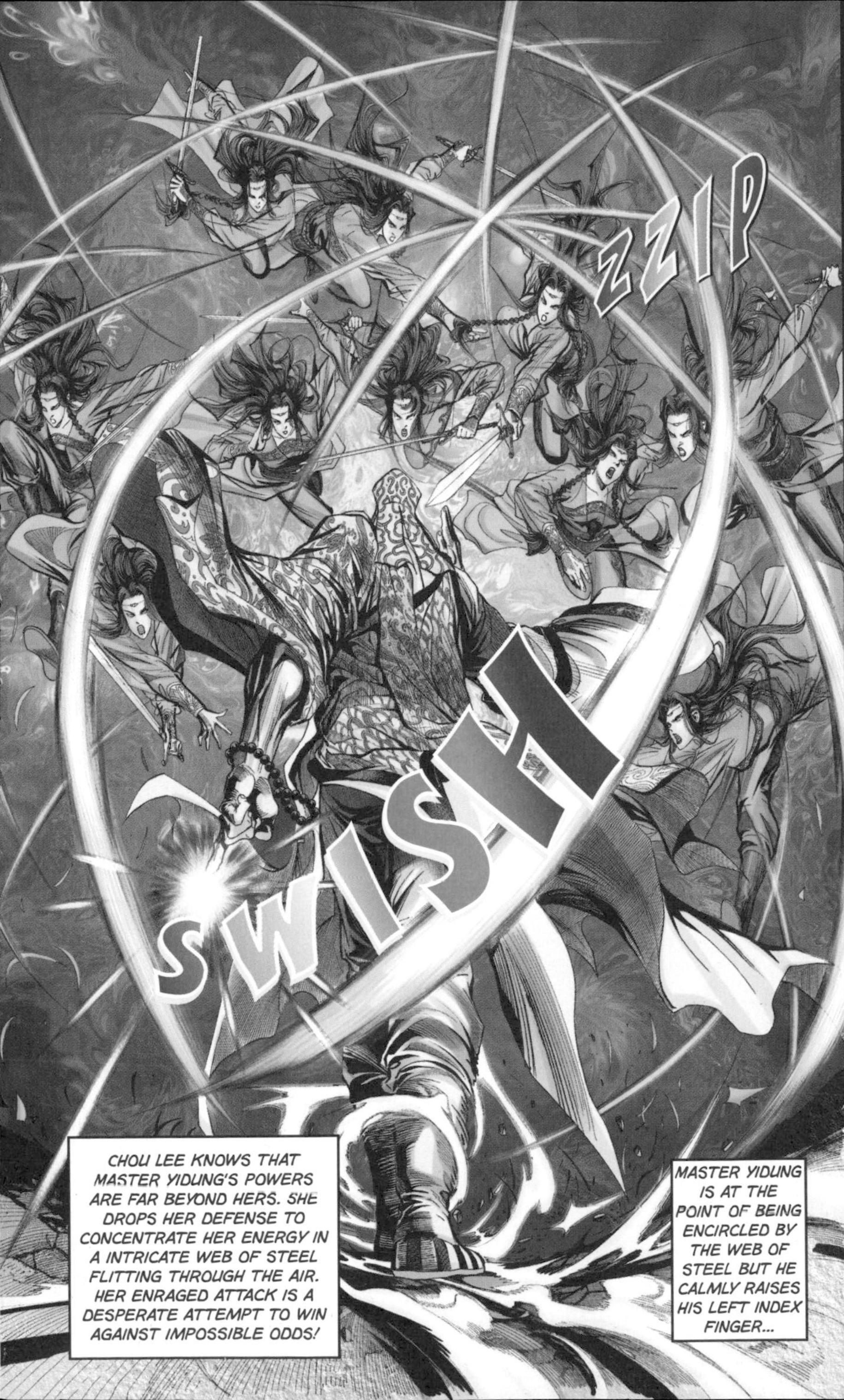
ZZIP
SWISH
CHOU LEE KNOWS THAT MASTER YIDUNG'S POWERS ARE FAR BEYOND HERS. SHE DROPS HER DEFENSE TO CONCENTRATE HER ENERGY IN A INTRICATE WEB OF STEEL FLITTING THROUGH THE AIR. HER ENRAGED ATTACK IS A DESPERATE ATTEMPT TO WIN AGAINST IMPOSSIBLE ODDS!
MASTER YIDUNG IS AT THE POINT OF BEING ENCIRCLED BY THE WEB OF STEEL BUT HE CALMLY RAISES HIS LEFT INDEX FINGER...

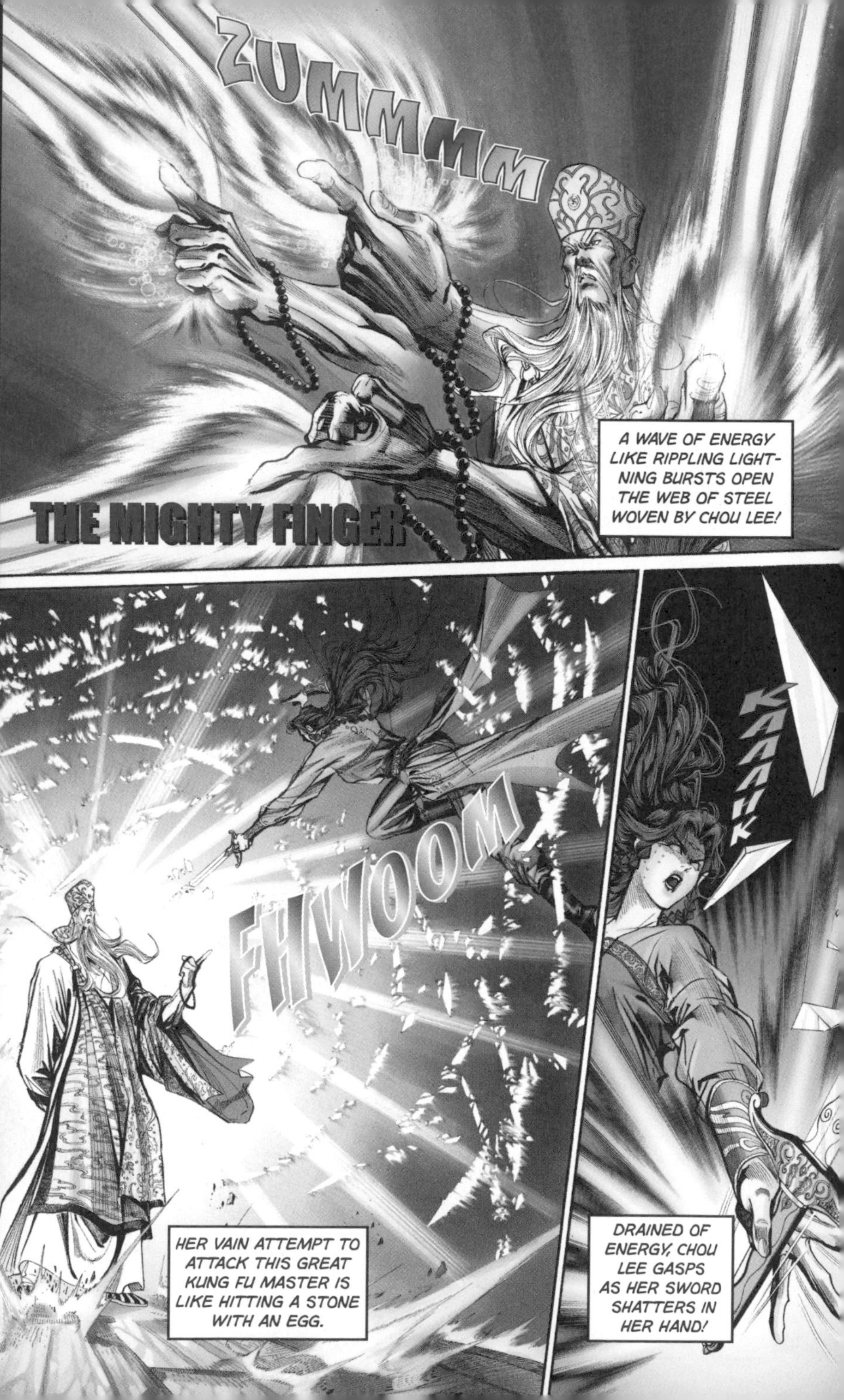
ZUMMMMM
THE MIGHTY FINGER
A WAVE OF ENERGY LIKE RIPPLING LIGHTNING BURSTS OPEN THE WEB OF STEEL WOVEN BY CHOU LEE!
FHWOOM
HER VAIN ATTEMPT TO ATTACK THIS GREAT KUNG FU MASTER IS LIKE HITTING A STONE WITH AN EGG.
KAAAHK
DRAINED OF ENERGY, CHOU LEE GASPS AS HER SWORD SHATTERS IN HER HAND!

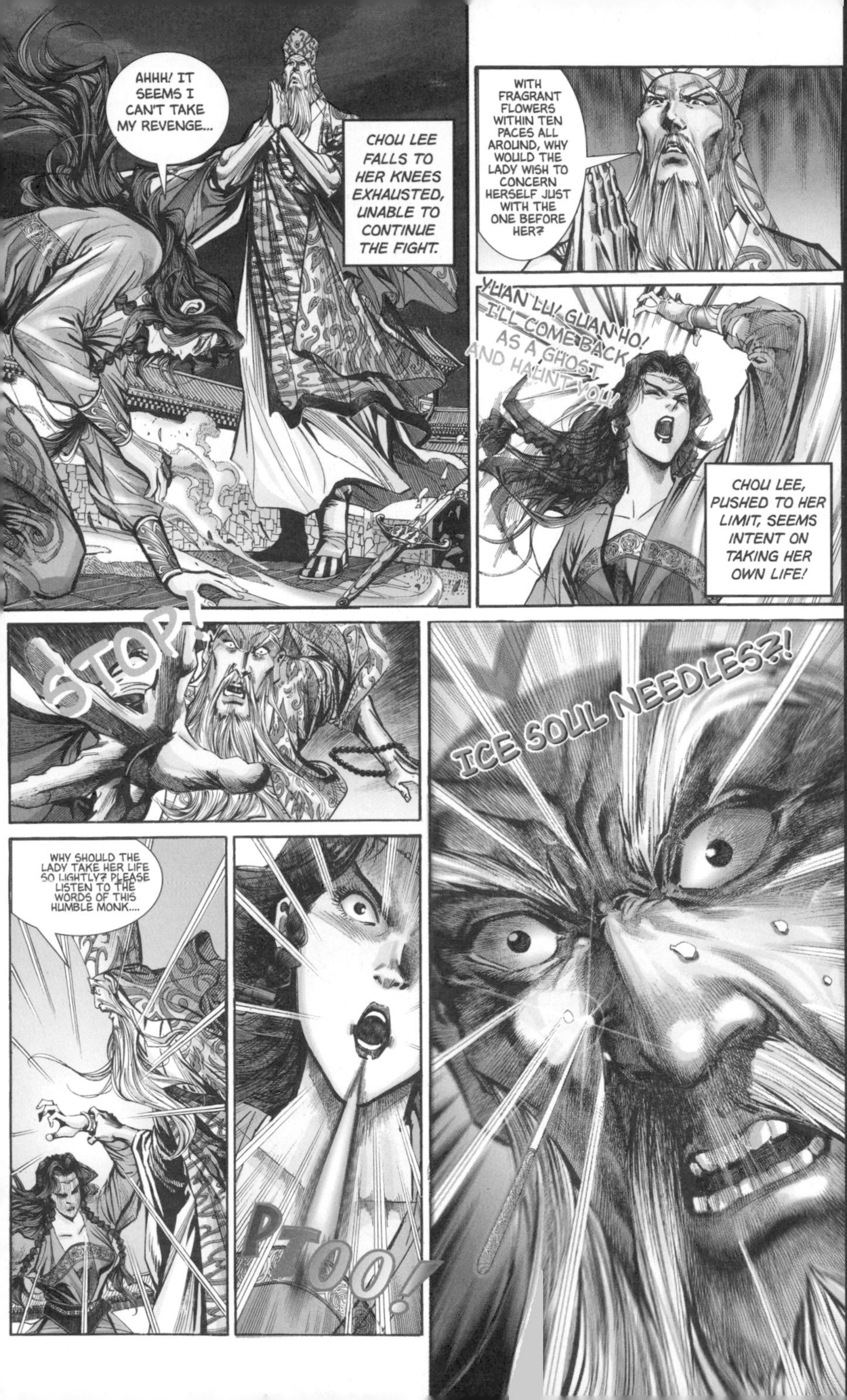
AHHH! IT SEEMS I CAN'T TAKE MY REVENGE...
CHOU LEE FALLS TO HER KNEES EXHAUSTED, UNABLE TO CONTINUE THE FIGHT.
WITH FRAGRANT FLOWERS WITHIN TEN PACES ALL AROUND, WHY WOULD THE LADY WISH TO CONCERN HERSELF JUST WITH THE ONE BEFORE HER?
YUAN LU! GUAN HO! I'LL COME BACK AS A GHOST AND HAUNT YOU!
CHOU LEE, PUSHED TO HER LIMIT, SEEMS INTENT ON TAKING HER OWN LIFE!
STOP!
WHY SHOULD THE LADY TAKE HER LIFE SO LIGHTLY? PLEASE LISTEN TO THE WORDS OF THIS HUMBLE MONK....
PTOO!
ICE SOUL NEEDLES?!

THE LEGENDARY COUPLE SAMPLE PAGE

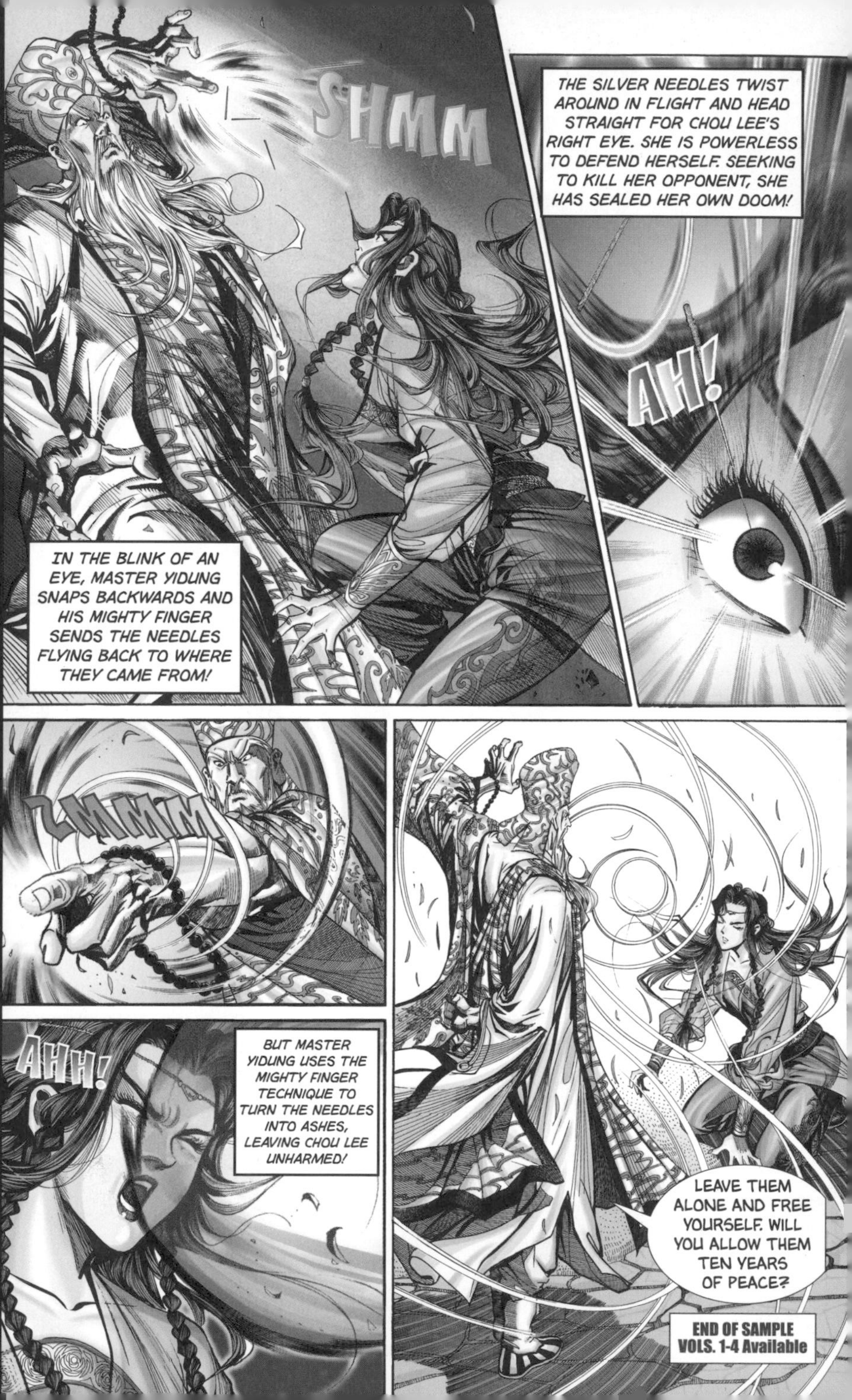
SHMM
IN THE BLINK OF AN EYE, MASTER YIDUNG SNAPS BACKWARDS AND HIS MIGHTY FINGER SENDS THE NEEDLES FLYING BACK TO WHERE THEY CAME FROM!
THE SILVER NEEDLES TWIST AROUND IN FLIGHT AND HEAD STRAIGHT FOR CHOU LEE'S RIGHT EYE. SHE IS POWERLESS TO DEFEND HERSELF. SEEKING TO KILL HER OPPONENT, SHE HAS SEALED HER OWN DOOM!
AH!
ZMMM
AHH!
BUT MASTER YIDUNG USES THE MIGHTY FINGER TECHNIQUE TO TURN THE NEEDLES INTO ASHES, LEAVING CHOU LEE UNHARMED!
LEAVE THEM ALONE AND FREE YOURSELF. WILL YOU ALLOW THEM TEN YEARS OF PEACE?
END OF SAMPLE
VOLS. 1-4 Available

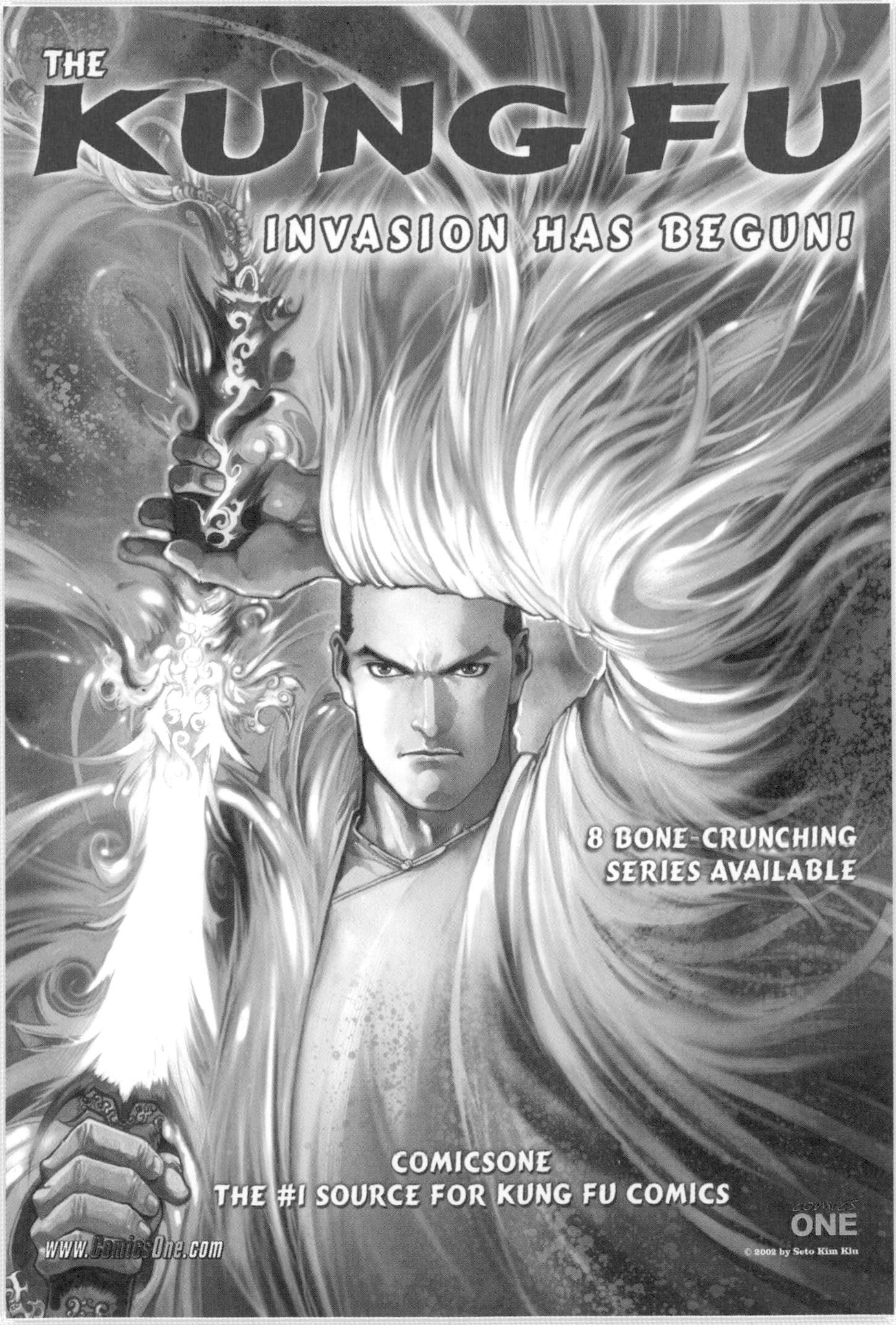
THE
KUNG FU
INVASION HAS BEGUN!
8 BONE-CRUNCHING
SERIES AVAILABLE
COMICSONE
THE #1 SOURCE FOR KUNG FU COMICS
www.ComicsOne.com
ONE
© 2002 by Seto Kim Kiu